Sarah Weddington

A Question *of* Choice

40th Anniversary Edition
REVISED AND UPDATED

THE FEMINIST PRESS
AT THE CITY UNIVERSITY OF NEW YORK
FEMINISTPRESS.ORG

Published in 2013 by the Feminist Press
at the City University of New York
The Graduate Center
365 Fifth Avenue, Suite 5406
New York, NY 10016

feministpress.org

Library of Congress Cataloging-in-Publication Data
Weddington, Sarah Ragle.
  A question of choice / Sarah Weddington. — 40th
anniversary edition, revised and updated.
    p. cm.
  Includes index.
  ISBN 978-1-55861-812-1
1. Abortion. 2. Weddington, Sarah Ragle. 3. Women
lawyers—United States--Biography. 4. Lawyers—United
States—Biography. 5. Abortion—United States. I. Title.
  HQ767.W38 2013
  363.4'6—dc23
                                                    2012043901

Contents

I first met Cecile Richards in Austin when her mother, Ann, was running for State Treasurer of Texas. Later, as a law student and Ann's campaign fundraiser in New York, I worked with Cecile to elect Ann Governor of Texas. We were both young Texas women, born and bred, deeply committed to social justice and enhancing the roles of women. I was inspired by Cecile's indefatigable determination and enduring commitment to the positive transformation of the quality of life for women everywhere.

Cecile is a nationally respected leader who serves with honor and distinction as President of Planned Parenthood of America and the Planned Parenthood Action Fund. Under her leadership the number of supporters of Planned Parenthood has doubled to more than 7 million people.

In the intervening years, Cecile has cleared many paths on national and international levels, working tirelessly for and on behalf of women and teens. She was the Deputy Chief of Staff to House Democratic Leader Nancy Pelosi. In 2004, she founded and served as President of America Votes, a coalition of forty-two national grassroots organizations working to maximize registration, education, and voter participation. Cecile began her career organizing low-wage workers in the hotel, health care, and janitorial industries in California, Louisiana, and Texas. In 2012, *Time* magazine recognized Cecile for her extraordinary work and brilliance as one of the 100 most influential people in the world. The best is yet to come!

Rebecca A. Seawright
Chair, Board of Directors
Feminist Press at CUNY

Foreword

A lifetime activist, teacher, lecturer, and leader, Sarah Weddington has chronicled the recent decades in the important and ongoing struggle for women's rights.

Forty years after the landmark *Roe v. Wade* decision, Sarah, who at the tender age of twenty-six successfully argued the case before the US Supreme Court, puts the continuing political fight for women's equality in perspective and looks at where women in America stand today with regard to reproductive health care access and rights.

At a moment when the right to legal abortion hangs by a precariously thin thread in the federal courts, and when many states have enacted burdensome restrictions on women, intended only to humiliate and shame those who seek to end a pregnancy, Sarah has brought us full circle from the early days when women routinely died in emergency rooms across America due to unsafe and botched abortions. Despite decades of a constitutional right to abortion, American politics and politicians are still consumed with the issue and likely will be for years to come.

My first chance to get to know Sarah was when I was in high school, when she decided at a young age to run for the state legislature, and my mother, Ann Richards, agreed to run her campaign. Sarah had just argued *Roe v. Wade* before the Supreme Court, and although the decision would not be announced for many months, she was already a well-known feminist leader in central Texas. And my mother, after patiently raising four kids, was ready to jump into the political fray.

With Mom as her campaign manager, Sarah's campaign became a family affair. Our dining room table was cluttered with precinct maps and canvassing plans. Weekends were spent going door to door for Sarah and handing out "Weddington" stickers at PTA gatherings and neighborhood carnivals. In a hard-fought race, Sarah ultimately won, and my mother went to work full time to run her legislative office. It wasn't much later that Mom decided to run for office herself, starting out as County Commissioner in Austin, Texas. Eventually she was elected the first ever pro-choice woman governor of the state. The experience Mom gained from running Sarah's first campaign held her in good stead in her own political career.

What Mom saw in Sarah is precisely what this book reveals—a driven, thoughtful woman committed to making the lives of all women better. The daughter of a Methodist preacher, Sarah has approached life with a kindness and openness, making a point of respecting her opponents, no matter how profound their disagreements. Sarah's generosity comes from the same place as her great conviction. Because for Sarah, this fight for abortion access is about the broader ability of every woman to make her own health care decisions and to have the safest possible medical care.

Texas has produced some memorable women political leaders. These trailblazers include the writer Molly Ivins, Lady Bird Johnson, Congresswoman Barbara Jordan, and Ann Richards. And any list of Texas women who changed history includes Sarah Weddington. Sarah didn't just spend her 20s fighting for women to have access to safe, legal abortions. She's spent her entire career making sure women can make their own health care decisions.

As a newly graduated lawyer, Sarah was asked by a group of university graduate students to advise them on helping young women access information about contraception and abortion. This community work was eye-opening—Sarah realized just how pervasive illegal abortions were in Texas, and just how many women across the state were ending pregnancies in unsafe conditions, risking their lives. Sarah's work with this group would inspire her to pursue *Roe v. Wade*, and she would go on to change women's lives in America forever, by winning the Supreme Court case that promises a future of legal and safe abortion.

There are still doctors who can recount their early medical days when in emergency rooms, women routinely died as a result of self-abortions and illegal abortions. But the memories of the women and men, doctors, religious leaders and activists who led the fight for legal abortion have too often been lost to history. For those who can remember those days, it is unthinkable that we would revisit a right established decades ago. And yet the political battles over the right of a woman to make her own decisions about pregnancy are as intense as ever before.

Since *Roe* was decided, rather than attack the right to abortion head-on, political activists who oppose women's rights have used tactics to make abortion much harder to access, passing hundreds of laws that put enormous burdens on women, doctors, and their families. Many laws are based upon a fundamental premise that a woman is incapable of responsibly making her own decisions. As a result, twenty-four-hour waiting periods, biased counseling laws, forced ultrasounds and mandatory medical scrips are becoming common in some states. For medical providers, the restrictions passed by state legislatures are intended to make abortion financially impossible to provide, with burdensome regulations on facilities and licensing, and detailed requirements that interfere with the doctor/patient relationship. Harassment of patients and doctors is common, with full-time paid picketers outside medical offices. Tragically, the murder of Dr. George Tiller in Kansas in 2009, and others before him, are constant reminders of the danger faced by medical professionals and by women every day who are seeking reproductive care.

Uniquely, women's reproductive care continues to be an obsession for some politicians. Each year brings a new political angle for those seeking to end legal abortion, with the "person-hood" movement being the most recent wave. This movement, which has petitioned for ballot measures from Colorado to Montana to Mississippi, seeks to have a fertilized egg gain equal rights with a person—threatening not only legal abortion but also in vitro fertilization, birth control, and cancer treatment for pregnant women.

The fight for birth control coverage by insurance plans has become a major national debate in presidential and local politics. And despite its legality, far too many women lack basic access to health care in the United States, including birth control and abortion. The US continues to lead the industrialized nations by a significant margin in the numbers of unintended and teen pregnancies as well as abortions.

Yet despite the toxic political environment, medical advances in women's health give us hope for the future. Mifepristone, or medical abortion, has been a major advance in giving women access to safe, early abortion without surgery. In the past fifteen years, Planned Parenthood has been on the forefront of introducing this important medical option for women in America. And in the area of birth control, we've come a long way since the pill came on the scene more than fifty years ago. Now women have many more ways of preventing unintended pregnancy, and we are seeking positive results. Emergency contraception, or the morning-after pill, is now available without a prescription, and is used safely and reliably by millions of women to prevent unintended pregnancy.

Sarah has been on the front lines with women for the last forty years. Her lifelong commitment to the advancement of women is inspiring not only to those of us who have had the good fortune to work alongside her, but to the next generation of young women and men who will lead this movement. There are reasons to be hopeful. Technological advances have improved women's health care options. They have also provided all kinds of new organizing tools that were unthinkable when Sarah began. Through the use of social media, young women and men can share their stories and can mobilize in a matter of moments. Recently when the Virginia legislature passed a bill requiring vaginal untrasounds, within hours women and men had physically surrounded the statehouse and captured the national news. When the US House of Representatives held a hearing to confirm that women didn't need insurance coverage for birth control, and only called men to testify, the photo exploded on social media and eventually the bill was defeated. The next generation of young women and men, armed with the ability to organize and activate in real time, hold promise that a small minority that opposes legal abortion, women's rights, and access to birth control will be unsuccessful over time.

Ever since arguing *Roe v. Wade*, Sarah has carried this movement forward. She understands this issue so well—and she never gives up. Sarah's passion is a source of great inspiration and a stalwart driver in the work we do every day at Planned Parenthood. Our nation is healthier, and generations of women are too, because of Sarah.

Cecile Richards
President of Planned Parenthood
Federation of America and Planned
Parenthood Action Fund

1. Beginnings

Three scenes summarize my life. Picture those the public knows: First, a triumphant young woman, five years out of law school, celebrating the victory of a Supreme Court case she has won, *Roe v. Wade*, which overturns the Texas anti-abortion statutes and makes abortion legal throughout the United States. Second, a worried mature woman, four decades later, writing and speaking with every ounce of energy to prevent what she hoped and believed American women would never again know: the horrors of a time when abortion was illegal.

This book tells the story of those scenes and of the years that surround them. It is the story of *Roe v. Wade*, which has been called one of the most significant Supreme Court cases of this century. It was won by the cumulative efforts of many, but the spearhead of the effort that legalized abortion in the nation began in Austin, Texas. The final outcome of the story of legal abortion in America will be written in the future, perhaps by one who has read this book.

But there is also a third scene for me, one I have in common with millions of women: a scared graduate student in 1967 who traveled to a dirty, dusty Mexican border town to have an abortion, fleeing the law that made abortion illegal in Texas.

MY MOUTH GOES DRY as I put myself back in those days in Austin when my period was late. I was in my third year of law school, going to school full-time and supporting myself by working several jobs. I was seriously dating Ron Weddington, who was finishing his undergraduate degree after returning from the army; he was planning to start law school the following summer. I had been celibate until our relationship progressed to the point that we were talking about getting married.

Each day I kept hurrying to the women's lounge in the law school between classes, hoping to find that something had happened; each day I was disappointed. I had to fight to maintain my routine, to work on my class assignments and to complete the demands of my jobs. I had to fight to keep my mind from being incapacitated by the questions that haunted me: What if I were pregnant? What would I do if I were? I had law school to finish and couldn't do that unless I was working. My parents were supporting two other children in college on a minimal income. I was not emotionally ready to commit to marriage. Even if we married, Ron had years of schooling ahead and I needed to work and shoulder our support. My parents would be disappointed in me. What would people who knew me think?

The only person who knew my dilemma was Ron. There were many reasons we were together. We had similar backgrounds; each of us spent our early years in Abilene, a flat, dry Texas town, and longed to be part of a wider world and experience more than the usual events in West Texas. I had led a very "proper" life, but Ron had seen more of the world. I enjoyed talking to him about my studies, his travels and military service, and politics. I loved his sense of humor and his eagerness to explore the world. It also pleased me that he was taller and smarter than I and that we had both been student leaders in high school. He had few stereotyped notions about appropriate roles for women; he did not think it at all strange that I, a woman, would want a career in law.

Ron went through those anxious days with me. He had already made it clear that he did not want children. I had no strong feelings either way and had told him that if we got married, whatever he wanted was fine with me. We began to go over the possibilities. Abortion was one, but we were worried about the risks of an illegal procedure. Ron said that he would help me, whatever I decided to do, and that the final decision was mine to make.

When I was in high school in Vernon, near Wichita Falls, Texas, and the Oklahoma border, I remembered there was a clinic near downtown where a doctor performed illegal abortions. The more adventurous teenagers would drive by late at night to check the license plates of cars in the area; they were from Oklahoma, Arkansas, and other nearby states. I remembered news stories from 1962 about Sherri Finkbine, a television personality and young mother of four in Scottsdale, Arizona, who had taken thalidomide while she was pregnant. When it was announced that the drug could cause mutations of the fetus— it might be born without arms or legs, for instance—she defied an Arizona court by traveling to Sweden to abort her severely deformed fetus. I thought what she had to go through was awful. Ron had heard stories of women who had had abortions, but abortion was something I had never talked about with friends or family.

If we decided on abortion, the next problem was: Where to go? There were no ads in phone books or newspapers; this was all undercover. You had to find someone who knew a name, a place—and I refused to tell anyone my situation. Fortunately, Ron was not as humiliated about this as I. He offered to make some calls and talk to a few acquaintances.

I made an appointment with a gynecologist under a false name; by the time I learned the test was positive, I knew I wanted an abortion. Ron had a friend who knew about a doctor in Piedras Negras, a Mexican town across from the border town of Eagle Pass, Texas; from its center to that of Piedras Negras was 2.6 miles. The doctor had some medical experience in the United States, spoke excellent English, and performed abortions. Abortion was illegal in Mexico, but the woman Ron spoke to told him abortions were done in many places; she assumed the doctors paid off the police to keep things quiet. She said several women she knew had been to this doctor, and that everything had turned out fine. He charged $400—cash only. My entire savings got us nearly there, and Ron made up the rest. He called for an appointment, made the necessary arrangements, and planned a weekend away. He obtained a powerful painkiller from his best friend who was a doctor's son, and the name of someone who might help if I ended up in medical trouble.

We left Austin early on a Friday morning, drove to Eagle Pass, checked into a motel, and went across the border to the meeting place. I was scared of the unknown, but mercifully I had been spared the horror stories I was later to hear from many women. In my mind's eye, I can still see Ron and me following a man in brown pants and a white guayabera shirt down dirt alleys to a small white building, two young Americans trying unsuccessfully to blend into the background.

I was grateful that the inside of the building was clean. I could not read what appeared to be a medical diploma on the wall, but it made me feel better. Besides the staff, we were the only ones there. Soon a nurse motioned for me to come through a door. Ron squeezed my hand, and I was on my way to put my life, my future, in the hands of strangers.

I was one of the lucky ones. The doctor was pleasant and seemed competent; this made me feel more at ease about being there. He explained the D&C (dilation and curettage) procedure, then motioned to the nurse and anesthesiologist to begin. I did exactly as I was told; when I felt the anesthesia taking effect, my last thoughts were: I hope I don't die, and I pray that no one ever finds out about this.

My first memory afterward is of waking up in our motel room with Ron by my side. It was the one time he had to play nurse for me. He told me that the doctor had reported to him after my surgery that everything had gone smoothly; I had walked out of the clinic and we had driven back across the border without incident. I was woozy but felt no more than the cramps the doctor had told me to expect. Ron checked; I didn't have a fever. I was filled with gratitude for that doctor and his assistants. Ron and I returned to Austin and plunged back into our usual routines. But the memories have always remained and been sharp and clear.

NOW I KNOW THERE were countless others living out their own private scenes when abortion was illegal. Some of them were not as lucky as I; they ended up in awful places, operated on by people who had no medical skills. Before abortion became legal in California in 1967, the county hospital in Los Angeles had a ward called the IOB (infected obstetrics) ward. It had about sixty beds for women suffering the results of botched abortions, and sometimes abortions they had performed themselves. Doctor and nurses who worked at public hospitals in the days when abortion was illegal remember women who died in their arms. Once, after I gave a speech in Dallas, a nurse told me about her best friend, who bled to death after her womb was perforated during an abortion. Another told me about a licensed vocational nurse who had five children and could not face having another one, who died from an infection resulting from an illegal abortion. From mid-1970 through 1972, nearly 350,000 women left their own states to obtain legal abortions in New York, one of the few states where abortion was then legal and available to nonresidents.

Increasing numbers of women have come up to tell me their own stories or those of people they love. I remember one woman who had learned of her mother's abortion; afraid that *Roe* would not survive the political onslaught of the 1990s, her mother had wanted her to know how terrible it would be if we ever went back to the days when abortion was illegal. Another woman told me about her grandmother, the sole support of five children, who self-induced an abortion when she found herself pregnant soon after her husband had deserted the family.

For me and the countless women who put their lives at risk to control their own destinies, the world changed in 1973 when *Roe v. Wade* became the law of the land. I hear it every day as I travel and speak. After a speech to doctors' spouses in Chicago, a woman in the audience told me of desperately wanting a child, of getting pregnant and then discovering the fetus was fatally deformed. She wanted me to know how much she appreciated the fact that she had been able to have a legal abortion so that she and her husband could begin again. In Jacksonville, Florida, a woman proudly showed me that she was pregnant. She said she had considered an abortion but had decided against it; she felt good about her choice and the fact that it was her decision to make. College students have told me how lucky they feel to be maturing at a time when abortion is legal. *Roe v. Wade* made the country a better place for women.

But I am getting ahead of myself. Let's return to the beginning of the story, to where and when *Roe v. Wade* began: Austin, Texas, in the 1960s.

2. Yearning for More Choices for Women

I ndira Gandhi is reported to have said, "I have felt like a bird born in too small a cage." That is just how many of us women born in the 1940s felt in the 1960s. We were born and grew up at a time when social and legal restrictions forced women into narrower roles than we longed to occupy. We were told "Women don't," "You can't," "That would be too strenuous for you."

Texans have always been an independent breed, and in the sixties and seventies many women in Texas began to reveal their own streak of independence. Ours is a state now known as one where "men are men, and women are elected officials." When I travel, people ask me how Texas has produced such strong women as Governor Ann Richards, former Congresswoman Barbara Jordan, press secretary Liz Carpenter who served former First Lady Lady Bird Johnson, writer Molly Ivins, State Senator Wendy Davis and President of the Planned Parenthood Federation of America, (referred to as Planned Parenthood throughout this book) Cecile Richards. I tell them that Texas is a place where the basis for acceptance is never who your parents are or where you come from. Instead what is important is a frontier ethic of individual worth and accomplishment. Women demonstrating those qualities are accepted. I sometimes use Molly Ivins' line that the chauvinism in Texas was so powerful that only strong women survived it. It is said we Texas women love riding horses because the only time we felt in control as youngsters was when we rode. Then we were in control of a huge animal of power and grace, and were free to explore the boundless acres spread out beneath the sky. Everywhere else, others sought to control us. When I was young I rode on the plains of West Texas, the land stretching to the far horizon with not another soul in sight. I wondered what lay beyond the world my eyes could see, the world in which I had grown up.

Texas did not become known for its women with can-do attitudes overnight. It took years of struggle and effort. There were many in the 1960s like me who were searching for new identities and who fought to push back the bars of their own personal cages.

My first quest for that wider world was in moving to Austin when I was nineteen. It became home in January 1965, when I arrived with my twelve-year-old brother, John, my 1945 two-tone-green Pontiac piled high with our clothes and household items. John and I had arrived in an oasis of beauty and liberal thought in an otherwise largely dry and dusty conservative state. I've since heard Austin called the "blue dot" in a red state.

We had come to work for the Texas legislature during its spring session. When the session ended, John would return home to the family and school; I was hoping to stay and enter the University of Texas law school.

I was born in Abilene and grew up in various West Texas towns—Wylie, Munday, Canyon, and Vernon, places so small many Texans have never heard of them. My father was a Methodist minister. I was the traditional preacher's daughter: I sang in the church choir, played the church organ and piano, gave Sunday devotionals and was a youth leader in the church community. The praise I got from church members and friends of my parents for those performances helped build in me a solid sense of confidence in my abilities to accomplish whatever I set out to do. However, I was nontraditional in that I did not envision marriage and children as my primary future, as my parents and friends knew.

Years ago I heard the following saying: "To be a leader, you must be comfortable feeling different." As a preacher's kid I always felt different; I was an independent thinker. I was not invited to participate in many of the activities of my peers. When I look back, it seems just as well. I grew up being an officer in the Methodist Youth Fellowship, the drum major (not a majorette) of the Canyon Junior High School Band, and president of the Future Homemakers of America of Canyon High School in my sophomore year.

At McMurry College, now McMurry University, a small Methodist liberal arts school in Abilene, I continued to be a leader. I was active in a social organization, participated in productions of the drama department, and was elected secretary of the student body. I followed a traditional route, graduating with secondary-education teaching credentials for English and speech, but I harbored the dream of going to law school. During my senior year, I went to talk about this with the dean, who told me I should not even think of it. His son was in law school and was finding it very difficult. No woman from McMurry had ever gone to law school. He said it would be too strenuous for me. That was when I decided I *was* going.

I had already begun to chafe under some of the other restrictions I faced growing up in West Texas. While I was growing up, women's basketball teams were composed of ten players, five on each half of the court. The players on one side of the court would work their way, two dribbles at a time, to the center of the court, where they would pass the ball to teammates three inches away, who would head for the goal two dribbles at a time. I could never understand why we could not run full court, or why it was considered travelling, a technical violation, if we failed to pass the ball after two dribbles. When I persisted, I was told that running full court would be too strenuous for women. A high school physical education instructor told us, "Young women must preserve their reproductive capacity; after all, it is their meal ticket." I took a silent vow that I would have a meal ticket other than reproductive capacity.

One day during an education class at McMurry, we were discussing the custom that if a woman teacher became pregnant she would quit, and if she did not she would be fired. My teacher wanted the class to consider whether a pregnant teacher had a moral responsibility to tell the principal as soon as she knew she was pregnant, or whether she could wait until the principal figured it out. I saw no reason why she should have to quit at all.

On another occasion at McMurray I led a small rebellion against school rules that prevented student government from sponsoring dances, even when chaperoned on campus. The administration finally gave in and allowed a "social function" with music; we students gave in and did not call it a "dance."

When I finished my college classes in December 1964, my brother John was wanting a job as a page for the Texas legislature. Our folks would not let him go by himself, so we worked out a deal that I would also apply for a job, and we would live together for the semester. Although his continued schooling was a concern, he—like me—had skipped two grades. Arrangements were made for him to be tutored in Austin.

Even before we unpacked, we drove from our furnished apartment in an unfashionable part of South Austin down Congress Avenue to the state Capitol. A magnificent building of the finest red granite, the Capitol then dominated the downtown skyline. Its dome soars 309 feet and is topped by a golden statue of the Goddess of Liberty. The statue makes the Texas Capitol the tallest in the country; it is even higher than the nation's. Our drive to the Capitol on the day we arrived was the first of many. But we never failed to experience a sense of excitement at its grandeur and its various moods created by the changing weather. As we drove, John and I talked of being explorers who had arrived to see the Texas legislature in action and to test our abilities to survive alone and far from home.

We drove over Town Lake, which meanders twelve blocks south of the Capitol. Today ducks, geese, and swans share its quiet beauty with people rowing, jogging and walking the onshore trails. In the spring the trails are lined with wildflowers and trees in bloom. The natural beauty of Austin was a sharp contrast to our former homes.

John and I passed the Capitol and circled through the university campus, where we would both later study and work. The campus, which begins five blocks north of the Capitol, is known to locals as the "Forty Acres" because it was originally a forty-acre tract donated to the state in 1883. UT was—and is—a research-oriented school with an influential, nationally known faculty, many of whom were educated at leading East and West Coast institutions. They brought new ideas and a sense of excitement and intellectual exploration to the campus and the city. The university soon had a reputation for students with strong beliefs and lusty behavior. It was the scene of protests during the Vietnam War, and environmentally conscious students sat in campus trees to save them when a regent ordered bulldozers to destroy the trees.

Austin's highly educated population, produced not only by UT but by four other schools as well—Concordia (Lutheran), St. Edwards (Catholic), Huston—Tillotson (one of the oldest universities in the state serving primarily black students), and Austin Community College—has helped create a liberal atmosphere. Many graduates choose to accept salaries lower than in other

Texas cities, for example, for the pleasures of living in the capital. Austin is a "live and let live" place, where one can comfortably go almost anywhere in cutoffs or boots.

Austin is the focus of Texas politics. During legislative sessions 150 House members and thirty-one senators descend like locusts upon the city. An old Texas saying has it that no person's life, liberty, or property is safe while the Texas legislature is in session. The state constitution was written to encourage the legislators to meet as little as possible. They do meet, in regular session, for 140 days every other year.

John was a page for the Enrolling and Engrossing Room (E&E), where I was a clerk/typist. We worked in an area dominated by a large room of typists. Because multiple copies of everything (one for the House, one for the Senate, and so on) were needed, and copy machines were not yet standard equipment, typists had to make nine sets of carbon copies of each page of legislation, and were not allowed even one mistake. If a mistake was made, the entire page had to be retyped. It was literally a dirty job, as we handled so many carbons. The typing skills I developed through that rigorous training were later to serve me well.

I alternated between typing and proofing the typed documents. The proofreaders, all women, sat together at a large table. One person would read from the text that had been amended or changed, while several others would read the newly typed version to be sure it was absolutely accurate, down to the last comma. I sometimes wondered why so many proofed the same document, but perhaps it was done in an abundance of caution: even a single word or punctuation change can significantly alter the meaning of legislation.

John and I took advantage of the opportunity of free time to watch the session. On my breaks and whenever my work was caught up, I would signal to my supervisor—I had a standard sign of pointing toward the House floor and mouthing "I'm going out"—and slip out to the balcony of the House of Representatives to observe. I was appalled. Most of the Representatives, all male except for Maude Isaacks, seemed to be paying no attention to the business of the House. They put their boots up on their desks and behaved in what I considered a crude manner. There are, as I had heard tell and was learning firsthand, two things one should never see being made: one is sausage, and the other is law.

THE SESSION ENDED in May, and I began the UT School of Law as a member of the June 1965 entering class. I was worried about being one of about forty women in a school of sixteen hundred students. I had heard horror stories about professors who refused to call on women students—who, they said, would quit practicing law to get married, thus denying an education to men who would stay in the profession—and about the rigors and irrelevant questions women endured in the search for jobs.

I did not know what law school would be like or whether I could do the work. I had never read a case. I did not know how to "think like a lawyer," as the professors kept urging but failed to explain. The Socratic method was foreign to anything I had experienced. Professors using this method do not ask about the cases assigned for reading but instead ask questions *beyond* the reading, demanding that students synthesize conclusions. I worried about whether I was smart enough to survive.

When I became one of five women among 120 men in that summer's entering class, I felt I was breaking new ground as a woman. The few women in law school tended to bond together to study and share information about classes, professors, and other students. Our gathering place was the women's lounge, a large room with couches, comfortable chairs with footstools, and a few desks and straight-backed chairs. We went there between classes to see friends, check our bulletin board (notes taped to mirrors), exchange information, or eat food brought from home. Linda Coffee, a Dallas resident who had graduated from Rice University in Houston and who was smart enough to be invited to join the law review, was one of the women I often studied with.

(When, two years later, the round of job interviews for the graduating class began, I interviewed for months but received no job offers. Since I was graduating in the top quarter of my class and was a hard worker, I believed the reason I could not get a job with a firm was that I was a woman. The women in my class commiserated about our lack of job offers. Additionally, we took umbrage at the fact that firms were paying for male students to fly to various cities for interviews, but they did not offer the same courtesy to female students. Eventually, Mettie L. Brown, the head of the University of Texas School of Law placement office, essentially told the law firms that she wouldn't let them use the law school facilities to interview students unless they provided transportation for both the men and the women invited for follow-up interviews. She and our Dean, W. Page Keeton, are due the credit for opening new opportunities for women. Each was a wonderful person to whom I continue to be grateful.

According to Ms. Brown, I was a "break-through:" the first woman from my law school to have her way paid to an out-of-town interview. The firm was in Dallas, which wasn't far, but the change in law firm policies was tremendous. However, I did not get an offer from that firm either. In fact, the senior partner in charge of the interview asked questions like, "Lawyers often have to work late but women have to be home to cook dinner. How could you do both?" He also told me, "To train a young lawyer we have to be able to cuss him out, but we couldn't cuss at you—you're a woman. How would we ever train you?" Eventually, the firm said that other candidates were better suited to their needs. Law firms by and large were not prepared to hire female lawyers.)

One of my professors saved me. John Sutton, a former FBI agent and attorney in San Angelo, was a man with a quick laugh, an incisive mind, and a willingness to spend extra time to encourage female students. I took as many classes from Sutton as I could. One day during my last semester—miracle of miracles—he offered me a job assisting his work with the American Bar Association's Special Committee on the Reevaluation of Ethical Standards. I jumped at the opportunity. The committee's task was to revise the Canons of Professional Ethics, the document that governed ethical standards for lawyers, into a new document called the Code of Professional Responsibility.

Ron finished his political science degree and started law school in June 1968. We married on August 25 and took a penny-pinching honeymoon, delayed by his summer finals, to Topolobampo, a sleepy Mexican fishing village. It was during those years when Ron was in law school and I was working for Sutton that I became involved in the Austin women's movement and in the effort to overturn the Texas anti-abortion statutes.

THERE ARE MOMENTS in your life—"aha" moments—when, for whatever reason, you suddenly see the same facts in a different light. I had always struggled against conventional wisdom, but none of my West Texas friends seemed to share my discontent. However, in law classes we discussed legal problems unique to women. Women law students wondered how to change the laws, but there was little talk about the overall patterns of discrimination women experienced.

I remember applying for a credit card after I became a lawyer. The man who took my application said it would not be complete without my husband's signature. I tried to explain my situation, that I had always supported myself, was providing more than half of the household income, and I was a lawyer, but the man insisted I needed my husband's consent. I refused to apply under that condition. For me, this type of discrimination or unfairness always got put in the category of "That's the way it is." I secretly resolved to find a way to fix things in the future, but it seemed a big waste of energy to throw a hissy fit over my own experiences.

My energy began to flow, however, when I sat with a consciousness-raising group and saw that many other women were experiencing the same injustices. Judy Smith, whom I had met through Ron's classmate Jim Wheelis, invited me along to one group meeting. Judy and Jim, among all of Ron's friends, had the most significant impact on my future as a lawyer.

Judy was an intense, extremely smart woman who had majored in chemistry at Brandeis and was studying molecular biology for her Ph.D. from the zoology department at UT. She got there in spite of a professor who—although Judy had made one of two A's in his class—refused to write a recommendation for her because, he told her, "I don't believe in giving recommendations to women." She preferred listening instead of talking, and with her formidable presence she was unlike anyone I had ever known. Judy was articulate in her dedication to causes; she was the first self-described feminist I met.

Jim was from Mart, Texas, a town even smaller than the ones I had grown up in. Incredibly bright, he had attended Harvard for a year, did not like it, dropped out, and completed his undergraduate chemistry degree at night school in Alabama while driving a truck and working for a veterinarian. He was always cynically insightful. Ron liked Jim because he was a soulmate in political causes. I liked him because he was a gentle person who always treated me with respect and listened to my opinions. He was well-read and never took himself too seriously. Jim and Judy wrote for Austin's underground counterculture newspaper *The Rag*. Judy was also active in a variety of women's activities, including the consciousness-raising group and an abortion referral project.

Bea Durden was another important participant in the women's meetings. Bea, who had a Ph.D. in biology from Yale, was in Austin with her husband, a science teacher at UT, and their two children. She was president of the Austin spider club and also wrote for *The Rag*, and she had an incredibly diverse storehouse of knowledge. Yet she was not able to find a job.

The consciousness-raising sessions had begun after someone brought to Austin a pre-publication mimeograph of *Our Bodies, Ourselves*, the women's health book. A group of women graduate students gathered to talk about the book, and the conversations went on to cover the general status of women in society. The group expanded to include a variety of women who, each in her own way, were searching for more choices.

Many of the women who participated in the meetings were writers for *The Rag*. At UT in the tumultuous sixties, the paper was a source of knowledge about happenings in the city and around the country. It described when the free health care clinic would be open, what to do if a person was arrested in a protest, where to find the best music in town, and when the next meeting of student and activist organizations would be. *Rag* staffers shared a sense of outrage; they saw the written word as an instrument for change and felt an enormous responsibility to their readers. Every writer could instantly list a multitude of societal changes that should be made.

In 1968 the UT Board of Regents banned *The Rag* from being sold on campus. The paper's staff considered this a violation of the First Amendment's guarantee of freedom of the press. They contacted David Richards, a local attorney interested in civil rights issues who was then married to Ann Richards who would be elected governor of Texas in 1990. Richards agreed to represent them, and Jim Wheelis and Ron were among those who sued the university. Jim sued as a writer who wanted to communicate with other students; Ron, who was not a *Rag* writer, as a student who wanted to read *The Rag*. The case, *New Left Education Project v. The Board of Trustees of the University of Texas*, went on to the US Supreme Court on procedural issues. David had previously won at the three-judge federal court level; he won again, and the university capitulated. The victory was interpreted by Austin activists to mean that the federal court system was a possible route for achieving justice.

Later that year women became involved in *Rag* editorial decisions. Their influence was immediately evident. Birth control information and devices were hard to come by at the time, but articles in *The Rag* told about the safest forms of birth control and how to obtain them. The paper became in effect a health class for many women.

Many of the discussions from the consciousness-raising meetings, which also frequently focused on contraception and abortion, found their way into *The Rag*. At meetings women talked of the need for more and safer contraceptives and for greater access. They talked about how they could not truly determine their own destinies in terms of education, employment, and physical and psychological health until they could control the number and spacing of their children. When contraceptives failed, one way of avoiding pregnancy was abortion. Yet Texas law made abortion illegal except to save the life of the woman. Others talked about the fact that women with money could go to states such as California for safe, legal abortions, but women who were poorer, younger, or less sophisticated often did not make it to those places and instead ended up in Mexico or in back alleys. Stories of abortion mills and self-induced abortions were uncomfortably common. Members of the consciousness-raising group wanted to find a way to keep women from the awful illegal places in Texas, Mexico, or wherever they were.

The first move for *The Rag* was to print public service articles about safe and unsafe abortion methods. One article listed three methods as safe when performed by a competent physician: dilation and curettage with anesthesia, vacuum aspiration, and hysterectomy. The message went on to warn against various other methods that involved excruciating pain and could lead to permanent disability, infection, or death. Often women would drink ergot, a poison, or take quinine sulphate. Neither achieved abortion; ergot could cause fatal kidney damage, and quinine sulphate could result in deformities in the fetus or death to the woman. Taking estrogen or castor oil, as some did, had no result.

The articles further cautioned women about the dangers of inserting solids or fluids into the uterus, including objects such as knitting needles, artists' paintbrushes, telephone wire, packing gauze, catheters, curtain rods, ballpoint pens, chopsticks, slippery elm bark, and coat hangers. These could pierce the womb and bladder, and often cause death from an infection or hemorrhage. Soapsuds, alcohol, potassium permanganate, lye, Lysol, pine oil, and other substances inserted into the uterus could cause severe burning of tissues, shock, hemorrhaging, and death.

Some women believed that air pumped into the uterus would cause abortion. However, *The Rag* articles warned, the result could instead be the introduction of gas emboli into the bloodstream, collapse of the uterus, and sudden, violent death. Similarly the paper warned against using a vacuum cleaner, which was *not* the same as vacuum aspiration, a safe procedure when performed by a physician; using a vacuum cleaner could extract the uterus from the pelvic cavity and was fatal almost immediately.

The Rag advised that physical exertion, such as lifting heavy objects and running, was useless; that throwing oneself down stairs often resulted in severe injury to the woman, but no abortion; and that only doctors or other specially trained personnel could safely practice methods of safe abortion. All other methods, it emphasized, could cause severe physical trauma or death.

Having already taken steps to educate women about harmful

procedures, Judy, Bea, and others organized a referral project to inform women about their bodies, about their rights, about available birth control, and about safe abortion. Before the referral project was set up, each of the participants had informally fielded calls from women seeking abortions. Judy, for example, had received calls in the middle of the night from young women saying they had been given her name and needed help. Judy would roll out of bed, get her notes, and start talking about the possibilities, but after hanging up she continued to worry about the women behind the desperate voices. If they could find no other alternative, she knew, some of them might take something like ergot. Judy wanted to find the names of clinics where women could be referred—places with safe, responsible doctors.

First, she and Vic Foe, another biology graduate student, found some safe, clean, nondegrading clinics in Mexico, where enforcement of the law against abortion was very lax. The standards were high, not just regarding sanitary conditions, but also in the attitudes of physicians and staff members toward patients. Once Judy and Vic located places that met their criteria, they began referring women who called them. Others volunteered to share the load of answering phones and giving advice. As their efforts expanded, more women were calling, and the volunteers gradually had more information to share. What began as individual efforts evolved to become an organized abortion referral project.

Women at the project, with some cooperating men, volunteered to help their sisters, even at personal risk. The first priority, unanimously agreed to, was to encourage women to avoid unwanted pregnancy. The volunteers at the project considered access to birth control and preventative measures just as important as information about obtaining a safe abortion. They also taught about sexually transmitted diseases and how to avoid them. But among their principles was the belief that every woman, whatever her income level, whatever her color or background, who wanted to terminate a pregnancy should have access to the safest services possible. The referral project had been set up to serve only women connected with UT, but word of its existence quickly spread throughout the Austin area.

After great debate over the pros and cons of doing so, the group placed its first ad for the Women's Liberation Birth Control Information Center in *The Rag* in October 1969. If a woman was pregnant or thought she was, or just did not know, she could call a hotline during certain hours and get a volunteer counselor's home phone number. Bea, whose number was often the one furnished, received numerous calls at home. Since she was afraid her phone was tapped, she would ask for the caller's number, go to a nearby pay phone, and return the call. Was she acting a little paranoid? In those days, as the saying went, you weren't paranoid if they were after you.

This ad, and those that followed, did not mention "abortion referral," because of the possibility of legal entanglements. The ads continued to warn against dangerous methods of abortion and sometimes cautioned women about lists of doctors' names in circulation that were "often obsolete or bootlegged" and led only to "quacks or the authorities [the police]."

Because the Texas law against abortion "unless necessary" to save the woman's life had never been definitively interpreted, a few Texas doctors were willing to perform abortions if they thought they might be saving a woman's mental life. Judy found such a doctor in San Antonio, and he gave the Information Center forms that read: "_____ (name of patient) needs an abortion for mental reasons." If a doctor or minister would sign the form, he felt he could win the case if prosecuted.

But sometimes the trip to San Antonio ended in disappointment. One young Austin woman, for example, was the sole support of her parents and her eleven brothers and sisters, when she discovered she was pregnant. If she continued the pregnancy she would lose her job, and the family would lose her income. She wanted an abortion. She called Judy late one night, and the call started in the usual way: "I was given your name, and they said you would help me." The young woman had little money. Judy and Jim, hoping the doctor in San Antonio would consider this case justifiable, drove the young woman there. When they arrived at the clinic, however, the doctor refused to do the abortion, for reasons they never understood. The young woman felt her world crashing down. After they returned to Austin, Judy never heard from her again. Jim remembers her sobbing. "It was just a screaming pain."

I never volunteered in the Information Center, which we called "the referral project" when talking to each other, but I did do legal research to answer questions for consciousness-raising groups and for the referral project. I looked up Texas laws on a variety of subjects, including abortion. As time went on, I answered other questions. When there were requests from groups for speakers on the legal aspects of current women's issues, including abortion, I was one of the two who helped out. The other was a law student, Bobby Nelson.

THE MOST IMPORTANT THING to remember—and today it is perhaps hard to—is that abortions were illegal in Texas. Doctors could be prosecuted for performing abortions and the volunteers at the referral project didn't know whether they could get into legal trouble by referring women for safe abortions. It was encouraging to hear that some ministers and rabbis were also providing problem-pregnancy counseling services. I was delighted that among them were Methodist ministers; one of them, Robert Cooper, was a friend of my father's. Cooper and Claude Evans were in Dallas, Bob Breihan in Austin. We thought the clergy would be less likely to be prosecuted than people working out of the referral project who also wrote for *The Rag*, so Judy approached Breihan and asked if he and those working with him would be willing to cooperate and share information with the referral project. He said yes.

Breihan had first heard about the Clergy Consultation Service on Abortion when he attended a National Association of Ministers conference in Michigan in November 1968. The Service was a national network of clergy who, "because of a common concern for humane and compassionate counseling for women with problem pregnancies," were committed to sharing information and having a standard of procedure for abortion referral. The Reverend Howard Moody, of the Judson Memorial Church in New York City, and twenty-one other Protestant ministers and Jewish rabbis had started the effort on March 7, 1967, to educate and inform the public so that a more liberal abortion law in New York and throughout the nation might be enacted.

The Clergy Consultation ministers agreed:

> A belief in the "sanctity of life" certainly includes helpfulness and sympathy to the woman forced by the present law into criminality. We are mindful that there are doctors who in their wisdom perform therapeutic abortions outside the present legal restrictions. When a physician performs such an operation, motivated by compassion and concern for the patient and not simply for monetary gain, we do not regard him as a criminal but living by the highest standard of the Hippocratic oath. . . . Therefore, to that end we are establishing a Problem Pregnancy Consultation service, including referral to the best available medical advice and aid to women in need.

The Clergy Consultation Service adhered to a strict code. Anti-abortion laws, the participants maintained, forced women to experience mental anguish, physical suffering, and even unnecessary death. Women were being driven into a criminal underworld or into the dangerous practice of self-induced abortion.

Evans and Cooper had attended the Michigan meeting with Breihan. An event a few months earlier had turned Evans into a proponent of abortion reform. A pregnant student named Mary had come to his office at Southern Methodist University asking for funds for an abortion. She said she was going to a "nurse in the community." Evans explained that abortion was illegal, that it would put her life in danger, and suggested that she talk the situation over with her parents. Mary had legitimate reasons why she could not talk to her family. Finally, against his better judgment, Evans said he would loan her the money, but only if she promised to call him if her temperature rose or she had any other negative symptoms afterward. She promised, and a couple of days later the phone rang. It was Mary's roommate. "Mary has a temperature of a hundred and four. What should we do?" Evans says he almost passed out. He knew that physicians were allowed to aid a woman after abortion, so he instructed Mary's roommate to take her to the hospital. The doctors dripped antibiotics into her. Within twenty-four hours she was out of danger; forty-eight hours later she was out of the hospital.

Evans realized that some women caught in problem pregnancies would risk anything—life, limb, parents, families, *anything*—to get an abortion. The only thing he could do was help women who came to him live through it in the most healthy way. After a pastor or rabbi cooperating with the Clergy Consultation Service counseled a pregnant woman, if the decision was to terminate the pregnancy, the clergyman would recommend places she might go to for either a safe legal abortion or a safe illegal one. The most important goal was to preserve the woman's health. Members of the Service at various times sent women to California, Puerto Rico, Mexico, and even as far as Japan. As abortion became legal in Hawaii, New York and other states around 1970, the list of possible places expanded.

The Austin chapter of Clergy Consultation and the volunteers at the referral project worked out a cooperative agreement so that through their combined efforts more women could be served and more clinics inspected. Women having abortions were given very specific instructions. They were told where to park their cars, where the building was and what it would look like, where the office was and what the doctor should look like.

Clergy Consultation had a system of quality control similar to the one Judy had set up. Evans and Cooper toured the clinics they recommended and kept files on each of the doctors. One of the many problems of referring women to clinics in Mexico was that people who were not doctors, but who wanted to get in on the money to be made from performing abortions for US women would set up clinics without the medical knowledge to run them. Clergy Consultation and the referral project were determined to keep women out of the hands of such quacks. Passwords and code words were used to ensure that the women were treated only by the prearranged doctors.

The ministers made follow-up a priority; they were concerned about the immediate health of the women and about continuing to counsel them if they so desired or needed. They knew the only way to guarantee quality and safety was by hearing from the women who had had abortions. Breihan attended referral project meetings to share quality assessment responses. The referral project did not keep statistics, but the Texas chapter of Clergy Consultation did. It referred about 6,000 pregnant women before 1973. The most unexpected finding was that the women who sought counseling were evenly distributed among religions and that their religious affiliation matched their presence in the community. If twenty percent of a community's population was Catholic, then twenty percent of the women seen by

Clergy Consultation were Catholic. If twenty percent of a community's population was Methodist, then twenty percent of the women seen were Methodist. Naturally, the ministers involved concluded that religious belief was not a factor in determining which women sought referral services.

A friend of mine, Claudia Middleton, was an American Airlines flight attendant based in Dallas. When she started flying, Claudia wondered why so many women were on Friday-morning flights to El Paso. An older attendant clued her in: those were the "abortion flights." Up to twenty women at a time were headed to El Paso to cross the border for an abortion.

In the 1960s many women were seeking to expand their boundaries, to be allowed to make choices in their own lives, and to meet the challenges that men had traditionally met in career and life patterns. Women sat in small groups across the country and talked about their role and status and about changing customs and laws they felt were unjust. In Texas, a group of volunteers, primarily women and male ministers, said their state abortion law was wrong. People could sense the intermittent possibility of dramatic changes. We thought it was just a matter of time.

3. *The Roots of* Roe v Wade

Roe v. Wade started at a garage sale, amid paltry castoffs. Raising money for the causes I was involved in took ingenuity and constant effort. Our groups solicited contributions large and small, often passed a collection plate, and sponsored everything from garage sales to bake sales. Looking back, I find it strange that members of a women's liberation consciousness-raising group were raising money via the traditional female methods of baking and garage sales, but the sales brought in much-needed money, so we did what we had to do.

Items for sale were displayed on the concrete driveway and in the garage of the half of the small stone house turned duplex that Ron and I had rented in September 1969. The place was old and well-worn, typical of inexpensive student housing, and it quickly became the staging point for a variety of activities. We were the only ones in our circle of acquaintances who had a garage, and I was an organizer. Donated items were stored in the garage, and I would gather volunteers to price, display, and sell them.

One bright fall Saturday, the kind of day that compels cheer and energy, Judy Smith and Bea Durden had signed up for the earliest two-hour work shift, and we were working in an easy rhythm, setting up and then handling sales as customers came and went. We must have seemed a strange trio: Judy, at five-eleven, larger than I, with long hair and no makeup; Bea, the shortest of us, with a bowl haircut and rough sandals; and me in my tailored pantsuit and hair in a ponytail. We may have been different in appearance, mannerisms, and life-style, but what we shared was a dedication to the protection of women and a goal of righting the wrongs we perceived.

As we worked, a more talkative Judy replaced her usually silent self. She had a lot on her mind. The referral project volunteers were worried about being involved in covert activity. They sometimes had a premonition that the police might burst in and close them down. The trips to illegal clinics, the use of code words, and the feeling that law enforcement authorities knew what they were doing added intrigue to their operation. They knew abortion in Texas was illegal; they were not sure whether their own activities were legal or illegal, or what penalties they were risking.

Their concern was easy to understand. Many volunteers had clashed with local authorities before, and they thought the police would happily use any excuse to cause them misery. An incident earlier in 1969 made them more nervous. A favorite UT professor had been fired because, rumor had it, he uttered the word "revolution" in class. When people gathered to protest the firing, the university regents closed the Chuck Wagon snack bar in the Student Union to anyone not carrying a student identification card. They wanted to keep Austin activists and protest organizers who were not students out of their usual gathering place at the Union. Instead the action riled students and activists, and the next day three hundred of them showed up for dinner without IDs. They took over the Chuck Wagon for several hours and sat singing peacefully. By the time the Texas Department of Public Safety arrived, all but one of the students had departed. Yet within a week twenty-one people had been rounded up and charged with instigating a riot. They became known as the "Chuck Wagon 21," and the incident was added to a list that made each side more suspicious of the other.

Other Union protesters had been arrested and jailed, at least briefly, in connection with antiwar protests. *Rag* staffers and members of other groups thought they were under surveillance. Barbara Hines, a participant at the referral project, was one of several who petitioned under the Freedom of Information Act years later and obtained edited copies of their FBI records. Barbara's read in part: *"Security Informants:* Barbara Hines has been involved with Women's Liberation and interested in Women's Abortion Action Coalition. She has a knowledge of the medical and physiological aspects of abortion. . . . Source stated that Women's Liberation is basically opposed to male chauvinism to the point of eliminating the wearing of brassieres and clean attire in order not to be a sex symbol. The group also favors abortions."

Referral volunteers were not sure they could get away with breaking the law if their activities were in fact illegal. Additionally, word of the referral project had spread, and the number of women seeking its services had grown so rapidly some volunteers were beginning to burn out. And because of the legal uncertainties, the project was finding it difficult to recruit new people to share the load. There were plenty of sympathetic individuals. But they were not willing to put themselves on the line.

Bea was more worried that the project was *not* reaching women with unwanted pregnancies. She fretted that because of the referral project's timidity in announcing its existence, many women were still ending up in unsafe places and then in emergency rooms—even though information and help were available in the heart of Austin. Yet advertising the availability of abortion information was incompatible with the strategy of avoiding conflict with the law by being circumspect and not inviting attention. To serve more women, the project needed to be more public;

yet some volunteers worried about the personal ramifications of changing the way they operated. They wondered whether the authorities would continue to leave them alone if they moved into the spotlight.

The frustration level rose as the volunteers counseled more and more women, learning their life situations and witnessing the roadblocks women had to overcome in their search for safe legal abortions. The Texas anti-abortion statute was obviously the culprit in the dramas of human struggle played out daily before the volunteers.

While we sorted our prized junk at the garage sale, Judy posed the primary questions that the volunteers wanted answered: Could they be prosecuted and/or convicted as accomplices to the crime of abortion simply for referring women? Would it make any legal difference if they sent women only to places where abortion was legal? Abortions in Texas or Mexico, although illegal, were often cheaper, especially because of lower travel costs. As a practical matter, there were both "good" and "bad" illegal places. What if volunteers referred women to the "good" illegal places?

I didn't know the answers. Abortion had never been a topic in any of my law classes, and I had not been involved in any criminal cases since becoming licensed as a lawyer. Earlier, when I had looked up the Texas law on abortion for the referral project, I had not researched the subject of referring women for abortion. The statute made it a crime to "furnish the means for procuring an abortion," but I didn't know whether that applied only to drugs and instruments, or information as well. I knew Texas also had a general accomplice statute that applied to a variety of crimes.

I told Judy and Bea I would be glad to do research. I wanted to help the project continue and succeed, so l began spending more time in the UT law library, meeting with project volunteers, and talking to law professors, law students, and other lawyers.

THE TEXAS ANTI-ABORTION STATUTE was passed originally in 1854. The primary provision made it illegal for a person to perform an abortion or to give a woman something to cause her to abort. The penalty was two to five years in prison; if the woman had not consented, however, the penalty was doubled.

Other provisions said that anyone who "furnished the means for procuring an abortion" was guilty as an accomplice; that the fine for attempting to perform an abortion—even if it failed—was $100 to $1,000; and that if a woman died because of an abortion or attempted abortion, her death was murder. It was legal to perform an abortion only if it was "procured or attempted by medical advice for the purpose of saving the life" of the woman.

No one knew exactly when the exception applied. If a woman said she would kill herself unless an abortion were done, would the abortion then be legal? Did it apply when her life would be shortened by continuing the pregnancy, or only when she would surely die in a very short time without one? Doctors did not want to risk a prison sentence or sacrifice their medical licenses to test the interpretation of the statute. As a result, in order to avoid the possibility of prosecution, almost no doctor would do an abortion, under any circumstances.

First I read cases decided under the Texas anti-abortion statute. But since there had been few cases prosecuting doctors and I could not find any that dealt with the referral issue, I still had no clear answer for the project volunteers. I expanded my research to the laws in other states, the general issue of abortion, and federal cases that might be relevant.

I found that there were three general types of abortion laws in the United States. Texas law was an example of the "restrictive" law, under which abortion was illegal in almost every situation. Then there were the "liberalized" laws. These laws were not really liberal; they were simply more liberal than the restrictive laws. In Colorado, Florida, Georgia, and Maryland, among other states, abortion was allowed in cases of rape, incest, or fetal deformity, or to save the life or health of the woman. Generally there were procedural requirements that had to be met, such as obtaining approval from a hospital committee of doctors. Even among states that had the same liberalized abortion law, enforcement could be very different: abortions might be fairly easily available in one and impossible in another. Finally, there were laws like those in California and New York, which as implemented, essentially allowed abortion as a legal alternative. If a woman were lucky enough to live in those states or had the money to travel to them, she could obtain a safe, legal abortion.

Reading about the history of abortion laws in the United States was my next project. I learned there were no laws against abortion for years after people came to America and established a nation. Under common law in England, our legal heritage, abortion was not a crime until "quickening," when a woman first felt fetal movement; abortion after that seems to have been a misdemeanor, or minor crime. When the first abortion had been induced was shrouded in the mists of history; women, it seemed, had always sought to limit fertility.

State laws against abortion were first passed in the United States in about 1828, twenty-six years before the Texas law. There was no evidence that they were passed to protect the fetus or maintain a principle about "when life begins." The laws were intended, simply, to protect women. Surgery was dangerous then because of the risk of infection; doctors did not know how to achieve antiseptic surgery. It was far more dangerous for a woman to have an abortion than to carry the pregnancy to term. Also, in the mid-1800s the medical profession was organizing itself and wanted to put out of business the midwives and homeopathic physicians who often did abortions. By 1900 every state had enacted a strong anti-abortion statute. But instead of ending, abortion went underground. (Years later, in 1970, the

Nixon Report on Crime listed illegal abortions as the third highest money-maker for organized crime.)

At the end of the day Ron and I would talk about what I was learning. I must have sounded like a broken record to him, because my focus was narrowed so tightly on the law pertaining to abortion. It helped me to talk with him and others about how to fit the isolated pieces I was finding into an overall pattern and which avenues of research I should pursue next. Sometimes I felt as if I were making *no* progress; every point I looked up seemed to lead not to an answer, but to another long page of more points I *needed* to look up.

People who knew of my research stopped by my office in the law school to check on my results. The office was in an out-of-the-way part of the school called "Boys' Town," where the young professors (then all male) had offices. I never got around to putting up pictures or decorating, so the place had no character—which seemed to fit the utilitarian nature of that back wing. But my office had everything I needed: a huge, old wooden desk with a large wooden table behind it, a built-in bookshelf, a filing cabinet, a telephone, and a typewriter. I could spread out my materials and type up my notes.

Soon I was finding US Supreme Court decisions supporting a position that there were certain personal decisions the government had no business making. I ran to find Ron after I read *Griswold v. Connecticut,* a 1965 Supreme Court case involving a challenge to the Connecticut law that made the use of birth control ("any drug or article to prevent conception") a criminal offense. The penalty was a fine of at least $50 or imprisonment from sixty days to a year, or both. I can hear myself now: "Can you *believe* that birth control was actually *illegal?*" Estelle Griswold, executive director of the Planned Parenthood League of Connecticut, and Dr. Lee Buxton, a prominent New Haven physician and Planned Parenthood's medical director, were arrested after giving contraceptives to a married couple. The state pressed criminal charges, and the two were convicted as accessories to the crime of using birth control. Each was fined $100; they appealed and won in the Supreme Court. The state law was declared unconstitutional.

In the majority opinion, Justice William O. Douglas wrote:

> We deal with a right of privacy older than the Bill of Rights— older than our political parties, older than our school system. Marriage is a coming together for better or for worse, hopefully enduring, and intimate to the degree of being sacred. It is an association that promotes a way of life, not causes; a harmony in living, not political faiths; a bilateral loyalty, not commercial or social projects. Yet it is an association for as noble a purpose as any involved in our prior decisions.

That opinion also made reference to prior opinions that built our country's legal tradition of privacy—aspects of family life in which, the Court had said, the government could not meddle. A concurring opinion written by Justice Arthur Goldberg, joined by Chief Justice Earl Warren and Justice William Brennan, cited former justice Louis Brandeis's analysis of the principles underlying the Constitution's guarantees of privacy:

> The makers of our Constitution undertook to secure conditions favorable to the pursuit of happiness. They recognized the significance of man's spiritual nature, of his feelings and of his intellect. They knew that only a part of the pain, pleasure and satisfactions of life are to be found in material things. They sought to protect Americans in their beliefs, their thoughts, their emotions and their sensations. They conferred, as against the Government, *the right to be let alone*—the most comprehensive of rights and the right most valued by civilized men. [Italics added.]

In the majority opinion, Justice Douglas clearly stated that the "right of privacy" had a scope wider than the words written in the Constitution. His opinion also said that the Constitution includes rights that are not specifically spelled out; that "liberty" includes rights that emanate from specific guarantees, but also protects the essential conditions for life in a free society; and that one of the requirements of a free society, consistent with the "totality of the constitutional scheme under which we live," is freedom from government intrusion in home, family, and marital relations.

My treasure hunt continued to yield rewards, and I found cases in which people had challenged state abortion laws and won decisions overturning those laws. In October 1969, by a four-to-three vote, the California Supreme Court held the state's anti-abortion law unconstitutional and reversed a doctor's conviction in *California v. Belous*. The case involved Leon Belous of Los Angeles, a doctor who had directed a young patient to a competent but unlicensed physician in California at a time when abortion was illegal there. Belous acted because the young woman was threatening to go to Tijuana for an abortion; he feared that she would end up seriously injured or dead. Belous was convicted of "procuring" an illegal abortion.

The California Supreme Court said the law was vague, since abortion was allowed "to preserve the life of a woman" but nobody could determine with certainty what that meant. I read the words from the opinion to Ron: "The fundamental right of the woman to choose whether to bear children follows from the Supreme Court's and this Court's repeated acknowledgement of a 'right of privacy' and of 'liberty' in matters related to marriage, family, and sex."

During my reading about *Belous*, I learned how abortion had come to be virtually legal in California. In 1967 the California legislature passed a law considerably more lenient than the one under which Belous was prosecuted; it allowed abortion to protect the *health* of the woman, which many doctors interpreted to include mental health. Despite opposition spearheaded by the Roman Catholic Church, the law was signed, reluctantly, by then-governor Ronald Reagan. California became a favored destination for many women seeking a safe, legal abortion. Travel between states for the purpose of obtaining legal abortion became so common that the term "abortion tourism" was coined.

Cases challenging state laws were springing up in federal courts across the nation, and cases from the District of Columbia, Illinois, New York, and Wisconsin were all pending in the Supreme Court. The DC statute allowed abortion "for the preservation of the woman's life or health." Dr. Milan Vuitch interpreted that phrase to cover a wide variety of conditions, and he performed scores of abortions. In 1969, after one of many instances in which the police arrested him for performing illegal abortions, he challenged the arrest. Before the criminal case went to trial, Federal District Judge Gerhard Gesell dismissed the indictments on the grounds that the abortion statute was unconstitutionally vague. The government appealed, and the Supreme Court granted a hearing. In April 1971, the Supreme Court ruled that the DC statue was not unconstitutionally vague.

THE ENCOURAGING CASES I was finding made it exciting to meet periodically with referral project volunteers and to share the information I was uncovering about efforts in other states to challenge the laws in court or change them through the legislative process. I took comfort in the knowledge that many other people around the country were as frustrated with the law as we were, and I began to see our efforts in Texas as one piece of a national patchwork. Although I still did not have an answer to the original question of whether the volunteers could be convicted as accomplices, Ron and I decided that a district attorney had the power to start a prosecution (whether it could be won or not) in almost any situation.

One day Judy Smith and Jim Wheelis asked me to meet them for coffee in the law school snack bar. Ron also joined us. The snack bar was a modest, serviceable room crowded with tables and chairs left in disarray as students came and went. We chatted casually at first, but the conversation quickly became serious when Judy announced that she wanted a lawsuit filed to challenge the constitutionality of the Texas anti-abortion statute. She explained why. Although legislative lobbying efforts had paid off in a few states, Texas was hopeless. During the 1969 regular legislative session, all of us had supported Dallas representative Jim Clark's bill to "liberalize" the Texas abortion law, but the bill went nowhere. Around the nation, the big advances seemed to be coming from courtrooms, not legislative halls. Shouldn't we be following the example of those who were winning, and file a court challenge?

A lawsuit was an obvious route, as I knew, but I was still buried in my expanding list of things to research and had not focused on the possibility of *our* filing a lawsuit. After all, my total legal experience consisted of a few uncontested divorces for friends, ten or twelve uncomplicated wills for people with little property, one adoption for relatives, and a few miscellaneous matters. I had never been involved in a contested case. The idea of challenging the Texas abortion law in federal court was overwhelming.

Ron and Jim were taking a class on federal procedure, and Judy had been listening to Jim discuss the concept of three-judge federal courts and the use of the federal court system. One night they stayed up late talking about the victory David Richards had won for *The Rag*. Jim clearly remembers the turning point in their conversation, when Judy said: "It will take forever to change the laws against abortion in a state-by-state legislative process. But if we could overturn the laws through the federal courts, that would apply nationwide. Is that a possibility?" They went to bed having concluded that if the legal system could work for *The Rag*, it might also work for abortion. Judy thought a federal lawsuit was the way to go.

She had already spoken to some referral project participants about lawyers they might approach. Frankly, she told me, they could not come up with the name of another attorney who might do the case for free. They were pleased with my research. They knew that I was inexperienced, and also that Ron and I would soon be looking for jobs and might be leaving Austin. But they felt strongly that a woman lawyer should do the case, and I was the only woman they knew licensed to practice. Besides, they knew me personally and felt secure that if I agreed to do it, I would give it my usual all-out effort.

"No, you need someone older and with more experience," I told Judy. "You need somebody in a firm, with research and secretarial backup." My mind whirred with all the reasons I was not the right person. What I didn't verbalize was that I could not stand the thought that I might try and fail. Then the idea emerged that any challenge we filed would simply supplement those pending in various states. We assumed one of the several cases already filed would be the icebreaker. We began to talk of a Texas effort as one to add to the momentum of the litigation strategy others had already put in motion. We might be able to help one of those cases get to the Supreme Court, since it generally accepts cases when decisions by different federal courts are at odds on the same issue. We never thought we were filing what would become *the* Supreme Court case.

I eventually warmed to the lawsuit idea, but I thought I was an unlikely person—and not the right person—to tackle it. In the end, however, it seemed I was the best free legal help available, and there were reasons I was inclined to accept the challenge. In private Ron and I discussed the possibility of helping others avoid what we had gone through and preventing any more of the sorts of horror stories we had heard from the project volunteers. We had been lucky: we were older, we had money, we had each other, and we had landed in the hands of a competent doctor. We both felt strongly that it was not the government's business to prohibit abortion, and we were deeply sympathetic to the personal tragedies that resulted from anti-abortion laws.

In addition, I was restless. I wanted to be more of a lawyer and less of a researcher. I relished my work with John Sutton; he was a fabulous boss and one of a rare breed of men who delighted in working with smart women. But the travel part of my work was essentially over, and the job would soon end. And I was not really practicing law. This was a source of frustration. My years of legal training were not being fully utilized. I was still chafing that I had not been able to get a position at a law firm. I had extra time, and Ron, Jim, and I had access to the excellent resources of the UT law library.

I also felt responsible to try to help others. Perhaps this had to do with my family. As a preacher, Daddy was not of the fire-and-brimstone variety; rather, his focus was the gospel of "Christian social concern," that we as Christians have a responsibility to look beyond our individual lives and act out of a concern for others. The United Methodist Church had publicly stated its opposition to laws making abortion a crime. Mother and Daddy had been supportive when I had challenged other societal restrictions on women; I assumed they would not object to my applying my legal training now. I wrote about my abortion-related work in letters home. They did not encourage me, but they did not object.

Ron and I agreed that we could afford for me to do the case pro bono. We were living in the minimal way students often do, so we had low monthly expenses. We had already saved enough to take us through the summer of 1970, when I would no longer have a job with Sutton's committee. I was in demand to type papers for law students since I could often correct errors in the papers as I typed, and that work brought in extra money. With Ron's GI benefits and part-time job, we were able to pay our bills.

Other factors nudged me along. My training at that point was in the theory of law. I did not know how to cross-examine a witness, but UT Law School has a reputation for teaching students to think well. That is what constitutional litigation is all about. Ron, Jim, people from the referral project, and some women law students were offering to be my backups. I thought several of my professors would help if asked, and Sutton, who had extensive trial experience, offered to walk me through trial procedures.

And perhaps my inexperience was a plus. I did not fully appreciate that the odds were stacked against our endeavor. If I had been older and more sophisticated, I probably would have thought, "Oh, the Texas law against abortion has been around for a hundred years. We are *never* going to get the Supreme Court to overturn it. And besides, think of all the problems there could be with depositions and interrogatories and all the other legal work required." As it was, none of us had any inkling of the long-term impact of what we were starting.

As our plans took shape, we became excited about what winning would mean for women. The final decision was made over dinner at Judy and Jim's apartment: I would file a lawsuit in federal court challenging the constitutionality of the Texas anti-abortion statute.

NOW THE ENORMITY of the task ahead began to overwhelm me. What if I lost? What if I let the group down? Ron told me to knock off the "what ifs" and take one step at a time. I finally perked up and went back to the library. Soon we were arranging meetings to determine how to structure the challenge, who to have as plaintiffs, and what other work had to be accomplished before we could file the suit.

Ron and Jim suggested the three of us consult Professor Bernie Ward, one of their favorite teachers and the most accessible expert on the legislation authorizing three-judge federal courts. Professor Ward was about five-six; he talked with a clipped accent, his black hair was beginning to disappear, and he often smoked a pipe. His office was a clutter of papers. We trooped there and asked his advice. Since he had previously taught at Notre Dame, I suspected that he was personally opposed to abortion, but he listened thoughtfully to what we had to say. He discussed with us how, in certain cases when a constitutional issue was being presented, the presiding judge in one of the eleven circuits or judicial areas of the country could appoint one judge from the circuit court and two federal district judges to hear the case (hence the "three-judge court"). The procedure was a wonderful way to get access to some competent intellectual resources within the federal judicial system. Presidents Eisenhower, Kennedy, and Johnson had made outstanding appointments of very talented legal scholars to the federal judicial system. Texas was in the Fifth Circuit, headquartered in New Orleans; Ward said this circuit had become progressive and responsive to constitutional challenges. We left feeling encouraged by his comment that our case would be appropriate for three-judge consideration.

As I started drafting the documents to file suit, it became clear that I needed additional help. Ron, Jim, Bobby Nelson, Diane Dodson, who was a law student, and others could do specific research, but I needed an attorney familiar with federal lawsuits to volunteer to assist me. I decided to ask my former classmate Linda Coffee. After we graduated, Linda had returned to her hometown, Dallas, where she clerked for Federal District Judge Sarah T. Hughes. Judge Hughes was a legendary Texas woman. A state legislator from Dallas in the 1940s, she was later narrowly defeated for a seat on the Texas Supreme Court. In

1961, President Kennedy appointed Hughes a federal judge. In 1963 she became known to people outside Texas for swearing in Lyndon Johnson on *Air Force One* to be the US President as the plane carried Kennedy's body to Washington. Linda was working for a Dallas bankruptcy firm, Palmer and Palmer. She had never discussed an abortion issue with me, but I knew she opposed other inequalities that affected women. I thought she would agree that abortion should not be a matter for legislative fiat. Because of her clerkship for Hughes, Linda was a storehouse of knowledge about federal procedure and trials. I hoped her firm would not disapprove of her helping me.

I called Linda in early December 1969 to explain what I was working on and asked if she would help. I was pleased that she was receptive. My goal was to overturn the Texas abortion laws, I told her, and I was willing to work in whatever way was deemed most efficient, whether that meant her taking the lead or our being co-counsel.

I asked her whether the referral project or a group of the volunteers could be the plaintiffs in such a lawsuit, or whether we would need to find someone else for that purpose. One of the principles of law is that a court will not render an "advisory opinion." It will not allow people to come to court with a certain legal issue and ask the court what it thinks about the issue. Instead, people who file lawsuits must have a "genuine case or controversy" and must be able to show that they are directly and significantly affected by the law in question. We needed someone who could show a personal, direct, significant impact of the Texas anti-abortion statutes. Often cases are filed with several plaintiffs in order to present a number of legal issues. Some of the project volunteers were willing to be plaintiffs, and they were willing to have the project itself file as a plaintiff. We discussed alleging that members of the project were fearful of being prosecuted, but none of them had been prosecuted or even threatened with prosecution, so we could not show whether or not the fear was justified.

When I spoke to Linda again, she was enthusiastic. Her firm had no objection to her working on the suit. She offered to check into some of the procedural points I had raised, but said she felt reasonably sure the organization would have the requisite standing to challenge the statute. However, the need to keep a low profile eventually made us decide against having the referral center as a plaintiff.

Linda and I met frequently in person and talked by phone in preparation for the lawsuit. As we drafted the complaint and lined up our legal points, our constant worry was about the right plaintiffs. After Linda did some research, we decided neither the Austin volunteers nor the referral project would be certain to have standing, so we started looking for individuals who could demonstrate a more direct impact.

OUR FIRST AGREED-UPON plaintiff was a woman we knew in Dallas who had heard Linda give a speech about the contemplated lawsuit. A brilliant women's activist with a Ph.D. in English, she felt strongly that the Texas anti-abortion statutes kept women from making decisions that were rightfully theirs. She had no children and was not pregnant, but she had a neurochemical disorder. Although pregnancy would not present a serious risk to her life, her doctor had told her it would be best if she avoided pregnancy until her condition materially improved. He also told her not to take the most effective means of contraception, the birth control pill. She and her husband offered to be plaintiffs on the basis that their normal marital intimacies were endangered because, although they were conscientiously practicing an alternative method of contraception, there was a significant risk of contraceptive failure and they knew that if she were to become pregnant, consideration for her health would suggest an abortion. In Texas, that would be illegal and therefore also dangerous to her health. Yet they did not wish to be a celibate married couple.

We also needed to find a pregnant Texas woman who wanted an abortion and would be willing to be a plaintiff. At one of the meetings with the Austin women, I was explaining the need for a pregnant plaintiff and asked "Are any of you pregnant?" "No," they said, "but if you need someone who is, just give us some time." In fact, it turned out to be a bigger problem than we anticipated. Several women who came to the referral project for information indicated they would be happy to help, but they were all at an early stage of pregnancy and had the money to get a prompt abortion—certainly the safest route for them. We did not know how long it would take for a court to act. It was best for them to go ahead and have an abortion. Our search would have to continue.

As an outgrowth of my work on the case, I had become involved in a variety of activities, including making frequent speeches about the plans for the suit. The more people who knew about our plans, the more likely it was that a suitable plaintiff would appear.

Then a woman went to Dallas lawyer Henry McCluskey, a friend of Linda's who knew of the proposed lawsuit. The woman said she was pregnant, did not want to be, and wanted an abortion. He told her he could and would handle an adoption if she chose that route. He also told her there was nothing he could do about the abortion, but he knew two young women who might be of help, and referred her to Linda.

Linda talked to the woman, and then called and asked me to come to Dallas to meet her. I flew there a few days later and met Linda at a place the woman had suggested, a pizza parlor. It was fairly large, and very clean, but without much decoration—plastic-topped tables and black-and-white checkered linoleum on the floor. Linda filled me in on her impressions of the woman, who was in her early twenties. Then the person who would later become Jane Roe arrived.

Lawyer-client privilege prohibits a lawyer from revealing information told by a client in confidence. However, I can share information that we filed in the public record of the court or that has since been printed in newspapers, magazines, and books as a result of interviews others have done with Jane Roe. In recent years, for example, Jane Roe has revealed her actual name, Norma McCorvey. But when I am talking about the case I still refer to her only as Jane Roe.

She was petite, with an upturned nose. She was wearing jeans and an oversize blouse that was not tucked in, peasant style. She was outgoing and talked easily. After initial chitchat, I told her about our ultimate goal: to be a part of the national efforts to make abortion a woman's choice and a safe medical procedure. I described the work of the Austin referral project and the research in progress, and let her know a little about the anti-abortion laws, and about our married-couple plaintiffs and the importance of a pregnant plaintiff.

She explained that she was pregnant and did not want to go through with the pregnancy. She had had a rough life: She already had one child and did not want another. Her mother had taken her daughter away from her and she seldom got to see her. She had never finished the tenth grade, was working as a waitress, and knew she would lose her job if the pregnancy continued. She could barely support herself, much less a child. I sympathized with her plight, and we agreed that it was unfair that many women—teachers, stewardesses, and others—lost their jobs if they became pregnant. That was something else we wanted to change.

Linda and I explained the Texas anti-abortion law and told her why we felt it was wrong. She had found an illegal place in

Dallas, she admitted, but she didn't like the looks of it. She had no money to travel to another state. As the conversation continued, Jane Roe asked if it would help if she had been raped. We said no; the Texas law had no exception for rape. It was just as illegal for a doctor to do an abortion for someone who had been raped as it generally was in other situations. I did ask, "Were there any witnesses? Was there a police report? Is there any way that we could prove a rape occurred?" Her answer in each instance was no.

Neither Linda nor I questioned her further about how she had gotten pregnant. I was not going to allege something in the complaint that I could not back up with proof. Also, we did not want the Texas law changed only to allow abortion in cases of rape. We wanted a decision that abortion was covered by the right of privacy. After all, women coming to the referral project were there as a result of a wide variety of circumstances. Our principles were not based on how conception occurred.

Jane Roe asked what being a plaintiff would involve. First, we told her, a minimal amount of time. In fact, she signed a one-page affidavit stating her situation. She never had to answer written or oral questions from the opposing lawyers. She did not attend any of the court hearings. Second, no money. Linda and I were donating our time, and we were covering the expenses.

Third, she could be anonymous. No one would know who she was unless she chose to tell them. Using pseudonyms or false names in legal cases was a long-standing tradition, and especially common in abortion cases, to protect the privacy of plaintiffs who did not want the "whole world" to know they had had or had wanted an abortion. On the other hand, doctors, social workers, and nonpregnant plaintiffs in abortion cases generally filed using their real names.

When Jane Roe agreed to be a plaintiff, I was grateful for her help. I found her street-smart and likeable. Her hard-luck stories touched a sympathetic chord.

Linda and I decided to file two lawsuits. A pregnant plaintiff has standing, but since our wife plaintiff wasn't pregnant, we were afraid the court would say she and her husband were not sufficiently at risk to have standing. There was another reason for filing two lawsuits: Since we would file the cases in Dallas, where Linda, Jane Roe, and the married couple resided, and where the federal court had a rotating docket, each case would be filed in a different judge's court. We hoped to increase our chances of having one of the cases filed in Judge Hughes's court; Linda thought she would be sympathetic. Our strategy then would be to ask that the other case be consolidated with it, so that we could try one case with the combined facts instead of two.

As we finished drawing up the necessary legal papers in 1970, Jane Roe's pregnancy was progressing. Linda spent the end of February on rough drafts of the documents to file. Our petitions were straightforward and only three legal-size pages in length. We asked the court to do two things: first, to declare or state that the Texas laws against abortion were unconstitutional on their face, that is, as one could see by merely reading them; and second, to enjoin, or stop, the enforcement of those statutes. In essence we wanted the court to say the Texas anti-abortion laws violated the US Constitution and to tell local law enforcement officials to quit prosecuting doctors under those statutes.

We still had to name our plaintiffs. We picked names that rhymed. I liked "Jane Roe." To me the name represented all women, not just one. We decided on "John and Mary Doe" for the couple.

IN LAW THERE ARE "magic words." If one of them applies to what you are challenging, you have a good chance of getting it overturned. Linda and I used all of the magic words that might possibly apply: The statutes were *vague* and uncertain on their face; they were *unconstitutionally broad* on their face in that they infringed upon plaintiffs' *right to safe and adequate medical advice* about the decision of whether to carry a pregnancy to term, upon the *fundamental* right of all women to choose whether to bear children, and upon plaintiffs' *right to privacy* in the physician-patient relationship; on their face they infringed upon plaintiffs' *right to life* in violation of the due-process clause of the Fourteenth Amendment; on their face they violated the *First Amendment* prohibition against laws respecting an establishment of religion; and on their face they denied plaintiffs the *equal protection of the laws.*

We asked that a three-judge court be appointed to hear each case, our justification being that our plaintiffs were alleging the statutes abridged their constitutional rights, and were seeking an injunction against enforcement of the statutes. We also pointed out that there was not a state forum or court in which their federal constitutional rights could be determined. A decision by a three-judge court, including a member of the circuit court and two district judges, would carry more weight than a decision by a single federal district judge.

We engaged in "alternative pleading," as lawyers often do: we gave the court several reasons to do what we were asking and set aside Texas law. First, we argued, there was a fundamental area of personal privacy secured by the First, Fourth, Fifth, Eighth, Ninth, and Fourteenth Amendments to the Constitution and the state statute violated that individual right of privacy. Second, we argued that the statute was vague and that doctors—although in danger of criminal prosecution, depending on their actions—could not read the statute and tell what was and what was not against the law. A criminal statute must say specifically what conduct is illegal, or it must be stricken as "vague."

The legal parts of the petitions in the *Roe* and *Doe* cases were identical. The statements of facts about the plaintiffs, obviously, were different. About Jane Roe we told the court:

— Plaintiff, Jane Roe, is an unmarried pregnant woman.

— Because of the economic hardships and social stigmas involved in bearing an illegitimate child, Plaintiff wishes to terminate her pregnancy by means of an operation, generally referred to as an abortion, performed by a competent, licensed physician, under safe, clinical conditions.

— Plaintiff's life does not appear to be threatened by the continuation of her pregnancy.

— Plaintiff [cannot] secure a legal abortion in Dallas County [Texas] because of the existence of the Texas Abortion Laws.

— Plaintiff cannot afford to travel to another jurisdiction where she could secure a legal abortion under safe, clinical conditions.

— An abortion performed by a competent, licensed physician under hospital or clinic conditions is a safe and simple procedure which presents less danger to the pregnant woman than ordinary childbirth.

— An abortion performed outside of the clinical setting by unqualified personnel is extremely dangerous and often results in death, maiming, sterility, or serious infection.

What the three-judge court would know of Jane Roe was limited to the information in the *Roe* complaint and what was later contained in her affidavit. There was no mention of how she got pregnant.

The petition for John and Mary Doe described their problems resulting from her neurochemical condition. It explained that the necessity of choosing among the alternatives to a safe abortion was "presently having a detrimental effect upon Plaintiffs' marital happiness." Because Mary Doe had helped some Dallas women find places for abortion and because we wanted to pose the questions about the legality of referral activities, we included comments about Mary Doe's wanting to refer women for abortion services and being unsure about whether she could do so legally.

We filed each suit against Henry Wade, the elected district attorney of Dallas County, the official responsible for law enforcement in that county. We wanted the court to tell Wade's office to leave the doctors alone.

In August 1985, *The Dallas Morning News* described the district attorney as follows: "Henry Wade drawls. He drops the endings from words and says 'cain't' for 'can't.' He chews cigars and spits tobacco juice. He plays a tough game of dominoes and prefers not to travel further than Forney. Pop the ruddy face, white hair and bulging waistline of the Dallas district attorney into a seersucker suit, and it's easy to picture him shuffling around a sleepy country courthouse."

But appearances were deceiving. Many thought of him as one of the most effective professional law enforcement men in the country. He served as DA for a total of thirty-five years and sent twenty-nine people to death row, more than half of whom were eventually executed. He prosecuted Jack Ruby for the shooting of Lee Harvey Oswald and was involved in many other famous cases.

ON MARCH 2, 1970, Linda and I spent the evening working on last-minute details and changes. When we finished, our first case was captioned: "In The United States District Court for the Northern District of Texas, Dallas Division—Jane Roe, Plaintiff, v. Henry Wade, District Attorney of Dallas County, Defendant." The next day it was docketed as cause number 3-3690-B. It became known as *Roe v. Wade.*

Our second case was captioned: "In The United States District Court for the Northern District of Texas, Dallas Division—John Doe and Mary Doe, Plaintiffs, v. Henry Wade, District Attorney of Dallas County, Defendant." The next day it was docketed as cause number 3-3691-C. It became *Doe v. Wade*.

On March 3, 1970, Linda walked to the federal clerk's office in the federal courthouse of Dallas and paid from her own pocket thirty dollars to file the two cases. It was a day when anything seemed possible. Women were insistently questioning restrictions and trying to change them. Abortion now symbolized the question of whether women would have decision-making power over the issues that most affected their lives. I had resisted traditional ideas and had become a lawyer, and this prepared me for a special role; I wanted to do whatever I could to change the Texas anti-abortion statutes. Time, place, and people had converged to create a legal challenge. *Roe v. Wade* had begun.

4 . Off to Washington

Two and a half months later, Linda and I were seated at a long wooden table facing the much higher bench where the three judges would sit. We were on the fourth floor of the Dallas Federal Courthouse, an imposing building that had previously been a post office, in a courtroom that was more utilitarian than elegant. We were waiting for the judges to file in and hear *Roe*. We were unabashedly excited, and as prepared as we would ever be.

We had had some very good luck and had accomplished a great deal thus far. One of our two cases landed in Hughes's court; the other in that of Federal District Judge William M. Taylor of Dallas. Federal Circuit Judge Irving L. Goldberg had been appointed to join Hughes and Taylor on a three-judge panel to hear our cases. After a pretrial conference in Hughes's office in April, our cases were consolidated; we now said just *Roe* when actually referring to both *Roe* and *Doe*. Taylor had a reputation for fairness and open-mindedness. Goldberg was reputed to be brilliant, but domineering in court proceedings. We did not look forward to his trial questions, which we knew would be tough and incisive, but we calculated that he was our best chance of a second vote in our favor.

Sitting with Linda and me in the courtroom were Fred Bruner and Roy L. Merrill, Jr., two Dallas lawyers who had joined our case on behalf of their client, James Hubert Hallford, a physician under indictment for allegedly performing illegal abortions. On March 19 they had filed an application for intervention asking that Hallford be included as a third plaintiff. Hallford had been a licensed physician since 1958; among the women who had come to him seeking abortions were rape and incest victims, women suffering from cancer, and women who had contracted German measles, a virus that can cause gross fetal abnormalities, while pregnant. We welcomed Hallford's participation because his problems added weight to our arguments that the statute was vague and could be interpreted in many different ways. We were skeptical that he would be recognized to have standing, however; very seldom do federal courts allow people with criminal charges pending against them in state court to escape from the litigation already in progress to a federal court.

At another table in the courtroom were representatives of DA Henry Wade and of the Texas attorney general, Crawford Martin. Judge Hughes had notified Martin of the suit because he was the elected official responsible for defending state laws. Linda and I were up against the combined forces of the AG's experienced legal force of some 130 attorneys and the DA's legal staff.

OF COURSE, we had done our homework. Once trial was set for May 22, 1970, we rushed to prepare and file two affidavits, notarized, signed statements used to prove important facts instead of having a witness testify in court. One contained facts about Jane Roe; the other was filed by Dr. Paul Trickett, the director of the University of Texas Student Health Center, and presented medical aspects of the abortion issue. The original Texas statutes had been passed to protect a woman's health in an era when doctors did not know how to prevent infection, and we wanted to show that now, at the time of trial, abortion was a safe procedure and medical problems resulted precisely because abortion was illegal.

Jane Roe's one page affidavit stated that she was over twenty-one, that because of her pregnancy she had experienced extreme difficulty in securing employment of any kind, and that she wanted to terminate her pregnancy because of the economic hardship it entailed and because of the social stigma attached to the bearing of illegitimate children in our society. We had trouble finding Jane Roe when we needed her to sign the affidavit. She moved frequently because of financial difficulties; Mary Doe was finally able to locate her. At Linda's office, Jane Roe signed one copy of the affidavit—a copy kept for only the opposing attorneys and the judges, should they ask to see it—with her real name and address. On the copy filed for public record her name and address were not given. Peggy Clewis, Linda's secretary, who notarized the document, had recently learned that she was pregnant, and she in particular noticed how *very* pregnant Jane Roe was. Peggy commented that she looked like a small woman carrying a *big* watermelon.

Dr. Trickett's affidavit stated that abortion involved only minimal risk to the patient, especially when it was done early (preferably during the first six to ten weeks of pregnancy), and that it was no more dangerous than a diagnostic dilation and curettage, a common, routine medical procedure. He described the general circumstances of many Texas women who had told him they wanted an abortion, and gave what he described as a conservative estimate that the UT Student Health Center diagnosed at least one pregnancy a day, and said that a majority of those pregnant women wanted an abortion. The affidavit also discussed patients he had seen after they had had illegal abortions and the medical problems they often experienced, which included "death, infection (which may lead to sterility or future ectopic pregnancies) and other medical conditions." According to Trickett, one cause of unwanted pregnancies was the unavailability of good methods of contraception. Since recent hearings in Washington about the dangers of the birth control pill, more women were choosing other, less reliable methods; these methods had a sixty- to eighty-percent effectiveness rate, leaving a twenty- to forty-percent chance of pregnancy. Trickett knew physicians who would be willing to perform abortions if the procedure were not illegal.

Linda and I had amended the complaints she filed to start the litigation to include class actions. A class action is a suit on behalf of all the individuals in a particular situation. It was then gaining currency as a technique for painting a larger picture than just the specific facts about one plaintiff. We had always thought of the suits as involving countless women who found themselves facing an unplanned, often unwanted pregnancy. From the beginning we considered the individuals who would be involved in the cases as ancillary to the primary focus on all women who, if pregnant, would want to have access to *all* options, including legal abortion. Ours were not cases about only Jane Roe or John and Mary Doe, although they were the vehicles for presenting larger issues. Technically, however, we had not filed our cases as class actions. We were aware of Jane Roe's personal circumstances and the need to hurry the process as much as possible. In our haste to get the suits started we had delayed researching the procedural requirements for filing class actions—defining the class, deciding who in a large group would have to be informed of the suits, and whether one plaintiff could fairly represent the interests of such a large class of plaintiffs. We knew we could amend the complaints before trial to include class actions.

George Schatzki, my former constitutional law professor, was the most accessible expert on class actions. Schatzki, a Harvard graduate, was a man of great energy. His shoulders were hunched from long hours spent poring over books at library tables. In class he seemed to be in perpetual motion. He would peer out from under bushy eyebrows to ask piercing questions. My proudest moment in law school came when I stumped Schatzki in class. I don't remember my question; I just remember his answer: "I don't know. Good question, I will tell you the answer tomorrow." And he did.

When I asked for help, Schatzki readily agreed. He told me that we definitely should convert the suits to class actions and told me how to structure them, offered a few other suggestions, and then talked with me about another concern Linda and I had: Jane Roe was due to give birth in a few months. When she was no longer pregnant would that give credence to the state's claim that the case was moot, a situation past the remedy being requested? What could we do to avoid having *Roe* thrown out of court? If we amended our complaints to include class actions, by implication we were saying there would always be pregnant women "out there" in Texas. Would that protect our cases? Schatzki thought it would, so Linda and I immediately expanded the cases to be class actions.

We filed a brief setting forth our positions in the litigation, with citations of cases that we thought backed up our arguments; then we began to prepare for oral argument. The Supreme Court's majority opinion in *Griswold v. Connecticut*, the birth control case, talked of the "penumbras" of the Bill of Rights, or emanations from those guarantees that help give them life and substance. The Court stated that various guarantees create "zones of privacy." One concurring opinion spoke of a concept of privacy supported in part by the language and history of the Ninth Amendment. Also mentioned were cases about personal rights and "liberties" protected from impairment by the states by the due-process clause of the Fourteenth Amendment. Linda and I were not sure how the three-judge court would respond to the various bases for privacy; we would have to walk a tightrope in arguing that privacy was protected by a combination of those provisions.

JOHN AND MARY DOE were at the hearing; Jane Roe was not. We did not know whether opponents of abortion would be demonstrating at the entrance to the court building or in the courtroom; since Jane Roe was obviously pregnant, she had decided not to attend. As it turned out, the few picketers who were there were backing us. Ginny Whitehill, an impeccably dressed woman in her mid-forties who had been a Planned Parenthood volunteer in Dallas for years and was a pro-choice activist, and a group of women from the local Unitarian church had come to give us moral support. The General Assembly of the Unitarian Universalist Association had passed a resolution in 1963 condemning restrictive abortion laws as an "affront to human life and dignity."

Linda spoke first. She presented the more technical aspects of our argument, among them that our plaintiffs were appropriate to raise the questions involved, that is, they had standing. One of her tasks was to demonstrate that there was no remedy for our plaintiffs in state court; otherwise the federal court would leave it to a state court to decide the matter. To establish the basis of our argument that the Texas law was unconstitutional, she started down the list of amendments we were relying on, the First, Fourth, Fifth, Eighth, Ninth, and Fourteenth. The First, she argued, protected the right of association; one of its aspects was the right of free association between a doctor and a patient, and the anti-abortion laws interfered with that right. Doctors did not feel free to advise their patients about abortion or to perform abortions when requested by patients, even when the doctors agreed such was justified.

The judges were not interested in hearing about the First Amendment; Hughes redirected Linda to the Ninth, which states: "The enumeration in the constitution of certain rights shall not be construed to deny or disparage others retained by the people." Linda responded quickly: "I don't think it makes any difference . . . whether you say that the rights involved are First Amendment rights or Ninth Amendment rights; I feel they are so important that they deserve the special protection that has been accorded to First Amendment rights. In other words, they involve fundamental human freedom, which I think recent cases have indicated are beginning to be given the same priority treatment that First Amendment rights have always afforded." Linda got a few other arguments in before Goldberg indicated that her thirteen minutes were up.

I had just been following the dialogue between Linda and the judges, listening for points to pursue or clarify. When it was my turn, I rose. I was twenty-five years old; I had never argued in a contested case, and it was my first appearance before federal judges. My voice quivered. Hughes looked down at me from the bench; she could see how nervous I was. She gave me a reassuring smile and a slight wink, as if to say, "Don't be nervous. Everything will be fine." I will always be grateful for that gesture. I did not interpret it as an indication of how she would rule in the case. Rather, I took it as an older woman lawyer's remembering what it was like when she was starting out.

I told the judges my argument would cover "the justification which the State alleges for the state abortion statute, that is, the protection of the life of the child" and aspects of the right of privacy. My plan was to pound the point that law had never treated the fetus as a person, but I started with a more subtle message: "I would like to draw to the court's attention the fact that life is an ongoing process. It is almost impossible to define a point at which life begins or perhaps even at which life ends. Certainly life in its very general matter is present in the sperm; it is present in the ova. The potential of life depends on a set of circumstances which must then occur." I went on to quote from former

Supreme Court justice Tom Clark, a Texan, who had written, "To say that life is present at conception is to give recognition to the potential rather than the actual."

I was ready to list cases in which state courts and federal laws had decided that a fetus did not have the legal rights of a person, when Goldberg asked me to assume that there was a Ninth Amendment right and to address the question of whether the state had *any* compelling interests in regulating abortion. He wanted to know whether the state would have sufficient justification for requiring that all abortions be done in a hospital or that they all be certified by one or more physicians, and whether there should be different standards for married and single women.

If the court found that a fundamental constitutional right was involved, I knew it would then require the state to prove a "compelling reason to regulate" before approving state restrictions. I agreed that a state might have some justification for very narrowly drawn regulations, such as prohibiting people who were not licensed medical personnel from performing abortions, but I added that I did not see any justification for regulating abortion when performed by a doctor; nor did I see how denying abortion to unmarried women would serve any compelling state interest. The judges pressed me on the constitutionality of other limits a state might adopt, and then my time was up.

First Bruner and then Merrill, Dr. Hallford's attorneys, rose to argue that the Texas law was vague and to discuss the problems doctors faced when defending themselves under the statute, since the exception for legal abortion was an affirmative defense; a doctor would first admit to performing an abortion and then have to prove that the reasons fit the exception. We had agreed in advance that Linda and I would not use our precious moments for the vagueness argument; Bruner and Merrill would concentrate on that. We would focus our argument on the constitutional aspects, the impact of illegal abortion on women, and the question of when legal rights began.

The hearing moved on to Jay Floyd from the Texas attorney general's office, who launched an attack on the right of Jane Roe to bring the suit. He pointed out that no woman in Texas had ever been sued for having an abortion, and that women could not claim to have been injured by the law. Further, he argued, the case was moot. None of the court papers made any reference to how far along Roe was in her pregnancy. But since the suit had been filed in March and it was now past the middle of May, and it was logical to assume she was a least several months pregnant when the case was filed, she was either no longer pregnant or too far along in her pregnancy to undergo an abortion even if abortion were legal. Her case presented no real controversy, Floyd said, and the judges should dismiss her claim. As to Mary Doe, he reminded them that she had never claimed to be pregnant. As far as everyone knew, she still was not pregnant. Fear of pregnancy, he said, was simply not enough to give someone the right to file a federal suit against the constitutionality of the Texas statutes.

The judges did not seem to respond positively to Floyd's arguments. Goldberg reminded him that some of the children involved in school desegregation cases had graduated from college by the times their cases were litigated. Did this mean that they were not entitled to attend desegregated schools? Hughes commented, "What would give them standing in a case like this to test the constitutionality of this statute? Apparently you don't think that anybody has standing." That *Roe v. Wade* was a class action suit gave us a strong response to Floyd's argument, because we represented women who were pregnant or who *in the future* might find themselves pregnant and want the option of a legal abortion.

Floyd moved to safer ground. He said he did not believe a right to abortion was found in the Constitution, and that it certainly was not in the First Amendment. Judge Hughes replied, "We agree with you on that." But Goldberg asked Floyd to address the Ninth Amendment and the issue of vagueness. Instead Floyd launched into his argument that the state had a compelling interest in protecting the fetus.

Hughes directed the discussion to a case Floyd had cited, *California v. Belous*. She pointed out that the California court had declared its state law unconstitutional on the basis that it was vague and indefinite. She wondered how Floyd could differentiate the Texas language. Goldberg in turn tried, unsuccessfully, to pin Floyd down on whether the imminent death of the woman might make abortion acceptable. Floyd declined to make what he viewed as an essentially medical judgment.

Floyd yielded the floor to John Tolle of the Dallas DA's office. His emphasis was on the state's right to make decisions. He did not disagree with my statement that no one knew when life began, but he went on to say that even in the absence of answers to this difficult question, the state had "a right to protect life . . . in whatever state it may be in . . . and if there is no absolute fact as to when life occurs, then it becomes . . . a legislative problem as to when [the legislators] are going to set up an arbitrary time." Tolle also argued "that the state's position will be, and is, that the right of the child to life is superior to that of a woman's right to privacy." That ended the hearing.

I was not happy with it, or my role in it. Because the judges had interrupted constantly, I did not feel I had been able to make my points as clearly as I should have; I had practiced summarizing my best remarks for the end, but instead I hurried and my conclusion was weak. My adrenaline had been pumping when I entered the courtroom; as I left I felt let down. When Linda and

I spoke with our supporters after the hearing, they tried to reassure us with their assessment that the arguments of our opponents were not strong or well made. We discussed the judges' questions and comments, but we could not predict what the court would decide. I was too inexperienced to know that a lawyer very seldom leaves a courtroom feeling confident about what the court's decision will be. When the case is heavily weighted on one side, the parties generally settle out of court. It is the close calls that make it to trial. Most lawyers leave the courtroom knowing they will simply have to wait for the decision. That is just the way it is. We began to wait.

A *DALLAS MORNING NEWS* story of May 24, 1970, headlined "Survival Rights of Mother, Fetus in Conflict," emphasized John Tolle's statements that the right of survival of the fetus was "superior" to that of the woman, and Judge Goldberg's comment that he saw nothing in the Texas statute on which the DA's office could base its argument of a "compelling interest" to protect unborn life. The article reported my comment, in response to questioning about the state's interest, that the state "could recognize life when the fetus is able to live outside of the mother," at twenty-two to twenty-six weeks after conception, or that another possible standard for life, used in organ transplants, might be considered: whether the brain was functioning. The article further noted that the courtroom was crowded "mainly with women." Given the subject, who could be surprised?

WHEN LINDA CALLED on June 17, her voice was so calm it took me a moment to realize she had important news. The three-judge court had released its decision. The good news was that the court had declared the Texas law unconstitutional. Jane Roe and Dr. Hallford, with the members of their respective classes, were found to be appropriate plaintiffs. The court said the Texas statutes were so vague that doctors could not tell when an abortion was legal or illegal; the parts of the opinion I was most interested in, however, had to do with the right of privacy.

The court agreed with our contention that the Texas abortion laws must be declared unconstitutional because they deprived single women and married couples of their right, secured by the Ninth Amendment, to choose not to have children. The opinion of the panel noted that, "freedom to choose in the matter of abortions has been accorded the status of a 'fundamental' right in every case" the court knew of where the questions had been raised. The judges wrote that "the burden is on the defendant to demonstrate to the satisfaction of the court that the infringement [by the Texas abortion laws] is necessary to support a compelling state interest," and concluded: "The defendant has failed to meet this burden."

We had won! I noted especially the court language about the "freedom to choose." I knew the State would probably appeal, but for that day we could celebrate. We had achieved a significant part of our goal: a declaration by a three-judge federal court that there was a constitutional shield protecting women and families from government interference with their most personal decisions.

Our celebration was dampened somewhat by the fact that the Does had been judged to lack standing and that the court had refused to order the DA not to prosecute doctors for performing abortions. The decision did establish a precedent that a pregnant woman should be included in future cases challenging anti-abortion statutes, but since the court recognized Roe and Hallford as appropriate plaintiffs, for our purposes that was a minor point. While not prohibiting the DA from prosecuting doctors, the court said it assumed Henry Wade would abide by its declaration that the law was unconstitutional. Linda and I felt the judges were incredibly naïve to believe that, if they did. Further, the whole point of the case was not to win a theoretical victory, but rather to make it legal for doctors to help women who were determined to end a pregnancy. Ron and I agreed that doctors would still sit on the sidelines, afraid to help for fear of prosecution. Linda and I would have to ask a higher court to look at the same issues. About our other constitutional claims, the court's opinion stated that aside from the Ninth Amendment, "these additional arguments are peripheral to the main issues. Consequently, they will not be passed upon."

Jane Roe and the Does were happy at the partial victory and pleased that we were planning to appeal the denial of an injunction against the DA's office and the denial of standing for the Does. But it was too late for Jane Roe; she gave birth early in the summer and placed the baby for adoption through Linda's friend, Dallas lawyer Henry McCluskey.

Henry Wade announced to the Dallas press that since the court had not ordered otherwise, he would continue to prosecute. As we expected, he also planned to appeal the decision. In Austin, Attorney General Martin said he too would appeal. Their statements were in fact a mixed blessing. Women still would not be able to obtain legal abortions in Texas; that was the bad part. Doctors in Dallas, for example, were afraid Wade would personally prosecute them if they performed any; UT students were told by student health center director Paul Trickett that center policy would remain the same, pending appeal; doctors in San Antonio and Galveston who taught at state medical schools and were in charge of care for the poor were told by local prosecutors that they could not provide abortion services.

The silver lining was that Wade's publicly stated position that he would continue to prosecute, regardless of what the federal court said, helped us to reach the Supreme Court in record time. Generally an initial federal court decision must be appealed to a circuit court before an appeal to the Supreme Court. Linda and

I were already planning our appeal to the Fifth Circuit Court, but she came up with the idea of also appealing directly to the Supreme Court. It was procedurally possible to go straight to the Supreme Court if a lower federal court had declared a state law unconstitutional yet local authorities continued to enforce the law. It was the one moment we cheered Wade: thanks to him, that was the exact situation here.

ROE STEPPED INTO the national spotlight because of the three-judge decision. On June 18, *The New York Times* carried a story titled "3 US Judges Rule Laws Invalid in Texas." The next day a *Dallas Morning News* editorial opened: "The controversy over abortion really boils down to a single question: 'Which comes first, the woman or the egg?'" A *Houston Post* story on June 23 quoted me:

> "It is not a victory, solely, of women's lib . . . Of course, many women are involved in the effort, but the real force is much broader than that. Physicians, people who work with children, who see the battered child who comes as the result of an unwanted pregnancy, many ministers who deal all the time with girls desperate for help—all these people have been involved in getting the change."

I laughed at the *Post's* concluding comment: "If their day in court proves anything, it certainly proves that genteel Southern ladies can indeed be very good lawyers." I knew that lawyers and interested individuals all over the country whose cases I had been following in the newspapers would now be following ours. We were linked by newsprint.

After the elation wore off, Linda and I found ourselves extremely busy. We were researching and preparing for our appeals, but our work was constantly—and usually pleasantly—interrupted by letters and calls from people across the country.

Linda heard from an Atlanta lawyer, Margie Pitts Hames, about her Georgia case, *Doe v. Bolton*, which was also being appealed to the Supreme Court because they too were denied injunctive relief. We did not know it then, but the Georgia case was to become a companion case to *Roe*; the two were argued the same day before the Supreme Court.

The Georgia anti-abortion statute was less restrictive than the law in Texas; it allowed abortion performed by a "physician duly licensed" in Georgia when, for example, continuing the pregnancy would endanger the life of the pregnant woman or seriously and permanently injure her health; when the fetus would likely be born with a grave, permanent, and irremediable mental or physical defect, or when the pregnancy resulted from forcible or statutory rape.

However, there was a string of further qualifications and conditions in the Georgia law, hurdles that women had to jump over in their determination to get an abortion. Included were a residence requirement and the stipulations that the doctor put in writing his medical judgment that an abortion was justified for one of the specified reasons, and have concurrence from at least two other state-licensed physicians on the basis of separate examinations of the woman; that the abortion be in a hospital certified by the Joint Commission on Accreditation of Hospitals; that there be advance approval by an abortion committee of no fewer than three members of the hospital staff; that there be certification in cases of rape; and that records be kept, and kept confidential.

The Georgia case was typical of others pending around the country in that it included plaintiffs from a variety of work and life situations; Margie Pitts Hames was trying to present a broad spectrum of interests for consideration. The Georgia plaintiffs included a married pregnant woman (given the pseudonym Mary Doe) with three children, two of them in foster homes and one up for adoption, who had been a mental patient at a state hospital; nine physicians, seven nurses, five clergymen, and two social workers; and two nonprofit Georgia corporations that advocated abortion reform. Defendants included the state attorney general, Arthur Bolton; the district attorney of Fulton County; and the Atlanta chief of police. In comparison, our case was much simpler. I couldn't imagine dealing with that many extra players.

The case had been presented to the US District Court for the Northern District of Georgia in Atlanta. On July 31, six weeks after the Dallas decision, the court issued its opinion, declaring primary parts of the Georgia law unconstitutional. Margie Pitts Hames contacted Linda to ask for copies of documents filed in our case since she was a volunteer lawyer for the American Civil Liberties Union and was also involved in appeals of parts of the Georgia case she failed to win.

None of us had any idea about which abortion case—if any—the Supreme Court would agree to hear. In addition to the Georgia and Texas cases, there were cases pending in Colorado, Illinois, Indiana, Kentucky, Michigan, Minnesota, New Jersey, North Carolina, Oregon, and Vermont. In 1971, the Court received thousands of appeals and accepted roughly 150. While the numbers are different now, it is still true that when a case is appealed the odds are heavily against the Court's agreeing to consider it. The justices vote on which appeals to accept, and four justices must vote yes before a case is set for the submission of briefs and oral argument.

We also heard from Roy Lucas, a New York City lawyer who identified himself as president of the James Madison Constitutional Law Institute. He said the institute was specializing in abortion cases, and offered to help on the appeal. Lucas sounded knowledgeable, and Linda and I welcomed assistance. Several people in Austin had already given us valuable advice or research time, and experienced help was a godsend.

Because the Fifth Circuit agreed to postpone consideration of our appeal there until after the Supreme Court accepted or rejected *Roe*, our first appeal deadline was October 13, when the Jurisdictional Statement, the initial small document asking the Supreme Court to consider a case, was due in Washington. Linda had a backlog of bankruptcy work at her firm. Ron and I were in the process of moving to Fort Worth, where he had a job with a small plaintiffs' firm and I would be an assistant city attorney. Lucas said he would be happy to get the Jurisdictional Statement submitted, and we gratefully accepted his offer without properly defining the terms and conditions of an agreement. The papers went back and forth, with Lucas in the lead on the Supreme Court appeal.

My new boss, S. G. Johndroe, Jr., turned out to be gruff and irascible but kindhearted and very competent. He took great pride in having hired me as the first female assistant city attorney. Our office intercom system consisted of Johndroe yelling from his desk. He would yell down the hall, "*Sarah*," and I would go scurrying to his office. Every boss has quirks; Johndroe always maintained that he yelled at me only so I would feel a part of the office: he called me the same way he called all the male attorneys. Above all, I admired Johndroe's absolute honesty and dedication to the city.

WORK ON THE abortion issue in Texas and elsewhere never followed a single track. We were always juggling several possible balls at the same time, pursuing every possible route to change the law. Linda and I had the lead in the court challenge and followed the progress of litigation around the country, but I was also very involved in political and legislative strategy and events. I was one of many speakers working to build public support for amending the laws. The abortion referral project and Clergy Consultation Service were actively finding the help women needed without delay and assisting with other channels. We identified a few dedicated doctors, such as Fred Hansen in Austin, Hugh Savage in Fort Worth, and Charles Powell in Galveston, to serve as our medical experts on pro-choice panels and in legislative hearings.

Writers at *The Rag* kept on publishing stories related to contraception and abortion. One article reported that there were more than a million illegal abortions in the United States every year: "The large majority are on married women. The large majority take place in back rooms, women are rushed in and out regardless of any complications, and the abortionist is often not a competent medical doctor." This piece also commented that "women should control their lives and their own bodies. We support the case . . . to abolish the Texas abortion laws." When I read another *Rag* story, complete with pictures, about menstrual extraction, a procedure for monthly removal of the lining of the uterus, I silently prayed women would never need to resort to that.

The Rag discussed not only overpopulation and birth control, but also the dangers that came with illegal abortion. Those who wrote for the paper and those who volunteered at the abortion referral project were often the same people; they felt a great responsibility to safeguard the well-being of women, sometimes by advising them who to stay away from. One article in *The Rag* warned women about an abortion provider whom the referral project volunteers disapproved of: "After talking with him at length, we decided not to work with him. We felt his attitude toward abortion and toward women in general was very destructive. We advised *The Rag* not to run an ad for his service; however, many other undergrad papers do. Watch out for them." Another article warned of "rip-off referrals" by people who demanded a fee to arrange a New York abortion, although women's groups were providing free information, and mentioned unscrupulous

New York taxi drivers who charged distraught women outrageous fares to take them to clinics.

The volunteers at the referral center were busier than ever. They sought new, safe places to refer women to, but leads often turned out to be disappointing. They heard of a hospital in Washington, DC, for example, that would allow abortions if a woman had a note from a physician saying that the abortion was necessary for her mental health. But the charge for such a note was $125, and the hospital fee $200. The combined cost of travel and medical procedure put that option out of reach for most Texas women. Indeed, cost was always a problem, even though friends might take up collections and some women might obtain money through student loans without specifying the need.

As Austin activists read and attended meetings in other states, we realized that thousands of people were working on multiple levels, trying to help women directly while simultaneously striving to change anti-abortion statutes. People throughout the country felt joined by a common dedication to the principle that women should be able to make their own choices.

That fall of 1970, I was following case developments across the country and planning strategy for the 1971 regular session of the Texas legislature. On November 18, a three-judge opinion in Wisconsin left intact only the section of the state law prohibiting abortion of a "quickened" fetus, one whose movement the woman could feel. We were always monitoring such decisions, which could help or hurt us in our own legal efforts. In a few months the Texas legislature would convene for its regular session; abortion would be an issue and we faced a dilemma. As in earlier sessions, some of our friends wanted to introduce a bill to make at least some abortions legal in Texas. If the Texas law changed, however, *Roe* might well be thrown out of court as moot. On the other hand, we did not want to rely on the Supreme Court to save women in Texas: what the Court justices would eventually do was a big question mark. We did not know whether we could get further in the courts or in the legislature, but it seemed important to pursue both the case and a legislative strategy.

There was in addition a conflict among pro-choice forces that I was moderating about which provisions to back in legislation. The conflict was between what was possible and what was ideal. The Texas Abortion Coalition, a blue-ribbon committee led by Ginny Whitehill, which included rabbis and ministers, Dr. Hugh Savage, head of Texas Obstetricians and Gynecologists, as well as several elected officials and many prominent women, felt the only bill with a chance of passing was a liberalized law. Judy Smith and the referral project volunteers in Austin wanted the repeal of all anti-abortion laws, or legislation more in conformity with the three-judge court decision we had already won.

AS 1971 LOOMED, Linda and I asked Santa Claus for good news from the Supreme Court; we wanted it to grant a hearing in our case. Ron and I used the holiday break to talk about what the New Year might bring and to make resolutions. I again vowed to achieve better balance between my professional and personal lives. We missed Austin and were thinking about ways to return, but we decided we couldn't make plans until the future of *Roe* became more certain. Ron guessed it had a good shot of becoming a Supreme Court case because of the mounting number of challenges and decisions on state abortion laws. But that seemed less likely when the new year brought headlines that the Supreme Court would hear *United States v. Vuitch*, the DC case. We were disappointed by speculation in the press that the Court might decide the abortion issue in that case and never hear another. But we were too busy with the legislative session to be unduly concerned about whether *Vuitch* might deprive us of an opportunity to appear before the Supreme Court.

On January 30, a few weeks after the legislative session began, all of the pro-choice Texas groups sponsored a "Citizens' Hearing on Abortion" on the UT campus. The room was packed. The star of the day was a Minneapolis doctor, Jane Hodgson, who had been convicted on November 21, 1970, for performing an illegal abortion. Minnesota law allowed abortion only if the life of the woman was threatened. Hodgson had a patient, a young housewife with three children, who contracted German measles in her first month of pregnancy; this condition was known to cause gross deformities in the fetus. First Hodgson filed a federal suit challenging the Minnesota anti-abortion law. When the court delayed, Hodgson acted. The fetus Hodgson aborted in a hospital was severely deformed. Nonetheless, after a lengthy trial Hodgson was convicted and received a thirty-day jail sentence and was suspended for a one-year probation period. (The Minnesota legislature later changed the penalty for performing illegal abortions to a life sentence.) We sat in awe as Hodgson spoke of her decision to put her medical license and her future on the line for a patient who deserved her help. She spoke eloquently against anti-abortion laws that prevented physicians from giving patients the highest standard of medical care. We applauded when she said that doctors must think of the quality of life rather than mere existence.

Bills were introduced in both the Texas House and the Texas Senate allowing abortion with the consent of the woman and her doctor if the woman were sixteen or over; if unmarried and under sixteen, she needed the consent of her parents; a married woman of any age would not need her parents' consent. In spite of our dislike of those provisions, we knew we had no choice of getting a better bill and only a slim chance of seeing those provisions passed.

The legislative hearings on abortion were characterized by great tension. For weeks prior to the hearings each side strategized over its testimony—whom to have as witnesses, what handouts to give the committee members. Just before the hearings were to begin, each side whipped its advocates up to a frenzy and again encouraged supporters to write or call their representatives in the legislature.

The process was complicated by frequent, unpredictable rescheduling. People would come to Austin for a hearing, wait and wait, and then learn that the committee had postponed the hearing. Witnesses had to be persuaded to come a second time, and even a third. The delays sometimes had unexpected results. On one occasion the anti-abortion folk bused children from parochial schools around the state to visit the capitol and be in the balconies for the abortion hearings. Instead, the hearings were postponed and the kids ended up observing a debate on something like pornography or liquor regulation.

Another complicating factor was that almost the last subject in the world that legislators wanted to deal with was abortion. Most legislators prized getting reelected, and they considered abortion a no-win issue. Whatever they did, plenty of people would be mad. Legislators were trying to duck the issue, and the majority were profoundly grateful to any among them who could devise a strategy that seemed to meet the issue head-on while in fact avoiding a vote.

Once a hearing was set, the staff of the committee considering a bill guaranteed both sides equal time for their formal presentations. The Texas Abortion Coalition was involved especially in planning the witnesses and outlining the points each should cover. In whatever time remained, testimony would become a free-for-all. Anyone in the audience could sign up to testify, and testimony would continue until all the committee members left. Pro-choice groups were urging members, friends, and other citizens to attend and show support.

Before the hearings began, one of the heated debates within

the pro-choice factions concerned whether or not to show enlarged photographs of women who had died from illegal abortions. Someone gave me a box of them; I have never forgotten one image of a dead woman on a black-and-white-tiled bathroom floor, her head on the floor and her hips in the air. The photographer left to one's imagination who had caused her death, but it was clear abortion was the reason. We expected the anti-abortionists to use grotesque and misleading photographs; they usually did. Some of our side felt we should show graphically the problems that resulted when abortion was illegal. Others argued that we would be sinking to the level of the opposition—a level we disdained—if we did the same. We decided to use reason instead of the pictures. But we included in the witness list women who could testify about what they had personally been through to obtain an abortion.

Senate Bill 553, our bill, would be before the Senate Public Health Committee on Monday, March 29, 1971. At six p.m. Sunday night two referral project volunteers, Bobby Nelson and Vic Foe, gave up sleep to get packets ready to distribute to legislators by nine the next morning. The packets were handed out to an overflowing crowd, people from all around the state who had come to voice their sentiments and buttonhole elected officials. Anti-abortionists and advocates of choice were giving out distinctive stickers or buttons for supporters to wear, each group trying to impress the legislators with its numbers. Tension was high.

Each side was allocated an hour and a half. The pro-choice time was split among Senate sponsors of the bill, me, three doctors (one a psychiatrist), a social worker, several women giving personal testimony of their abortions, two ministers (including the Reverend Claude Evans), and Richard Lamm, a Colorado legislator who later became that state's governor. Lamm was the male star for our side; he had sponsored the bill that liberalized the abortion law in Colorado. His district was predominantly

Catholic, yet he had been reelected twice. One point of having him testify was to demonstrate that legislators could vote pro-choice *and* be re-elected.

The most moving testimony was given by women who had had illegal abortions, or induced an abortion themselves. One was an unforgettable, gutsy woman, the sole provider for her two children, who knew that another child would have made it impossible for the family to survive. She would have lost her job and would not have been able to support the three children financially. "I could not have that baby," the woman said in a steely voice, tears streaming down her face. People at the referral project were willing to help her, but she didn't have the money for an abortion, in or out of state. Her only option, she felt, was to induce one herself.

The hearing room was completely silent as she told how night after night, when her children were asleep, she would take the heaviest book in the house and whack her stomach repeatedly. For hours she would sit and pummel her belly. And now she relived those nights in her testimony, her face cringing in pain. She said the only thought that went through her mind then was the well-being of her existing children. I can still see her with her eyes closed, crying, her fists clutched in front of her as she jerked the imaginary book toward her body. With each strike, she recalled, her body would cry in agony, but she was determined to succeed. She described the welts that resulted on her stomach and the bruises on her skin. She continued the beating until one night she felt cramps; at the cost of great pain and suffering, she had succeeded.

Among those testifying against the bill was Joseph Wither-spoon, who had been my jurisprudence professor in law school. He would get red in the face and very agitated whenever he talked about abortion. A few weeks earlier, when I was visiting former colleagues at the law school, Witherspoon had stopped me in the hall to tell me how distressed he was that I was trying the *Roe* case; after all, I had received an award for the best grade in his class. He simply could not believe that a student who did so well in his class would then go on to use her skills against the abortion laws. During his testimony, Witherspoon turned to me and said in a passionate, angry voice, "You should be ashamed, Sarah Weddington, you will *never* win. I know it."

Also in opposition, and very much in evidence, were the Solid Rock Mothers, who were from an evangelical religious group and seemed to feel God was personally on their side. Zealots like these scared me then; they scare me now. I respect the importance of religious faith, but I am skeptical of people who are certain they have the one "true" way and who freely throw God's name around in support of their own beliefs.

In spite of our intense efforts, it was discouragingly clear by early May that no new abortion bill was going to pass that session. No matter how hard we worked, or how many pro-choice people wrote or called, or how well we presented information at the hearing, the legislators did not want to deal with abortion. They wanted the subject, and us, to go away. We despaired of ever changing the situation for women in Texas through the legislative process. Linda and I once again felt the pressure to win in the courts.

The plus of the 1971 legislative session, though, was that I got to know Ruth McLean Bowman Bowers, a woman about twenty years my senior and a longtime supporter of Planned Parenthood in San Antonio, and her husband, Bill. Our mutual belief that abortion should be a woman's decision drew Ruth and me together. I admired Ruth's savvy, and her knowledge of the world, derived from foreign travel and experiences I had never had, and the fact that she was a wonderful friend and down-to-earth person. We often spent days together at the Capitol doing pro-choice lobbying. Later she supported the *Roe* litigation.

ABORTION MADE NATIONAL headlines that spring when Richard Nixon, who opposed it, took advantage of his role as president and commander in chief to end the practice of abortions in military hospitals. While we were seeking to make abortion legal for all, politics had closed access for one group of women. The use of presidential power against us was new then, but it would become a repeated pattern in the 1980s.

The spring was ending on a down note, when lightning struck. On May 21, the Orders of the United States Supreme Court included the following:

Probable Jurisdiction Noted or Postponed

No. 808. ROE ET AL. V. WADE. Appeal from D.C.N.D.Tex. Probable jurisdiction postponed to hearing of case on the merits. Reported below: 314 F.Supp. 1217.

No. 971. DOE ET AL. V. BOLTON, ATTORNEY GENERAL OF GEORGIA, ET AL. Appeal from D.C.N.D.Ga. Probable jurisdiction postponed to hearing of case on the merits. Reported below: 319 F.Supp. 1048.

Our Texas case, along with the Georgia case, would be heard sometime in October or after. I exulted. We had lost in the state legislature, but we had a chance to win in the US Supreme Court. A new Court term begins the first Monday in October and ends the following June or July. All cases argued during the new term are decided before the Court adjourns around July 4. We would have answers from the Supreme Court by then.

Ron and I speculated that the Court accepted those two cases because each involved a type of statute adopted in several states, Texas having the "restrictive" law and Georgia the "liberalized." By deciding those two cases, the Court would be commenting on laws in effect in almost every state. Also, *Roe* seemed the one case where the issue of a woman's right of choice was front and center, unencumbered by other questions except those raised by Dr. Hallford involving a doctor's ability to provide the best service to patients.

I immediately called those who were closest to the case. Linda and I had an excited "Can you *believe* this?" conversation. The Austin referral project volunteers were elated. John and Mary Doe said immediately that they, along with Mary's mother and grandmother, would go to Washington to watch the hearing. Eventually I was able to find a number for Jane Roe and call her. She said she was doing okay—and although her response to the news was placid, she seemed proud. My parents too were proud of my professional accomplishments. When I invited them to come to DC for the hearing, Daddy said he had to stay home, but he encouraged Mother to go; she was excited about the possibility.

During the next few days it really hit me to what extent *Roe* and the Georgia case were the focus of national attention. I was flooded with calls from pro-choice activists and attorneys in other states. My first contested case was going to the United States Supreme Court! The little case that Linda and I had started as volunteer lawyers in response to questions from women at the referral project might well become the vehicle for protecting reproductive rights and freedom of choice for every American woman. The thought was overwhelming—and humbling. Reality set in as I thought of the responsibility of the case and the disastrous consequences and despair that would follow if we lost.

I looked at the names of the Supreme Court justices and wondered how each would vote: Justice William O. Douglas had written the majority opinion for *Griswold v. Connecticut*, which recognized the right of privacy; I felt comfortable he would be on our side. Three other justices, John Harlan, William Brennan, Jr., and Byron White, had voted in the majority on *Griswold*, but I did not know if they would be willing to extend the right to the issue of abortion. Justices Hugo Black and Potter Stewart had voted against *Griswold*, so I was very uncertain of them. Then there were the three newest justices: Thurgood Marshall, Henry Blackmun, and Chief Justice Warren Burger. I considered Marshall, a Lyndon Johnson appointee and a brilliant legal mind; I felt comfortable he would side with us. Since Burger and Blackmun were appointed by Richard Nixon, I was not so sure of them.

The Supreme Court's orders provoked speculation and discussion around the country, yet the wheels of the Court kept turning. A memo from the clerk's office gave the schedule for the preparation of the case: it would be calendared, or set for argument, in the October 1971 session of the Court; certain papers and our brief would be due June 17; the State's brief would be due thirty days thereafter. A docketing fee of fifty dollars had been sent to the Court on May 6 by Roy Lucas at the Constitutional Law Institute.

Ron and I now had to make a decision about our future. I was excited about the Court's action and talked about it at work. My boss asked me if I planned to be involved, and I said, "Of course." The next day he yelled for me. After a short visit, he scrawled a note in blue ink across a sheet of yellow legal pad, tore it off, and handed it to me. I can still see the words clearly: "No more women's lib. No more abortion." It may have been that members of the Fort Worth City Council, our highest bosses, were giving him grief about my activities. Johndroe has since died, and I will never know for sure.

I had to choose between continuing employment for the city and continuing involvement in the case. I could not bear the thought of not being involved in the Supreme Court action, and Ron wanted me to have that experience. We both said we would never forgive ourselves if we failed to give the case our best shot. And we were both ready to return to Austin. We had lived frugally and had saved money while in Fort Worth, so we decided to quit our jobs, move back to Austin, and start our own law practice. We found a two-story wooden frame house in the downtown area. It needed a lot of work, but that made it all the more affordable to rent, and we planned to do most of the repairs. We could live upstairs and start our practice below.

When I called to tell Roy Lucas the news, he said he had been thinking of opening other offices and would be happy for me to work part-time with the Institute. Ron and I completed our move, and I returned to work on the case by gathering information about the problems faced by poor women who could not obtain abortions. But I was worried to see no progress from the Institute; the deadline for submitting the brief was upon us. I decided to go to New York and see for myself what was happening there.

As a young woman, I had ridden the plains of West Texas on horseback and tried to imagine the world beyond the horizon. Now, as an adult, I was on my way to the Big Apple. Anti-abortion laws had become emblematic of the laws and customs that imprisoned women. Without the ability to control their reproductive capacity, women could not fully control education, employment, family size, or their own physical and psychological well-being. I went to a new adventure determined to set the stage for a victory for all women.

5 . *Preparing for Supreme Court Argument*

N ew York was overwhelming, and my arrival was not auspicious. The airline lost one of my bags and by the time I filled out all the necessary papers, I had missed the last bus from the airport to the city and had to take the more expensive alternative, a taxi. The first taxi ride of my life was in a car with a bulletproof partition between the passenger and the driver, a sign that said the driver did not carry more than five dollars in change, and an enclosed money bucket in the floor of the front seat, welded to the transmission. My first night I stayed with an acquaintance; the day before, a stewardess had been murdered three blocks away.

The next day I saw my summer home. I was not favorably impressed. The Women's Medical Center, where I would be living, was a former abortion clinic in a four-story brownstone at 70 Irving Place, near Union Square in the lower third of Manhattan, a disreputable but not seedy part of the city. The building had a worn-down look. During the day it was used as a counseling center, where women seeking abortions might be referred to another location. At night it was home to four of us from the Institute and two renters.

I was housed in the switchboard room. There was no air-conditioning, so I slept with the windows open; still, the summer air was hotter than the hinges of hell. The unfamiliar noises of the city kept me from sleeping soundly until I managed to acquire a window unit. My bed was really a crude wooden chaise longue, with a gaudy, flowery cushion mattress; it had previously been the resting place for women after they had had abortions. The only other furniture was a dresser and a red bean-bag chair. I would have found my circumstances depressing if it had not been for the fact that the accommodations were free (Roy Lucas was on the Women's Medical Center board and did its legal work) and the others from the Institute, with whom I shared a kitchen and a bathroom, went out of their way to be kind to me.

The building did have a place on the roof where we could sit late at night and catch whatever breeze there was. I remember admiring the lights of the city from that vantage point. Now I realize the view was one to which many a New Yorker would not give a second glance, but it was the first time I had ever stayed in a place with access to the roof. The building had security problems, though. We were burglarized twice while I was living there; at night I took to latching a variety of fierce-looking locks.

The James Madison Constitutional Law Institute, where I would be working, was located at No. 4 Patchin Place in Greenwich Village, next to the grim tower of the Women's House of Detention. No. 4 was a long, narrow three-story house. Roy Lucas lived on the top floor. Its claim to fame was that it had once been the home of the writer e. e. cummings. My desk and typewriter were set up in the pleasant and sunny coffee room at the rear of the second floor. But the Institute was chaotic. In school I had studied Abraham Maslow's hierarchy of needs. Maslow's theory was that there are various levels of personal needs that must be satisfied before one can move to the next step of emotional growth and eventually become self-actualized; first come food, clothing and shelter. That summer I learned how much Maslow's hierarchy applies also to organizations. Good work simply does not get done until the basics are in place.

For most of the summer I was the only woman working at the Institute. I do not remember any particular discussion about the oddity of that given the focus on abortion cases. When the secretary quit, soon after I arrived, I took over as typist. I was easily the best typist in the building and was willing to do anything to speed up the preparation of the legal papers. I just wanted to get the brief done and go home. Nick Danforth, vice president of the Institute, was the only one who commented sympathetically on my doing most of the typing. That was typical of his admirable sensitivity; earlier he had established counseling for the men who sometimes accompanied their partners to the Women's Medical Center when abortions were performed there.

ON JUNE 8, Roy Lucas had requested an extension of time to file our *Roe* brief. Shortly after I arrived in New York in mid-June, the deadline was moved to August 1. Not a word on the brief had been written; Lucas explained that he was planning to use passages from various briefs he had already written for other purposes. But the work on *Roe v. Wade* was behind several other commitments he had made. He had agreed the Institute would file a jurisdictional statement in a North Carolina case; the appeal brief on Dr. Hodgson's case in Minnesota was several months past due and she was frantic; and the staff had just started on an *amicus* curiae brief on medical issues for the Georgia *Doe v. Bolton* case. (An *amicus* brief is one submitted by a "friend of the court" or by a person or group who, though not a participant in a lawsuit, has something to say to the court about the subject.) I pitched in to get some of the items with immediate deadlines out of the way, in hopes that everyone could then focus on the *Roe* brief. I especially wanted to help Dr. Hodgson; I had admired her ever since hearing her in Texas. The staff worked diligently to get the backlog cleared away, but each time we finished one project, something new—other than *Roe*—came up.

Soon it was clear to me that the *Roe* brief would never be ready on time. The deadline was approaching, and we had neither a brief nor, as yet, another extension. I could imagine our being thrown out of court for having failed to file the brief. Lucas finally agreed we would have to ask for another extension and I breathed a sigh of relief when the Court gave us until August 17.

That scare was a blessing. I realized I had to stop being pulled into other projects and start organizing. Linda and I talked by phone about the lack of progress, and what to do about it, but the living and working conditions were so unpleasant that I hesitated to ask her or anyone else to come help. Also, Linda had a paying job in Dallas; I assumed it would be impossible for her to leave Texas for an indefinite period.

So I called my partner. I told Ron at length about the problems, which he already knew in part, and asked if he would come. I needed him to help me research and write. Of course he would be working for free, but it would get me back to Austin sooner. Luckily, we did not have any ongoing cases there. Ron was in the middle of remodeling our house, and I thought it would be simple for him to lock the door and come stay in New York until my job was finished. He gave me a hard time about having been so naive about Lucas in the first place. But I was appropriately contrite, and he agreed to come. He moved into the switchboard room with me. We moved from the chaise to the floor. As I wrote my parents, our bed was "three cushions from loungers under two so-called mattresses with the stuffing coming out." These were uncomfortable and cramped quarters; on the other hand, they have made every place I have stayed in since seem luxurious by comparison.

Before the Institute staff got to the brief, we had to file

another document with the Supreme Court and furnish copies to the opposing attorneys: this was a 139-page record, each page measuring 6 by 9¼ inches, with wide margins. It contained a copy of all of the documents previously submitted in *Roe*, along with the transcript of the arguments presented in the three-judge court hearing and a copy of that court's opinion. Two colleagues from the Institute and I had worked like crazy earlier in the summer getting the record printed and delivered to the Supreme Court. It has very strict rules regarding the format for materials submitted, and none of us had been involved in a case at this level before. We found a woman at Record Press on "Printers' Row" in Manhattan who had, and she advised us on what to do. The fact that Record Press was a twenty-four-hour-a-day operation was critical, as we were always behind and rushing to meet deadlines.

Lucas suggested that a Supplementary Appendix, an unusual item for a Supreme Court case but one that seemed to me a good idea, also be filed. We wanted to be sure the justices and their clerks had a collection of relevant legal, medical, and social science articles at their fingertips. Included was a table showing the types of statutes regulating abortion in the United States, the most recent proposals on abortion legislation from well-known legal groups such as the American Law Institute, technical medical journal articles that backed up points we wanted to make, and a variety of statistical materials. Lucas had a good many of the articles in his files, and several staff members set about to organize and supplement them. This appendix ended up at almost 500 pages, 8½ by 11 inches.

The next task was organizing the brief. Each side in a Supreme Court case submits a brief limited to about 150 pages. Like the record, it too had to measure 6 by 9¼ inches. Given the myriad aspects of the abortion issue, there was no way for one brief to cover everything that needed to be said. Our brief would touch on all major aspects of abortion, and other groups would file *amicus curiae* briefs expanding on them.

Our brief would mention the medical aspects of abortion, and then medical groups would file a friend of the Court brief strictly about medical details. We would mention the legal aspects, and law professors and lawyers would file a brief further delineating legal considerations. We would mention the impact of pregnancy on women, and women's organizations and individual women would furnish a supplementary brief. The same strategy was worked out for religious, psychiatric, and other aspects of abortion. The *amicus* effort would also present to the Court names of prominent individuals and groups who opposed the current law. We wanted the Court to be aware of the breadth of support for changing the laws.

Jimmye Kimmey, Executive Director of the Association for the Study of Abortion, who at first glance seemed an upper-class Texas lady out of the Emily Post school, agreed to undertake the task of organizing the *amicus* brief effort. She turned out to be one of the most efficient people I have known. She had access to funding from John D. Rockefeller III and Cordelia Scaife May, a Mellon heir, and she had collected almost every article ever written about abortion. Her association's primary role had been to sponsor information-gathering conferences and provide reprints to other organizations in support of educational efforts. Jimmye knew experts in related fields who could provide valuable information and suggestions.

When Ron arrived in New York, he and I went over the points of the primary brief and divided up the writing responsibility. Other Institute staff offered help, and friends back in Austin were also willing to do research. Some books were available at the Institute, but not nearly as many as were at the UT law library. We combed through Lucas's various materials to see what we could use.

Ron agreed to organize the part of the brief that concerned procedural and technical points; I would do the part on the merits. Our strategy had two elements: we would set out our own best arguments, and we would try to anticipate and parry the State's arguments. Since the State's brief was not due until thirty days after ours, we would have to guess about its contents. We could, however, use the State's arguments before the three-judge court as a guide.

Another project we divided up was a study of the individual justices on the Supreme Court: how they had voted in past cases, how they might be likely to vote in *Roe*, and how to organize our arguments to appeal to each as much as possible. We began to refer to them as "The Supremes." There was a feeling that the Burger Court, as distinct from the Warren Court of the 1950s and 1960s, was sending a message that it would not meddle with the other branches of government, state or federal, if it could avoid doing so. That seemed a bad omen for our case. We circulated articles around the Institute, such as one from the June 21, 1971, issue of *Time* entitled "The Supreme Court: End of an Era." The article described Chief Justice Warren Burger as the ceremonial leader of the Court but said he had "not yet assumed the Court's intellectual leadership." It also commented that an old friend and philosophical ally of Burger's was Justice Harry Blackmun. It said the key to the new Court's direction was with the four centrist justices, Potter Stewart, Byron White, John Harlan, and William Brennan, Jr., "whose shifting alliances frequently tip the balance on close constitutional questions."

The article said Stewart, fifty-six, epitomized the centrist position. "Pin-striped and polished, he writes careful opinions that cannot be easily categorized." We later heard that Stewart's wife was a Planned Parenthood volunteer; we hoped that was a good omen. At fifty-three, White was the youngest justice. *Time* characterized him as tough on crime, strong on civil rights, and flexible on just about everything else. Rumor had it that he and his wife had had difficulty having children. I wondered whether it was true and, if so, whether personal experience would have an impact. Would he think, How can women have abortions when my wife and I struggled so hard to have children? Brennan, sixty-five, was usually a stalwart of the Warren Court's liberal activist wing, but he seemed to be inching rightward to join the present center. Still, we hoped we might win his vote.

William O. Douglas, seventy-three years old, was the only justice we felt sure would vote for us. He had written the *Griswold* opinion, which emphasized the right of privacy. I talked by phone to Dag Hamilton, an Austin friend and lawyer who had once worked with Douglas, about how to frame our argument to appeal to him.

THERE WERE A FEW breaks in the relentless pace of work. Ron and I were anxious to explore New York before returning to Texas. We rode the Staten Island ferry and gawked at the Statue of Liberty. We took the Circle Line boat around Manhattan for three dollars. We went to the American Museum of Natural History and the Museum of Modem Art. We bought half-price tickets and saw *Oh! Calcutta!* and *1776.* For a dollar we swayed to Kris Kristofferson and Mary Travers singing in Central Park.

One weekend, to get away from the city's oppressive summer heat, we drove to Lake George with two friends from the Institute. The family of one of them, Nick Danforth, had a lake house there, which we imagined, in the normal Texas connotation, would be a rough two-room building with a big porch, so run-down you could put your feet up anywhere. It turned out to be somewhat more elegant: the Danforth family had bought a scenic plot of land by the lake two generations before and established a family enclave. It was reminiscent of the gilded age, and late-nineteenth-century luxury. There were actually five houses along the shore, all owned by Danforth relatives. There were tennis courts, motorboats, sailboats, and hills to climb. The opposite shore was protected parkland.

One of my favorite parts of the weekend was simply sitting in the back of Nick's beautiful turn-of-the-century redwood motorboat on the lake. Ron did some fishing, without results, and then tried out a Sunfish, while I was content to relax, read, and enjoy the surroundings. And sleeping in a real bed was a treat after our nights at Irving Place!

On Saturday we cooked dinner and raised toasts to the contributors who had just come through to keep us afloat through the last push to complete our work. A Boston businessman and philanthropist, Thomas Cabot, had contributed $15,000, and a gynecologist from Harlem had sent money and a letter describing the suffering he had seen after botched abortions; he was the only physician to respond to our huge mailing requesting financial help. One check was large and one was small, but together they paid our bills and nourished our spirits.

The other Institute staffers and I were fortunate to become involved with some of the stars of the pro-choice movement during the summer. They wanted us to win and so were willing to help whenever asked. One of the staff members interviewed Dr. Christopher Tietze, the head of the World Population Council, a founder of the Association for the Study of Abortion, and an internationally known demographer and collector of reproductive health statistics. I later met Tietze and I remember him as brilliant, gruffly speaking into his beard, and seeming to know the answer to every question about abortion statistics.

I also met Harriet Pilpel, the primary lawyer for the Planned Parenthood Federation of America, for the first time in person. I had spoken with her by phone the previous summer when she called to offer assistance for the appeal. She had an elegant mind and, with a twinkle in her eye, told wonderful war stories about

Griswold v. Connecticut and other cases she had been involved with. I felt privileged sitting in her office in a big New York law firm, talking with someone who had made history.

Another star was Alan Guttmacher, the head physician for Planned Parenthood and later the founder of the Alan Guttmacher Institute, a continuing source of excellent information on abortion. In 1967 he had advanced the movement for reform by writing *The Case for Legalized Abortion Now*. We consulted him in connection with the medical portion of the brief, and Guttmacher shared a wealth of information. When I met him I saw a distinguished gentleman with refined features and a warm personal manner.

THE AUGUST 17 DEADLINE loomed. Kitty Schild, a UT law student, sent me a memo on the question of whether the case was moot. The State was arguing that since Jane Roe was no longer pregnant she could no longer challenge the abortion law. We were arguing that the case was a class action and that at any specific moment there were pregnant women in Texas who wanted the option of abortion. It would be unreasonable to ask a woman to stay pregnant until a case could get to the Supreme Court— the law didn't work as fast as biology. Kitty put together a series of cases to help us make the argument that our case was not moot.

David Tundermann did a memo on legislative purpose. One of our arguments was that the original anti-abortion statutes were adopted because of a lack of medical techniques to prevent infection, but that abortion in early pregnancy was now statistically safer than carrying a pregnancy to term. We wanted to show the Court that the original basis for the statute was no longer valid.

Diane Dodson and other UT law students were adding cases, checking footnotes, and filling in holes for us. (Diane still enjoys telling the story of her Family Law final that summer. Professors often ask questions about important pending cases. Hers asked about abortion; because of her volunteer work for us she was able to ace the question.) Bea Durden did not have a law degree, but she was very resourceful; she found a murder case in which a pregnant woman had been killed and the fetus had also died, but the case was not ruled a double homicide. In another instance, a man kicked his estranged pregnant wife and killed the fetus; the court held that he was not guilty of murder.

Dr. William J. McGanity, the head of obstetrics and gynecology at the University of Texas Medical School in Galveston, combed the medical library there for helpful information. The hospital associated with the medical school was the state-run hospital providing indigent care. McGanity agreed to give me an affidavit for the Supreme Court, as did Dr. Paul C. MacDonald, chairman of the department of obstetrics and gynecology of the UT Southwestern Medical School in Dallas and the head of obstetrics and gynecology at Parkland Memorial, a city and county hospital responsible for providing area indigent care. Dr. Joseph Seitchik, the head of obstetrics and gynecology for the San Antonio-Bexar County public hospital and UT San Antonio Medical School, also helped. We hoped their comments would have a special impact with at least Justice Blackmun, who had been counsel to the Mayo Clinic before joining the bench, and we thought all of the justices would have a special respect for the opinions of other professionals.

Seitchik, for example, said his colleagues and students in 1970 had treated about five hundred patients for the after-effects of abortion, including about one patient per week "moderately to desperately ill" as the result of induced abortion. Seitchik's comments underlined the medical problems caused by illegal abortion.

In the end, our primary brief consisted of sections that

included a statement of the case (facts about the plaintiffs, the decision by the district court, and the difficulties caused by the denial of injunctive relief, i.e., the court's refusal to tell the district attorney not to prosecute doctors); relevant medical facts about abortion; a section on legal and medical standards relating to induced abortion; details on the relationship between contraception (and the fact that failproof contraception was not available) and the need for abortion; and a summary of our arguments. We ticked off the points we had to make: why each of our plaintiffs, not just Roe and Hallford, should have standing; why the three-judge court should have granted an injunction; and why the provisions of the Texas law were unconstitutional.

We made every argument we thought the Court might find persuasive. We discussed fundamental personal rights secured by the First, Fourth, Ninth, and Fourteenth Amendments, including the fundamental right to marital and personal privacy, and the right to seek and receive medical care. I thought the Supreme Court was likely to decide in our favor under the Fourteenth Amendment, although the lower court's decision was based on the Ninth, and I certainly did not want to say that was wrong.

In the summer of 1970, Henry Wade had stated that he would continue to prosecute doctors under the Texas law. I wanted something from him in writing to submit to the Supreme Court. Our direct appeal to the Court, bypassing the Fifth Circuit, was based on the fact that although the lower federal court had declared the Texas law unconstitutional, law enforcement authorities were continuing to enforce the law. I contacted John Tolle, Wade's assistant DA in Dallas, and he sent me a letter I could file with the Court, which stated that the DA's office was continuing to enforce the Texas abortion laws in all cases in which indictments were returned by the Dallas County grand jury.

We decided to expand the section of our brief that covered

ways in which the government had not regarded the fetus as a person. Glen Wilkerson, a UT law student who had worked with me for Professor John Sutton, did research on that. Some points were so simple and obvious that Ron and I debated about whether to include them when we worked this research up into the brief. Our footnote 96, for example, read: "Section 1 of the Fourteenth Amendment of the United States Constitution refers to 'all persons born or naturalized in the United States.' There are no cases which hold that fetuses are protected by the Fourteenth Amendment." This would in fact be one of the most important parts of the brief. The government, we argued, had not treated the fetus as a person in other ways. A pregnant woman who sought out a person willing to perform an abortion and who consented to, if not pleaded for, the procedure was guilty of no crime in Texas. Women who traveled to another state for an abortion were guilty of no crime. Self-induced abortion had never been treated as a criminal act.

We stated further that the unborn fetus was not legally a "human being" and that therefore killing a fetus was not murder or any other form of homicide. Homicide in Texas applied only to the killing of one who had been born. A fetus was not considered by the law equal to a "human being." As Ron wrote, "The State does not require that a pregnant woman with a history of spontaneous abortion go into seclusion in an attempt to save the pregnancy. No pregnant woman having knowingly engaged in conduct which she reasonably could have foreseen would result in injury to the fetus (such as skiing in late pregnancy) has ever been charged with negligent homicide."

We pointed out that no legal formalities of death were observed regarding fetuses, at least for those of less than five months gestation. Property rights were contingent upon being born alive. There had never been a tort (personal injury) recovery in Texas as the result of an injury to a fetus not born alive.

No benefits were given prior to birth for arrangements such as workman's compensation, where benefits are normally allowed for "children."

We admitted that there were some decisions better left to a representative process, but the decision on abortion was exactly the opposite. "A representative or majority decision-making process has led to chaos. Indeed, in the face of two difficult, unresolvable choices—to destroy life potential in either a fetus or its host—the choice can only be left to one of the entities whose potential is threatened." The woman, we argued, was the appropriate one to make the decision.

Lawyers who had been preparing *amicus* briefs began filing theirs in August, and they soon received press attention. To me they were fascinating and invigorating, and I was grateful for the time and expertise of the attorneys involved, and for the support of the groups and individuals who signed. Surely the Court would pay attention to such a mountain of credible statements and evidence.

Among the *amicus* briefs filed, one representing "millions of American women" and prepared by Los Angeles attorney Norma G. Zarky bore the signatures of US Senator Maurine B. Neuberger of Oregon, authors Marya Mannes and Elizabeth Janeway, anthropologist Margaret Mead, former Miss America Bess Myerson, and current DC Representative Eleanor Holmes Norton. The seven organizations supporting the brief included the American Association of University Women, the Young Women's Christian Association, the National Organization for Women, and the Professional Women's Caucus.

Harriet Pilpel filed an *amicus* brief for the Planned Parenthood Federation of America and the American Association of Planned Parenthood Physicians. Zero Population Growth filed a brief with several concerned California groups. Nancy Stearns of the Center for Constitutional Rights in New York wrote a brief for a variety of women lawyers and some women's health organizations.

A religious brief in our favor was written by the lawyer, social activist, and philanthropist Helen Buttenwieser and filed on behalf of the American Ethical Union, the American Friends Service Committee, the American Jewish Congress, the Episcopal Diocese of New York, the New York State Council of Churches, the Union of American Hebrew Congregations, the Unitarian Universalist Association, the United Church of Christ, and the Board of Christian Social Concerns of the United Methodist Church, among others.

There were also *amicus* briefs filed to support the State of Texas, including one by the attorneys general of Arizona, Connecticut, Kentucky, Nebraska, and Utah. A variety of groups and individuals who opposed abortion also filed, including Mothers for the Unborn and a Catholic group, the Association of Texas Diocesan Attorneys.

The documents for *Roe* stood more than a foot high once our brief and all the *amicus* briefs and those for the State were combined. I cannot believe there was anything pertinent to the case that was not in one or more of the briefs. With a great sense of relief, Ron and I put the finishing touches on the *Roe* documents and packed for Austin.

In late August, before we went home, we took the train to Gloucester, Massachusetts, to visit Cyril Means, a professor at New York University Law School, and his wife, Rosalind. Although he was American, Professor Means fit my conception of what an English barrister would be like. He was a leading theorist on the legality of abortion and was in the process of preparing a law review article on the history of abortion laws to submit to the Court. Ron and I went both to see the Massachusetts coast and to talk to Means about his research and our preparation for oral argument.

The Means home was a wonderful place, a typical New England three-story house with a screened-in porch and a view of the beach. I spent late afternoons with Rosalind Means and the Means children catching crabs and lobster. I had never eaten either, so I had to be taught how to conquer each—you cannot find those on the plains of West Texas! After dinner Professor Means, Ron, and I would sit on the porch, with the sound of ocean waves as the backdrop for our discussion of the points in the brief and the various people involved in the national effort. Means knew a great deal about the people; it was fascinating to hear his answers to our questions.

UPON OUR RETURN to Austin, Ron and I arranged get-togethers to show our written materials and report on our progress to the women from the referral project and others who had helped. I now had to face the question of who would present the oral argument to the Supreme Court. While I was in New York, Lucas had pressed the point that he was more experienced and knowledgeable than I. Always the peacemaker, I was searching for ways for both of us to be involved. Unbeknownst to me, Lucas had written the Court during the summer that he would be arguing *Roe*. As the fall began, I continued to assume that we would both be involved in the oral argument. Linda, our backup, would be sitting at counsel table. While in Washington for a meeting of the National Association for the Repeal of Abortion Laws (NARAL), the predecessor to what would eventually become the NARAL Pro-Choice America. I went to the Supreme Court to listen to some arguments and get a sense of how things were done. I retained the hope that Lucas and I could find a solution.

My first effort was to seek a full hour for our presentation. Each side in the DC case, *United States v. Vuitch*, had been granted an hour. I felt that since two consolidated cases (*Roe* and *Doe*) were actually involved here and the pertinent issues were so numerous and complex, they could not be covered in so short a time as the usual thirty minutes per side per case. My second effort was to seek permission for Lucas and me each to present half of the argument. I knew it would take a miracle for the Court to grant either request; it particularly frowned on divided presentation. It definitely preferred for one attorney to present the entire argument for each of the two sides per case. Further, if the justices wanted to allow additional time for argument, they could do so at the conclusion of the original presentation rather than provide for it in advance.

Lucas maintained that he was the better choice to present the case. But women attorneys (including, I believe, Rhonda Copelon and Nancy Stearns from the Center for Constitutional Rights) were calling and saying that no matter how sympathetic a man might be, he simply could not understand the fear of pregnancy or the resentment of the limitations that the law placed on women, or the other implications for the lives of women that pregnancy involved. This uniquely woman's case should be argued by a woman. The debate raged through the autumn. I was admitted to the Supreme Court bar (with Judge Sarah T. Hughes on record as the signer of the certificate), continued to do research, and practiced for the presentation "just in case."

On October 12 the Court denied the State's request for additional time to file its brief. Jay Floyd of the Texas attorney general's office filed the State's brief on October 18, and I read it several times for points that should be countered during oral argument. I found no surprises. In preparing for oral argument, I continually updated the information that had previously been submitted in writing to the Court. We collected statistics on births to pregnant teenagers. We kept up with a stream of events in other legal challenges to anti-abortion statutes. A Texas criminal appellate court had upheld the constitutionality of the Texas anti-abortion law in *Thompson v. State*; I read the case to see how to distinguish it from ours and argue that it was wrongly decided. I hoped the opinion of a lower state court would carry less weight than that of a three-judge federal court.

Moot court sessions took a major amount of time. Lawyers, law students, referral project volunteers, and interested friends would play the roles of Supreme Court justices. They would ask me questions they felt the justices might ask, and I would answer. Then we would critique my answers and work on improving them. We generally met in my conference room, where many of the participants had to sit on the floor. Other moot courts were held in a more formal setting at the law school, where a number of professors contributed their time. Looking back, I am not sure whether all of them wanted me to win, or whether they just enjoyed pretending they were on the Supreme Court.

THAT FALL I HEARD a frightening rumor that the State would have Charles Alan Wright presenting its oral argument. Wright, a UT law professor who specialized in federal courts and procedures, was one of the prospects for the seat Harry Blackmun eventually took, and he personally knew a majority of the justices. He would be a formidable opponent.

My showdown with Lucas came when oral argument was set for December 13, 1971. The Court wrote me asking for the name of the lawyer who would argue *Roe;* I sent a copy to Lucas; he said something to me that I interpreted as intimating that his efforts had "bought" him the right to argue. My back went up: neither Linda nor I would ever have "sold" the case. Then I got mad at Lucas when the Clerk's Office at the Court told me that they knew who would be arguing for *Roe* for the plaintiffs. "You do? Who?" I asked. It turned out that Lucas had written the Court saying he would be the one. He had never mentioned that to any of the others of us working on the case.

The clients in a case have the final say-so about who argues.

I talked to Linda, John and Mary Doe, and Jane Roe; each said, "You do it, Sarah." Each of them knew me but none of them had worked with Lucas. Linda wrote a letter to the Court on November 24 stating that I would be presenting oral argument. She sent a copy to Lucas and to Hallford's attorneys. Two days earlier, Jay Floyd wrote the Court that he would be representing the State of Texas. I was relieved that I would not be facing Wright.

On November 30, the Court clerk confirmed that I would be listed as counsel. At last I could concentrate totally on preparing for oral argument. I preferred to rely on myself, rather than take a chance on someone else; no one had spent more hours on the case than I, and my gender and youth might be an advantage. The older men sitting on the Court might listen more carefully simply because of the novelty. In addition, because of the experience in Mexico, Ron and I cared deeply about doing away with anti-abortion laws.

That same day Jay Floyd sent a Motion to Postpone Argument and Submission. He pointed out that there were two vacancies on the Court and asked that oral arguments be rescheduled for when the Court had its full membership. President Nixon had nominated Lewis Powell and William Rehnquist to fill the posts of Justices John Harlan and Hugo Black, who had retired, but as of the end of November neither had been confirmed. Even if their confirmation preceded the date of oral argument (as actually happened), they wouldn't be sworn in early enough to hear it, and thus could not participate in the decision.

I could see the logic to Floyd's motion, but I considered it a delaying tactic. If the case were postponed, the status quo would be maintained and women still would not have access to legal abortion. That was fine from Floyd's point of view, but it was not what I wanted. I wanted the law changed—and the sooner the better! As I completed legal preparations, a few other tasks also needed attention—those of preparing a statement, obtaining seats in the courtroom for a number of people who wanted and deserved to be there, arranging my notes for oral argument, and deciding what to wear to court.

First, my statement. The primary purpose of oral presentation is to answer the justices' questions. But I wanted to write out in advance a statement I could rehearse, in which all of my key points were included and perfectly phrased, and to memorize words to begin and end my allocated time. I intended to practice the points in advance but not take my notes into the courtroom. Once there I did not want to read a speech; I wanted to converse with the justices.

Next, seating. There were not enough seats in the courtroom for everyone who wanted to witness the presentations. Many Texans, pro-choice lawyers from other states, and Institute staffers would be going to Washington for our argument. The Court normally allocates six seats to each attorney arguing a case, so those six would automatically be allocated for me to designate. But I wanted to be sure that other lawyers like Harriet Pilpel and Cyril Means, who planned to be there, would have seats. I petitioned the Court, made a call to the Congressman in my parents' district, and sought out people who knew any of the justices or people who worked at the Court to ask their help in guaranteeing seats for others. In addition, Bill Bowers called Larry Temple, an Austin lawyer who had once worked for a Supreme Court justice. Larry called his former boss and arranged seats for Ginny Whitehill and Ruth Bowers in the section reserved for family and friends of the justices.

Linda would sit to my left at counsel table. I wished Ron could be there as well, but I felt an obligation to keep a place for Lucas. I knew I would have a seat for Ron through my parents' Congressman, if I could not finagle a better one.

Arranging to get people into the courtroom increased my awareness of those who were important to the issue or important to my life who would be there watching me before the Court. Dr. Hodgson, for example, would be in the courtroom. If I won, she would be free; if I lost, her medical license and her future would remain in jeopardy. I wrote the Court asking to designate twelve seats; it granted my request.

Now I turned to another task—arranging my information for the oral argument. I did not want to be shuffling through cards searching for the answer to a justice's question. Eventually I tailored a system for easy access to answers: Overlapping index cards would be taped inside a legal folder starting at the bottom left and right and continuing to the top of the folder. At the lower edge of each card, in big letters for easy reference, would be the subject the card covered—standing, mootness, First Amendment, and so on. I could see the entire top cards and the subject of each card beneath; and since the cards were taped in one at a time, they could all be flipped, so that information typed on each side was readily available.

Finally, I had to decide what to wear in Washington. Dress for argument in the Supreme Court is traditionally very formal. The marshal of the Court wears striped pants and a coat with cutaway tails. When the solicitor general, the government's top lawyer, appears there, he wears a morning coat. My best suit was a conservative dark blue three-piece with a high neck and long sleeves. It was appropriate for the oral argument.

As the court date approached I kept double-checking late cases. I thought I might get a question about the *Vuitch* case, so I asked Texan Terry O'Rourke, who was clerking for a DC judge, to check a few details; he supplied thorough, exact answers. (The first question I was asked by a Supreme Court justice was about *Vuitch*, and I knew the answer cold.)

A couple of days before argument I was still working with a list of pro-choice activists who wanted guaranteed seating in the courtroom. I called the Texas Attorney General's office and learned it had six seats it had not designated and that it would be willing for me to designate those seats. I sent the Attorney General a fervent thank-you note and I sent six more names to the Court.

WHEN I RECEIVED the Supreme Court's "Hearing List for the Session Beginning December 6, 1971," I looked at only two entries:

No. 70-18. *Jane Roe et al. v. Henry Wade.*
Appeal from the U.S.D.C. for the Northern District of
Texas.
For appellants: Mrs. Sarah R. Weddington, Austin, Tex.
For appellee: Jay Floyd, Assistant Attorney General of
Texas, Austin, Tex.
(1 hour for argument.)

No. 70-40. *Mary Doe et al. v. Arthur K. Bolton, as Attorney
General of State of Georgia, et al.*
Appeal from the U.S.D.C. for the Northern District of
Georgia.
For appellants: Mrs. Margie Pitts Hames, Atlanta, Ga.
For appellees: Mrs. Dorothy T. Beasley, Assistant Attorney
General of Georgia, Atlanta, Ga.
(1 hour for argument.)

I was remembering my experience in Mexico and hoping that finally the terror of illegal abortion would end. It was a moment of personal reflection, as well as professional pride. When some had laughed about two young, inexperienced lawyers as modern-day Don Quixotes, Linda and I just kept putting one legal foot in front of the other. After working on the case for two years, soon we would be before the United States Supreme Court—it was an awesome thought.

On December 7, the Court denied the State's motion to postpone oral argument, thereby ending any speculation that it might delay hearing *Roe* until there were nine justices on the bench. The standard forms from the clerk's office notifying us of this had "Dear Sir" printed on them; someone had had the sensitivity to change the notice sent to me to read "Dear Madam."

Cyril Means delivered proofs of his law review article to the Court on December 9 and simultaneously had copies delivered to each of the counsel involved in *Roe* and *Doe*. He wanted to ensure that there were no objections to mentions of his research during the proceedings.

Reporters were searching for stories in anticipation of the hearing. The day before oral argument the *Dallas Times Herald* ran a story headlined "Young Women Take Abortion Case to Supreme Court." The lead was: "The mothers of Sarah Weddington and Linda Coffee will witness one of the most tense hours of their daughters' lives Monday when the two attorneys argue the Texas abortion case before the US Supreme Court." The story went on to include a comment I'd made: "The first thing my mother asked was whether she could take a tape recorder and a camera with her to record the arguments. Isn't that just like a mother?" I had to tell her neither would be allowed in the courtroom.

Ron and I went to Washington a few days before the hearing. We had made arrangements to stay with Bill and Martha Hamilton, friends who had once lived in Texas. They were used to a steady stream of Texas visitors and reserved their foldout living room couch for us for as long as we wanted to stay.

My anxiety increased each day I was in the capital. I visited the Supreme Court to observe another case presentation—and thereby make certain I knew what I was supposed to do. I also spent time in the Supreme Court library. One woman at the checkout desk whispered to me that many staffers were rooting for my side to win.

I was feeling a heavy responsibility. I owed my best effort to the women who would continue to be forced to seek illegal abortions if we lost, to those who would otherwise risk self-induced abortions, to all the people who had helped me along the way, and to anyone who supported the right of choice. I wanted to justify their faith in me. I did not want any mistake of mine to let them down.

The day before my oral argument, Ron and I moved to the Capitol Hill Hotel to be within easy walking distance of the Court. We had dinner that night with Margie Pitts Hames and her husband. Margie and I wanted to coordinate our strategy for oral argument, since she would be arguing the pro-choice side of the Georgia case as soon as the Texas presentation ended. The four of us mulled over the latest gossip about the justices and how each was leaning, and reviewed tips about how to be successful the following day.

Supreme Court personnel were referring to December 13 as "Ladies' Day." Three of the four attorneys who would be arguing on that day were women. Jay Floyd was representing Texas, but Georgia was sending a woman assistant attorney general named Dorothy Beasley. Someone wondered out loud how Margie would handle it if it turned out that Beasley was pregnant and began her comments to the Court by saying, "Your Honors, I am here to argue on behalf of myself and Junior." As it turned out, Margie didn't have to face that situation.

After dinner Ron and I visited with Ruth Bowers to thank her again for her help regarding the case. Then it was time for some rest. That day I had yet again reviewed the most important documents and outlined over and over in my mind the critical points I had to make before the Court. I was prepared in every way I knew, but my mind just would not turn off.

I would lie down and think, "What if the Court asks about *Griswold*? I had better check the wording." And I would get up and review it. I would go back to bed and think, "Now how should I phrase the issue about when life begins from a legal perspective?" And I would get up to look at my notes again. Then I would try to sleep. It seemed only minutes until the alarm sounded.

Others have told me I appeared "calm and cool" that morning. If so, I concealed a bundle of surging emotions inside me. I was intense, concentrating on what I had to accomplish; I wanted to win more than I had ever wanted anything. I could not imagine how I was going to answer whatever questions the justices had *and* get across what I wanted to say in only thirty minutes.

Thirty minutes to reach across a three-foot abyss between the modest lectern behind which I would stand and the long bench where the justices would sit in their black robes. Thirty minutes to find a way to touch the hearts and minds of those men. Thirty minutes to make them hear the voices of women who had been through illegal or legal abortions and the eloquence of their strivings to deal with life's struggles. Thirty minutes to convey to the justices the legal reasoning and theory on my side and the accumulated expertise of many in various fields who said the Texas law should be overturned.

I was facing the biggest challenge of my life. I knew the hopes and prayers of millions of women, and men who cared about them, would walk into that courtroom with me.

6. A Great Day in Court

The weather was crisp and clear on the morning of December 13, 1971, and there was electricity in the air. Those on their way to the Supreme Court had a sense of the historic proportions of the moment. Betty Friedan made a visit to the Supreme Court that day; she says her "historical Geiger counter" was clicking madly, and she was determined to witness history in the making.

I was up and dressed early. As accessories for my suit, I chose a single strand of pearls, pearl earrings, and black heels. My strawberry-blond hair, which fell to beneath my shoulder blades, was down. Ron was in a black suit with a striped tie. As we were having breakfast in the hotel restaurant, a steady stream of people who were in town for the argument stopped by our table to extend their best wishes.

John and Mary Doe and her relatives walked down First Street to the Court with us; my parents' Congressman, George Mahon, would be driving my mother later. At the last minute Linda's mother was unable to come. We arrived at the Supreme Court before nine, more than an hour before oral argument was to begin. I wanted to be sure that arrangements were in order for those designated by me for special seating, and I wanted a few minutes to review my notes one last time in the lawyers' lounge. I also wanted to be early to avoid being distracted by any anti-abortion demonstrators. I am five-seven, Ron is six-four; we joked that he might have to help me get through. Then we decided they would never guess someone so young would be doing the argument.

As we approached the Supreme Court building, my adrenaline was pumping, but I felt a calm produced by months of preparation. I had a sense that all the pieces had already been set in motion; we were simply playing out the final scene. Demonstrators were not yet active, but there was a line of people out the front door and around the side of the building, all waiting to hear the oral arguments. A few people in line who knew me murmured, "We're pulling for you," and "Go get 'em, Sarah." We paused after ascending to the sixteen-pillared white marble front entrance. On either side were allegorical statues representing law and justice, and above us were chiseled the words "Equal Justice Under the Law."

We entered the towering front doors of the Court building and walked down the spacious central marble hallway, our steps echoing as we proceeded. I barely noted the marble busts of former chief justices as I passed them.

Our first destinations were the clerk's and marshal's offices. At the clerk's office, I picked up a card authorizing me to take into the courtroom the items I wanted with me for oral argument, my folder of index cards and the copies of documents submitted in the case. The instructions said in part:

> Remain seated at reserved table behind Counsel's table *throughout* the argument of the case immediately preceding your case on the calendar, unless special arrangements have been made with the Clerk.
>
> When Counsel's turn comes for argument he will proceed

to the rostrum without being called. *He should not begin until he has been recognized by the Chief justice,* then [should] open his argument with the usual, "Mr. Chief Justice, and may it please the Court—"

Counsel should compute their remaining time during argument. *Do not* make inquiry of the Chief Justice.

I hoped those forms would not always refer to lawyers as "he."

At the marshal's office, the office in charge of seating, I began to see the people for whom I had reserved seats. Several staff members from the Institute were there, as were Roy Merrill and Fred Bruner, the attorneys for Dr. Hallford. Jane Roe and Hallford were not.

I ran into Dennis Horan of Chicago, one of the most active anti-abortion attorneys of the day. He had filed an *amicus* brief in support of the state laws. We had met before at meetings where we argued opposite sides of the issue. We visited briefly about the day's proceedings, and as we parted he said, "It will be a sad day for this country if you win today. I am counting on your losing."

Linda, Ron, and I visited the lawyers' lounge, which is reserved for members of the Supreme Court bar. It is a room with pictures of former justices on the walls, sparsely furnished with chairs, reading tables, and lamps. We spoke with a few other attorneys there before I retreated to review my notes. By now the justices would have read the briefs, their clerks would have prepared memorandums about the case, and each justice would likely already be leaning one way or the other. Cases are seldom won in oral argument, but they can be lost. That is what I wanted to avoid.

While in the lawyers' lounge, I discovered one disconcerting fact: The only restroom facilities were marked "Men." To find facilities for women I had to hurry to the basement. (When I visited the Court on April 22, 1992, for the *Planned Parenthood of Southeastern Pennsylvania v. Casey* hearing, I again looked to see whether that had changed; it hadn't.) It wasn't until 1993, when Justice Ruth Bader Ginsburg was appointed to the Court, and joined Sandra Day O'Connor there, that a women's bathroom was installed in the lawyer's lounge.

At a little after nine-thirty I entered the courtroom. The space inspires reverence; it is very formal, yet it also creates a feeling of intimacy. Twenty-four marble columns line two sides of the room; thirteen different types of marble appear throughout the room. Its high, ornate ceiling is painted in a sea of color, with gilt and vivid reds and blues. The eighty-two-by-ninety-foot courtroom has about 350 seats, 298 in the public area, with some seventy of those reserved for lawyers.

Most people enter at the back of the courtroom through heavy maroon velvet curtains; these are meant to cut down on noise as people come and go during deliberations. Past the curtains is seating divided into three sections of what look like church pews with a minimal amount of fancy fabric cushioning. The section to the far left is the three-minute section; tourists sit here for three minutes and then are replaced by a new group. That process continues throughout oral argument. The other two sections are for those with reserved seats and those who have been standing in a first-come, first-served line. They may remain as long as they choose. The strict decorum of the Court was described by one writer:

> All First Amendment rights are suspended when one enters the hallowed halls of highest justice: bags are searched; one may not wear any [political] buttons, one may not speak, [or] sit leaning forward or with one leg crossed beneath the other or with an arm thrown across the back of the seat; one may not take notes—or carry a pad—unless one has a [court] press card and is seated in a special press section.

An aisle of three or four feet and a gold railing separate those in the pews from lawyers admitted to Supreme Court practice. Small chairs are reserved for the seventy or so lawyers who wish to sit and observe. I noted that the lawyers tended to sit behind the side they were championing; it reminded me of the bride's-side and groom's-side seating custom for weddings. This lawyers' area is divided by a central corridor; on either side of that area, closest to the high bench for the justices, are two large library tables.

The Court normally hears two arguments during each session; the morning session begins at ten and concludes at noon, and the afternoon session begins at one and ends at three. Each attorney who is to make a presentation during a specific session must be in place when that session begins.

Since *Roe v. Wade* was the first case and *Doe v. Bolton* was the second scheduled for the morning session, my place was at the front table on the left of the center aisle, in the seat closest to the aisle. At my place was a handmade goose-quill pen—a custom dating back to the time of Thomas Jefferson and Justice John Marshall; the pen would be mine to take as a souvenir for having made a presentation to the Court. (Until the late 1980s the pens were made by a Virginia man. When he died a female assistant took over and continued the custom.)

To my left was Linda, then Roy Lucas. Ron was sitting in the front row of the lawyers' section. Across the aisle to my right were the attorneys representing the State of Texas. Behind me were the plaintiffs' attorneys for *Doe*, Margie Pitts Hames and her co-counsel. Across from their table was the table for the advocates of the Georgia attorney general. Linda was surprised at how close we were sitting to the justices.

To the right of the counsel tables was a VIP section, thirty places primarily for family, friends, and acquaintances of the justices. That morning the section was absolutely packed. To the left of the tables was the press section; its eighty-five seats were filled to capacity.

I would stand to present my case at a small lectern positioned between the front counsel tables, just a few feet from the Chief Justice. On the lectern was a "cheat sheet," with a diagram of the justices' seating arrangement. The chief justice sits in the center, to his right the justice with the greatest seniority, to his left the second most senior, and so on, alternating down each side to the end of the bench. The two newest justices are always at the far ends. I would be facing, from right to left, Harry Blackmun, Byron White, William Brennan, Jr., Chief Justice Warren Burger, William Douglas, Potter Stewart, and Thurgood Marshall.

Lawyers must not exceed their allotted time for argument. A clock hangs prominently behind the chief justice to show one's thirty minutes ticking by. Instructions are also conveyed by lights on the lectern— green for "Speak," white for "Few Minutes Remain," and red for "Sit Down."

Beyond the justices' bench is a set of heavy velvet curtains through which the justices enter and exit the courtroom. Cabinetmakers craft an individual seat for each justice, so the chairs reflect the builds of the justices—short and squatty for Brennan; tall and thin for White. (I've been told that Justice Clarence Thomas has a comfy chair and that he is usually leaning back with his eyes closed during oral argument. That confirms what I've observed when I've attended oral arguments at the Court.)

Instead of using all thirty minutes for an initial presentation, a lawyer can reserve some time for rebuttal after the other side speaks. I chose to save five minutes for rebuttal, and walked from my place past the VIP section to arrange the appropriate signals with Court personnel. A woman sitting in that section in front of Ginny Whitehall and Ruth Bowers had been telling her companion who everyone was and explaining all of the Court traditions in a loud whisper. Ginny and Ruth thought she was probably a justice's wife. When her friend asked who I was, the woman replied, "I don't know. Must be a new secretary." Ruth, Ginny, and I later laughed about how surprised she must have been when that "secretary" got up to argue.

As I returned to my place I paused to shake hands with Jay Floyd and the other members of the attorney general's group, including Texas Attorney General Crawford Martin, and to thank them for the courtesy of allowing me to designate who would use seats they did not need. No one said anything like "And may the best man win," thank goodness.

The room was filling up. Jimmye Kimmey waved at me from the front row of pews. I visited a few minutes with Harriet Pilpel and Cyril Means, who had claimed seats in the attorneys' section. Pilpel wished me well. Means asked if I had my copy of his law review article; I did. He reiterated that he had furnished copies to the Court and other counsel, and that I should feel free to refer to it.

Margie Pitts Hames and I lingered between our tables, sharing last-minute details and good luck wishes. The room was full, but some people outside were still hoping to get in. The room grew quieter as the hands of the clock neared the hour.

PROMPTLY AT TEN the marshal announced with a whack of his gavel: "The Honorable, the Chief Justice and the Associate Justices of the Supreme Court of the United States!" A hush fell upon the room and we all rose. The velvet curtain beyond the bench parted and the justices were silhouetted in their black robes. As they filed in, the marshal continued: "Oyez, oyez, oyez! All persons having business before the Honorable, the Supreme Court of the United States, are admonished to draw near and give their attention, for the Court is now sitting. God save the United States and this Honorable Court." A friend later told me there was organ music playing in the vestibule. I know that is not true, but it would have seemed appropriate for the solemn and dramatic opening moments of the session.

After the justices were seated, the gavel fell again and everyone else in the courtroom sat. Clerks placed the appropriate briefs and papers in front of the justices; two attorneys were introduced and admitted to the Supreme Court bar. At 10:07 a.m., Chief Justice Burger, looking almost kindly with his white hair and placid demeanor, peered down at me and said, "Mrs. Weddington, you may proceed whenever you are ready." I approached the lectern.

Before that moment I had been extremely nervous. Once I was in motion and into the argument, I was fine. I have heard sports figures talk about the adrenaline surge they experience before an event and how hard it is to control until the event starts; then they are in motion, and the adrenaline levels off. I have seen horses put in stalls before a race exhibit that same pent-up energy, which is put to productive use when the bugle sounds, the gates open, and the race begins.

The transcript of the hearing does not indicate the names of justices who asked questions. Some of them I remember, others I do not. I remember that it was Chief Justice Burger who asked the first question. I had begun to go over the history of the case, but after only a minute or two he interrupted to ask about the relevance of the *Vuitch* case. I had to explain how the Supreme Court's consideration of that case had not decided the issues in *Roe*. I tried to return to the points I knew I had to make and win, but the justices kept interrupting. Finally I was given a few minutes to point out in the most passionate yet professional way I could the varied impacts of pregnancy on a woman's life. I stressed that legal abortion in early pregnancy is eight times safer than carrying a pregnancy to term. I concluded that portion of my presentation by saying that to a woman, pregnancy is perhaps the most determinative aspect of her life: "It disrupts her body, it disrupts her education, it disrupts her employment, and it often disrupts her entire family life. And . . . because of the impact on the woman, this certainly, in as far as there are any rights which are fundamental, is a matter . . . of such fundamental and basic concern to the woman involved that she should be allowed to make the choice as to whether to continue or terminate her pregnancy."

As the hearing progressed, it was obvious that the justices had read the written documents and were thoroughly prepared on the case. In fact, some made references indicating they had read a substantial portion of the *amicus* briefs. Undoubtedly their clerks had outlined the pertinent arguments and cases for them.

I was able to cite Mean's article, which documented that at the time the Constitution was adopted, there was no common-law prohibition against abortion and abortions were available to the women of this country.

Justice White called me on one of the items that we had gone over repeatedly in moot court sessions, namely, my equivocation about the constitutional basis I was arguing. I noted that the Court in *Griswold* was divided as to the basis of its opinion, and said, "I'm a little reluctant to aspire to wisdom that the Court was not in agreement on. I do feel that the Ninth Amendment is an appropriate place for freedom to rest. I think the Fourteenth Amendment is an equally appropriate place, under the rights of persons to life [and] liberty . . . In as far as liberty is meaningful, that liberty to these women would mean liberty from being forced to continue the unwanted pregnancy."

White came back: "You're relying in this branch of your argument simply on the due-process clause of the Fourteenth Amendment?"

I responded, "We originally brought the suit alleging . . . the due-process clause, [the] equal-protection clause, the Ninth Amendment, and a variety of others."

"And anything else that might have been appropriate," White cut in. I had to laugh and say yes. The truth was that we had included every argument we could think of.

We had not emphasized the equal-protection clause when we filed the suit in 1970, because the Supreme Court had not yet applied it to gender-based discrimination. The first time it did so was days earlier in 1971, in *Reed v. Reed*, an Idaho case.

One justice asked about the state's interests and any legislative history as to why the Texas statute was passed. I told him there was no legislative history documented in Texas, although there was some in other states, which we had documented and provided to the Court. I was also able to tell him that Texas cases under the statute had referred to the woman as the victim. Self-induced abortion in Texas was not a crime. In fact, the woman was guilty of no crime even if she sought out a doctor, consented, participated, and paid for the procedure. Also, the penalty for abortion depended on whether or not the woman's consent was obtained; the penalty was double if the doctor failed to get it.

I pointed out a variety of ways in which the state did not treat the fetus as a person with legal rights, as I had already done in the three-judge hearing in Texas. Abortion was not murder. There was no requirement of a death certificate, no formalities of birth. The products of conception were handled as a pathological specimen.

A justice interrupted to ask whether the Texas statute made a distinction on the basis of the period of pregnancy in which the abortion was performed. My answer was no. The justice then asked whether I made any distinction. It was another question I had given a great deal of thought to. I knew that everyone, me included, was uncomfortable with the idea of abortion in the later stages of pregnancy. But I had been looking for a legal peg on which to hang an answer. There simply was not such a peg until birth. I answered accordingly.

"No, sir. . . . I feel that the question of a time limit is not strictly before the Court, because of the nature of the situation in which the case is [presented]. Certainly I think, as a practical matter, though, that most of the States that do have some time limit indicated still permit abortions beyond the time limit for specified reasons, usually where the health of the mother is concerned."

As the justice continued to push me, I felt I had to stick to my basic answer that legal rights generally began at birth, while recognizing that the emotional, rather than constitutional, response to abortion was different for late pregnancy. As questions continued, I finally answered, "The Constitution, as I read it, and as interpreted and documented by Professor Means, attaches protection to the person at the time of birth. Those persons born are citizens. [Under] the enumeration clause, we count those people who are born."

A fair amount of the remainder of my thirty minutes was spent talking about the interests of doctors and whether Dr. Hallford was an appropriate party to the litigation. But we also returned to the question of the fetus.

One justice posed the question: "Does Texas law, in other areas . . . give rights to unborn children [I should have picked up on that reference to "children", but I don't remember that I did] in the areas of trusts and estates and wills . . . ?" "No, Your Honor, only if they are born alive," I replied. "The Supreme Court of Texas recently held in one case that there is an action for prenatal injury at any stage prior to birth, but only upon the condition that [the child] be born alive. The same is true of our property law; the child must be born alive. And I think there is a distinction between those children [who] are ultimately born, and I think it is appropriate to give them retroactive rights; but I think that's a completely different question from whether or not they had rights at the time they were still in the womb."

"What about the unborn child who is, as a result of an accident, killed—or whatever word you want to use . . . ?" the justice asked. When I indicated that there had been no litigation like that in Texas, I was asked about the rest of the country. I mentioned an Iowa case involving a stillbirth, in which the mother was found to have a cause of action for her injuries but not for the fetus.

I kept waiting for Douglas, the one justice whose vote I felt confident of, to ask me a question; he never did. Instead he continued to write furiously, with one ear cocked to the courtroom proceedings. Occasionally he would give a note to a messenger, who would go scurrying off and return with a book.

The red light at the lectern went on and the chief justice said, "Thank you, Mrs. Weddington. Mr. Floyd."

Floyd, the lawyer representing the Texas Attorney General, began by saying, "It's an old joke, but when a man argues against two beautiful ladies like this, they're going to have the last word." No one laughed. I think it unnerved him somewhat, but he went on to attack the standing of the plaintiffs.

He argued that Jane Roe did not have standing because she was no longer pregnant. A justice interrupted: "It's a class action, isn't it?" (I gave silent thanks to Schatzki for helping us amend the petitions.) Floyd admitted that it was. The justice continued, "I suppose we could almost take judicial notice of the fact that there are, at any given time, unmarried, pregnant females in the state of Texas." There was laughter in the courtroom, and Floyd agreed that the Court could, yet he persisted that as to Jane Roe, it was known that she was pregnant on May 21, 1970, but Linda and I had admitted she no longer was. The Court, he was saying, should not consider the case unless the plaintiff was still pregnant.

The justice then asked, "What procedure would you suggest for any pregnant female in the state of Texas ever to get any judicial consideration of this constitutional claim?" Floyd answered that he did not believe it could be done: "There are situations in which no remedy is provided. Now, I think she makes her choice prior to the time she becomes pregnant. That is the time of the choice. It's like, more or less, well, the first three or four years of our life, we don't remember anything, but once a child is born, a woman no longer has a choice; and I think pregnancy makes her make that choice, as well."

The justice responded, "Maybe she makes her choice when she decides to live in Texas!" Again there was laughter in the courtroom, and Floyd said, "There's no restriction on moving, you know." He went on to discuss the State's position that the appeal should have been to the Fifth Circuit, not the Supreme Court, and a variety of other matters.

A justice prodded Floyd about the fact that Texas did not attempt to punish women who attempted or performed self-induced abortions, and Floyd agree that was so but added, "Why not punish for murder?" The justice pointed out that the statute as it was did not equate abortion with murder. Later, when Floyd mentioned "life from the moment of impregnation," a justice asked him for scientific data to support that. Floyd responded that there were "unanswerable questions in this field"—again provoking courtroom laughter—and the justice responded, "I appreciate it, I appreciate it."

I had a short rebuttal, and at eleven minutes past eleven, the presentation was over. There was a short break while those of us involved in *Roe v. Wade* switched places with the attorneys in *Doe v. Bolton*; Linda and I carefully put away our souvenir goose-quill pens before moving. I had a wonderful view from the second set of tables and could watch the justices more calmly during the next argument. I kept trying to figure out from every slight smile or raised eyebrow what a justice was thinking or how he was reacting, and I replayed mentally what limited snippets I could remember from the previous hour.

THE *DOE* CASE PRESENTATION had not finished by noon, so a lunch recess of one hour was called. We all stood while the justices departed. I went with Ron, Linda, and others of our group to eat in the Supreme Court cafeteria one floor below, then hurried back to the courtroom for the remaining minutes of the presentation. When it was over, people seemed reluctant to leave the Court building. They stood in groups reviewing the justices' questions and trying to guess the outcome. Then people would form new groups and talk about the same things again. No one was certain of the outcome.

I had been concentrating so hard during the thirty minutes I stood before the Court that afterward I could remember only a little of what had been said. Linda and Ron had to review it for me. A Court staffer told me that a tape of the argument would be available through the National Archives—three years later. How I wished I could sneak a listen right then! To the best of my memory, there were no television cameras or reporters doing interviews after the hearing ended; most reporters hurried back to their offices to write their stories.

Ruth Bowers, who had arranged an informal get-together at the Hay-Adams Hotel for about twenty of the people most directly involved on the pro-choice side of the cases, remembers Ron grading me on my presentation as we left the Supreme Court in a taxi headed to the hotel. To her, Ron's comments seemed sarcastic as he pronounced a B-plus; she thought that perhaps he was a little jealous of my getting so much attention. But I knew that was an excellent grade in law school, and that was more likely his frame of reference. Later in the afternoon Ron, Mother, and I met at Congressman Mahon's office to thank him for his help. A staff member snapped a picture of the four of us. It is my best visual memento of the day.

That night Ruth hosted a dinner for more than thirty at the Steakhouse—appropriate for a Texas hostess and case—a restaurant in Arlington, Virginia. We were joined by John and Mary Doe, Ginny Whitehill, Dr. Jane Hodgson, Cyril Means, Nick Danforth and other players in the drama whom I especially liked. Again and again, we reviewed the day's events and speculated about the results. There was a sense of euphoria, maybe from relief at having made it this far, and through a day at the Supreme Court that went as well as could be hoped.

The next morning Ron and I gathered whatever newspapers we could find and met in the hotel coffee shop to read the stories with others who had attended the hearing. The *Washington Post* headline was "Texas Defends Anti-Abortion Law in Court." For *The New York Times* it was "Two Suits Contest Bans on Abortion." We would read items out loud to each other, exclaiming "Listen to *this* . . ." and "Can you believe this comment . . ." or "I wonder why the justice asked that question." Then it was time to pack and head for the airport.

If the justices followed custom, the Friday after oral arguments they would have their first conference to discuss a decision on *Roe* and *Doe*. They would determine whether they had jurisdiction and, if so, how to decide the cases on the merits. Ron and I, by then back in Austin, could only wait and wonder about the results of that conference.

AFTER SUCH A high-pressure year, which climaxed in December with the trip to Washington, 1972 began with a whimper. For weeks before the Supreme Court hearing I had been able to think of nothing else. But during the holidays I was spending time doing unexciting maintenance tasks and cleaning up what I had neglected in my preoccupation with *Roe*. For obvious financial reasons, Ron and I needed to begin our law practice in earnest. We rushed to have announcements of the opening of our law office printed and ready for mailing in early January.

Although I had a long list of things to do, I was having a hard time getting "ginned up." As a Texas friend of mine says, I felt like I'd been rode hard and put up wet. Ron and I were both suffering from the holiday blues. My sadness was due in part to marital problems: Ron and I were growing apart. I was always so busy; he had his activities and I had mine. He wanted me to be available, sometimes on the spur of the moment, to go sailing or see a movie, but I always had a heavy schedule. He felt as if he had to make an appointment to see me. Our value differences too were beginning to intrude. I would get mad if he stayed out occasionally, drinking or going to what I called "girlie bars." He would remind me that he had agreed to stay married as long as we were happy, but that what he considered my nagging was making him unhappy. It is hard to say how big a role it played, but it was also true that while Ron had helped with the *Roe* case, I was getting all the attention. He had always been very support-ive, but I had seen other marriages flounder when the husband felt eclipsed.

Each of us needed something stimulating to replace *Roe*. For Ron that became the campaign of Frances (Sissy) Farenthold for governor. Before we married, Ron had run for state repre-sentative against an incumbent in Abilene. Even though he had lost, Ron still loved being involved in the fervor of a liberal Texas campaign. So when Sissy asked him to become a paid member of her campaign team, he accepted with enthusiasm.

Change was in the air in Texas politics because of a recent scandal in which several state officials were accused of accept-ing bribes to pass a bill that would favor the owner of a bank in Sharpstown. Voters were disgusted with the people in office; the accused in the Sharpstown scandal were all white males. New ethics legislation was a major topic of conversation, and there was increasing talk of organizing support for women and minor-ity men to run for office. Eighteen-year-olds had just gotten the vote, and that was important in a college town such as Austin. All of these factors, it seemed, would help Farenthold.

My new challenge came when some women friends of mine in Austin began to discuss the possibility of a woman's running for Travis Country state representative. The incumbent, Republican Maurice Angly, had decided to run for state treasurer. The county had never been represented by a woman.

My friends and I had lobbied the Texas legislature to pass an equal legal rights amendment to the Texas Constitution and to change the abortion laws; the constitutional amendment would be on the November 1972 ballot, but so far no progress had been made regarding the abortion laws. Lobbying had been a frustrating experience for all of us; it was generally impossible to set up appointments to meet with most legislators, because they wanted to avoid our issues. Many were so skillful at ignoring us that we felt all but invisible at the Capitol.

We could not predict the outcome of *Roe*. If we lost we would have to try again in the political arena. We needed more champions and favorable votes in the state legislature, and the best way to direct attention to the broad spectrum of issues of special interest to women—including rape-law reform, access to credit, pregnancy leave, employment equity, and others—was to elect women to the Texas Senate and House of Representatives. My friends and I had recently been involved with others in forming women's political caucuses nationally and in Texas, and we were encouraged by the sense of shared political goals. We felt connected to a groundswell occurring nationwide to elect women, and we were tired of begging male legislators for help.

One evening after dinner at my house, a group of friends— Caryl Yontz, Susan Roberts, Linda Anderson, and Patty McKool —and I decided there was only one way for women to be elected officials: they had to run and they had to win. Since most men were skeptical of women's ability to win and generally would not devote time, energy, or money to women candidates, we had to learn how to run successful campaigns. We decided the best way to do that was to find a candidate and run a campaign.

All of us were in our twenties. Most of us had had prior experience as receptionists, secretaries, and assistants to men in political campaigns. None had served in a policy-making role. Caryl Yontz had worked in campaigns for Ralph Yarborough, a former US senator, and Dan Yarborough, a Democratic candidate for Texas governor. Susan Roberts had worked for Jake Pickle, a Travis County congressman. Linda Anderson had worked in efforts for Ralph Yarborough. Patty McKool, an undergraduate at UT, had helped in her father-in-law's successful campaigns for state senator from Dallas.

One of us had to be the guinea-pig candidate; I was "volunteered" to run for the state House of Representatives. Any member of the group could have served capably, but I was the only one with a law degree, a traditional qualification for men in politics. The house where Ron and I lived and worked could also serve as a campaign headquarters, and I was willing to pay the $100 filing fee from my savings. My knowledge of the legislative process had begun when I spent the spring of 1965 as a clerk/typist; having seen the House in action, I was hardly intimidated by the idea of being a legislator.

Together we decided I would run, despite not having taken any of the usual preliminary steps. We never ran a poll to see if I could win. The results probably would have been discouraging, if not disastrous. We never talked to city leaders; they probably would have found the idea of five political novices running a campaign quite amusing. In a burst of youthful enthusiasm we just decided to try. We were not talking about winning; as Susan Roberts said, "Of course Sarah can't win, but it is a great cause."

We thought we could force new issues to the forefront of public discussion, and that this exercise would teach us how to run winning campaigns in the future.

What impact would my involvement in the abortion issue have the five of us wondered. I did have some visibility and name identification, and my strong supporters might make an extra effort to help in the campaign and make contributions. On the other hand, voters who opposed legal abortion were likely to go out of their way to oppose me. The Hispanic vote in Austin was fairly important, and there was the possibility that the Roman Catholic hierarchy would urge voting for one of my opponents. Still, all in all, we decided my stand on abortion was a plus.

Caryl Yontz and Patty McKool contributed a key idea: I should have lunch with Ann Richards and ask her—convince her—to help us. Patty knew Ann because she was a close friend of Patty's mother-in-law. Years earlier Ann had been active in Young Democratic and Dallas politics. We met her at the Alamo Hotel in Austin, an unpretentious place that was Caryl's favorite watering hole, and she, Patty, and I laid out our plans. I liked Ann instantly, and she knew so much. Maybe she was swept away by our idealism, our enthusiasm, and our obvious need of help. Politically, I was a babe in the woods, and she could imagine the political wolves circling to devour me. She agreed to help.

I OFFICIALLY ANNOUNCED my candidacy for the Texas House on February 7, 1972. There were three other candidate in the Democratic primary race: a lobbyist, Durward Curlee; a young lawyer named Joe Garrison; and Hugh Hornsby, an insurance salesman. Our slogan was "Sarah will work in the House for You." We got a union printing shop to print our campaign stationery and stickers. Our logo, with the words "Elect Sarah Weddington State Representative Place 2," was purple and white, colors no one else had, in the shape of a flower. Our yard signs were impossible to read from a passing car, but once people knew what that purple-and-white flower symbolized, they did not need to read it.

The demands of a low-budget, grass-roots campaign are endless. We held an open house at campaign headquarters to solicit supporters, volunteers, and donations. We collected names and addresses of people willing to let me put my signs in their yards. Ron painted signs to mount on top of cars, "moving advertisements" for my campaign. People had get-togethers in their homes where I could meet their friends and neighbors. The expanding volunteer staff celebrated each time we got an endorsement.

Patty McKool, the only paid campaign worker, received the grand sum of fifteen dollars per week, plus plenty of grapefruit from my parents, and all the Mrs. Weaver's brand pimiento cheese she could eat. Ron's father, a wholesale grocer, could get things like pimiento cheese and sandwich meats for us at very low cost. Ron and I, along with the campaign volunteers who were often at our home at mealtime lived on the food he provided.

Money was a constant worry for the campaign. We had agreed never to spend money we didn't have, but we were anxious to get on radio and television. Campaigning was expensive. One column inch in the newspaper cost $5.88, a thirty-second radio spot $10, and a thirty-second TV spot an average of $80. We made most of our money through five-dollar suppers featuring chili, chips, and beer, and we raised enough to get a few spots Ron wrote, directed, and produced on radio and television.

Ann Richards and her children, who volunteered to hand out my literature, were invaluable. Ann's ideas were marvelous, such as the one for a Democratic fair. This was to include food, music, speeches, and a chance for voters to meet the candidates for public office running on the Democratic ticket. All of the candidates would sponsor a booth where voters could come to meet them and from which they would vie for attention. My campaign volunteers knew the other, better-funded candidates would be handing out personalized emery boards, balloons with their pictures on them, and other paraphernalia that I could not afford. Ann came up with the idea of putting my bumper stickers on cheap white paper sacks. All I had to do was sit and autograph the sacks and hand them out for people to put all that other stuff in and keep the environment clean. It was a great success. While one of my opponent's two cute children were dressed as clowns and offering balloons to people of voting age, we had people waiting in line to get an autographed white paper bag.

Our campaign was poor, but personalized. We went from door to door in neighborhoods, knocking and asking to speak to anyone of voting age. I passed out brochures in front of cafeterias, on downtown streets, and anywhere we knew there would be a crowd. It was hard to hand a brochure to a stranger only to see the person walk a few steps and discard it, as often happened. But some people offered a smile and kind words; those were the sugar pills I needed to keep going.

The primary was held on May 6; I wound up in a runoff against Hornsby. Our campaign celebrated briefly, then tried to calculate the odds. Hornsby was from an old Austin family and would be able to raise far more money than I. However, he was having trouble running against a woman. He would not call me by name, generally referring to me as "that sweet little girl." His condescending attitude made me mad—and it had the same effect on many other women who would vote. He was the odds-on favorite, but I had a chance to come from behind.

My physical appearance entered the campaign. Hornsby accused me of changing from the short dresses and long hair I had worn while campaigning on the UT campus to "lengthened skirts and a mature upswept bun." My purpose was to "confuse the voters," he alleged, but people thought that a ridiculous allegation. Furthermore, Hornsby said, Ron and I had lived in Fort Worth for nine months and had been back in Austin for less than a year; I had not grown up in Austin. He said I was therefore something of a "transient." My campaign volunteers figured, however, that the many people who had come to Austin to attend college and decided to stay after graduating, as Ron and I had, might be offended by Hornsby's tactics. If only those "transients" would vote for me, I could win.

Rumor had it that as Hornsby called on leaders in the community, he made them more inclined to support me. He talked about his many "volunteer hours of service to Travis County," but it turned out that he was including hours spent on his own campaign.

The abortion issue did turn out to be a net plus. While I lost some votes because of my role in *Roe*, many people supported me specifically because they agreed the Texas law should be changed. And some who did not agree said they liked a person running for office who would stand up and say what she really believed about a controversial topic.

The campaign brain trust redoubled its efforts for the runoff. We had to figure out how to make the highest impact for the fewest dollars. I walked through state office buildings and shook the hand of every worker I could find and asked for support. I went where the crowds were to push my brochures and hear what people were saying. We taped leaflets on the mirrors and over the toilet-tissue dispensers in every ladies' room in town.

We took advantage of the ideas of new volunteers such as Betsy Kusin, Cathy Bonner, and Jane Hickie. Betsy, a young advertising graduate, had joined us after having been let go by the advertising firm handling Hugh Hornsby's campaign (because she wasn't one of the boys). It was her brilliant idea to use a new service of home-delivered advertising to get my literature out to many more homes than volunteers could reach on foot. Betsy might not have been one of the boys, but she sure was a winner. Through all the ups and downs of the campaign, Caryl Yontz consistently maintained that I would win; I was sometimes in the ranks of doubting Thomases.

As the June 3 primary runoff approached, we worked for endorsements from every group we could think of, and printed postcards for people to mail to their friends and acquaintances asking people to support me. Everyone involved with my campaign faced election weekend with incredible resolution. That Saturday morning I voted, then hit the pavement looking for all the voters I could find. At seven that night I returned to headquarters to join campaign workers awaiting the results.

At about eight, the phones started ringing. The early returns looked good. I began calling volunteers to tell them the news and set the grapevine in motion. Hornsby conceded within an hour. The official tally was Weddington, 47,620; Hornsby, 37,713. Some of his financial supporters were heard to ask, "How was it you spent so much more money than she did, and that sweet little girl still beat you?" I would face Dwight Wheeler, the Republican candidate, in the general election the following November, but I felt confident that the difficult race was behind me. Democrats had an outstanding record of winning in Travis County.

DURING THE CAMPAIGN SEASON abortion had continued to be a topic of conversation and correspondence; the media covered it widely, and it still claimed my time and attention. People from around the country wrote and called wanting to talk about the Supreme Court hearing and the likely outcome. They often sent press clips; I was disappointed that so few of the journalists described the legal arguments accurately. It reminded me of how difficult expressing the intricacies of legal concepts can be.

I continued to speak about *Roe v. Wade* in Austin and elsewhere in Texas. I went to San Antonio to tape a radio program on abortion and wrote my parents, saying, "It's a long way to go for a few minutes, but San Antonio needs help so desperately . . .

because the Catholic bishop there really does have the legislators under his thumb." I was also writing about the issue—among other pieces a review of a planned position paper on abortion for the Texas synod of the United Presbyterian Church.

Because of my loaded schedule of speeches, I tried to keep up with stories in the newspapers; those were the things I was most often asked about during question-and-answer sessions. What the opposition was doing was of interest too, as sooner or later I would have to face their tactics or lines of argument. People looked to me for expertise on legal developments, so I paid special attention to information about court cases; one never knows which cases will turn out to be significant, and it is prudent to stay on top of any that are relevant.

That spring a Vermont court had overturned the state's abortion law and also instructed the state attorney general not to prosecute doctors performing abortions. Doctors could now terminate unwanted pregnancies there. In February a three-judge federal court had voted two to one to strike down New Jersey's 122-year-old abortion law on two grounds: vagueness and invasion of privacy. A bachelor professor of law at Fordham University, a Jesuit school in New York City, requested and received from a local court designation as special guardian of all human fetuses between the fourth and twenty-fourth week of gestation scheduled to be aborted in the city's municipal hospitals; a higher court overturned that action. In Florida a motion for retrial had been filed on behalf of a woman convicted in July 1971 of having had an abortion.

Ruth Bowers, Ginny Whitehill, and I were working once again on legislative strategy, this time for the 1973 session of the Texas legislature. Just as in 1970, we still did not know whether we would win or lose in the Supreme Court, so we wanted a backup strategy. Ruth hosted various meetings and luncheons— in Dallas, Houston, Galveston, Corpus Christi, San Antonio, Austin, and elsewhere—to coordinate a political focus for women. Ginny was organizing the Texas Citizens for Abortion Education, a tax-deductible group.

In March a presidential study commission had formally recommended that all states liberalize abortion laws and permit doctors to perform abortions at patients' request. The report, issued by the Commission on Population Growth and the American Future, whose guiding force was John D. Rockefeller 3d, also called for government to fund abortion services for poor women and urged that abortion costs be covered by health insurance. When she read newspaper coverage of the report, Ginny asked me to urge pro-choice people to write the president to implement its recommendations. There was, however, little chance Nixon would really do so.

The report lifted my spirits nonetheless. To me it was a sign that increasing numbers of people in power understood the problems of illegal abortion and wanted to do something about them. The commission based its recommendation on a solid foundation: "We are impressed with the fact that availability of abortion on request causes a reduction in the number of illegal abortions, maternal and infant deaths, and out-of wedlock births, thereby greatly improving the health of women and children." But I was getting worried that the Supreme Court had not yet announced its *Roe* decision. It seemed a bad sign.

WHILE THE CAMPAIGN STAFF was still celebrating the victory in the runoff, I received a notice about *Roe v. Wade* from the Supreme Court. Dated June 26, 1972, it informed me: "This case is restored to the calendar for reargument." At the bottom it read: "Mr. Justice Douglas dissents." *Doe v. Bolton* was also set for reargument.

The attorneys in each case were going to have to return to DC and play out the same roles and procedures once more. Arguing the same case twice is *very* unusual. The Court generally decides cases during the term in which they are argued. When a case is set for reargument, the Court generally asks the attorneys to address a specific issue. In this instance the justices gave us no idea what they were specifically interested in. Linda and I began to exchange the rumors from Washington.

One rumor was that the Court wanted all nine justices to participate in the decision. Only seven had been on the bench in December 1971; now Nixon appointees William Rehnquist and Lewis Powell had been confirmed and there were nine. Another story was that Nixon, who was opposed to abortion, did not want the Court—called by some the "Nixon Court"—to decide the case while he was running for his second term as president.

Yet another rumor was that Blackmun, the justice with the best background in medical-legal issues, who had been appointed by Chief Justice Burger to write the opinion, had asked for more time. The rumor added that Douglas was dissenting to the reargument probably because Burger had designated Blackmun to write the opinion. By Court custom, if the chief justice is on the majority side during the postargument conference, then he designates the justice who will write the opinion. If the chief justice is *not* on the majority side, as was rumored in this case, then the justice with seniority on the majority side makes that designation. The rumor was that Douglas, the senior justice on the majority side during the postargument conference, was upset by Burger's action to step in and appoint Blackmun, which contravened tradition. (Later, in their book *The Brethren*, Bob Woodward and Scott Armstrong confirmed that rumor.) Speculation was that Burger felt he would have the most influence with Blackmun and that an opinion Blackmun would write would be more conservative. There was also media speculation that we had in fact won the case five to two, but Burger was in dissent and used his position to force the Court into setting it for reargument. If that was true, it meant we would win if we simply held those five votes, regardless of how the new justices voted.

Unbeknownst to us, as *The Douglas Letters*, edited by Melvin Urofsky, revealed in 1987, Douglas had written Blackmun on May 19, 1972:

> In No. 70-18-*Roe v. Wade*, my notes confirm what Bill Brennen wrote yesterday in his memo to you—that abortion statutes were invalid save as they required that an abortion be performed by a licensed physician within a limited time after conception.
>
> That was the clear view of a majority of the seven who heard the argument. My notes also indicate that the Chief [Burger] had the opposed view, which made it puzzling as to why he made the assignment at all except that he indicated he might affirm on vagueness. My notes indicate that Byron [White] was not firmly settled and that you might join the majority of four.
>
> So I think we should meet what Bill Brennan calls the "core issue."
>
> I believe I gave you, some time back, my draft opinion in the *Georgia* case. I see no reason for reargument on that case.
>
> It always seemed to me to be an easier case than *Texas*.

On May 31, according to the same book, Douglas wrote Blackmun again:

> I have your memorandum submitted to the Conference with suggestion that these cases be reargued.
>
> I feel quite strongly that they should not be reargued. My reasons are as follows.
>
> In the first place, these cases which were argued last October have been as thoroughly worked and considered as any cases ever before the Court in my time.

I know you have done yeoman service and have written two difficult cases, and you have opinions now for a majority, which is 5.

There are always minor differences in style, one writing differently [from] another. But those two opinions of yours in *Texas* and *Georgia* are creditable jobs of craftsmanship and will, I think, stand the test of time.

While we could sit around and make pages of suggestions, I really don't think that is important. The important thing is to get them down.

In the second place, I have a feeling that where the court is split 4-4 or 4-2-1 or even in an important constitutional case 4-3, rearrangement may be desirable. But you have a firm 5 [Douglas included himself, Blackmun, Brennan, Marshall, and Stewart] and the firm 5 will be behind you in these two opinions until they come down. It is a difficult field and a difficult subject. But where there is that solid an agreement of the majority I think it is important to announce the cases, and let the results be known so that legislatures can go to work and draft their new laws.

Again, congratulations on a fine job. I hope the 5 can agree to get the cases down this Term, so that we can spend our energies next Term on other matters.

But the cases were set again for argument, in spite of Douglas' strong objection.

ALL I KNEW for certain was that we had to go back to Washington. I did not know what I could say during a second presentation that would be more persuasive than the arguments I had presented during the first. I would be busy in the fall, campaigning for myself and other Democratic candidates and trying to elect a pro-choice president. For weeks before the first argument I had done nothing but prepare for those thirty minutes; now squeezing in preparation time would be difficult. Luckily, Ron and I had hired a crackerjack experienced secretary, Martha Davis, so this time I wouldn't have to type everything.

By the end of the summer, reargument had been tentatively scheduled for October 10; it was later postponed by one day. Linda and I had a deadline of September 15 to submit a short supplementary brief; national Planned Parenthood and a few other groups were submitting *amicus* briefs. It was hard to settle down to work on the brief and prepare for oral argument with the fall campaigns in full swing.

We did manage to submit a seventeen-page brief. We reported that since the district court had not granted injunctive relief and so had refused to tell the district attorney not to prosecute doctors who performed abortions, Texas physicians were still refusing to perform them. During the last nine months of 1971, a total of 1,658 women from Texas had gone to New York to obtain abortions. We mentioned that the American Bar Association House of Delegates had approved a Uniform Abortion Act, which would allow termination of pregnancy up to twenty weeks; abortion was also allowed thereafter for reasons such as rape, incest, fetal deformity, and endangerment of the mental or physical health of the woman. We cited the Rockefeller Commission on Population Growth and the American Future, which had recommended that the matter of abortion be left to the conscience of the individual concerned, and several recently decided cases supporting our positions on standing and the substantive issues.

Another section of the brief stressed, yet again, the fact that Texas had never treated the fetus as having the rights and dignity of a person. We cited an 1889 decision which held that in order to obtain a murder conviction, the State must prove "that the child was born alive." We mentioned that under the rules of the Texas Welfare Department, a needy pregnant woman could not get welfare payments for her unborn child; that a federal court in

Pennsylvania had held that the embryo or fetus is not a person or citizen within the meaning of the Fourteenth Amendment or the Civil Rights Act; and that a New York State court had concluded that the Constitution does not confer or require legal personality for the unborn. We pointed out that the constitutional clause establishing a decennial census required that "the whole Number of . . . Persons" in each state be counted, but from the first census, in 1790, to the present, census takers had counted only those born. We ended the brief by again arguing that the Texas statute was vague and placed on the doctor an unconstitutional burden of proof, namely, that the abortion performed was within the exception to the statute.

I set aside a few days to review and prepare for argument. Martha Davis remembers numerous phone calls, many from Austin but also many from across the country. When she explained why it would be better not to interrupt me, callers would respond, "Fine. We just want her to know we're thinking about her and rooting for her to win." Martha says I didn't talk much before I left; that's my usual reaction when I am most under stress. At midnight the night before I was to leave for Washington, she was still typing and some half a dozen people were in my conference room, drilling me on key points.

On October 6, Ron and I loaded our things into the car of Carol Castlebury, a friend and campaign volunteer who was coming to D. C. with us, and drove to Dallas to pick up Ron's sister Cathy; the four of us then headed for Washington. (I had invited Patty McKool to go since she was thinking of law school, but she stayed for her classes at UT. Now that she's a lawyer, she wishes she had said yes.) Our drive was through the Shenandoah National Park, my first time to experience the beauty of fall foliage. The day after we arrived in DC, the others went sightseeing while I worked on the case. I spent the morning of the tenth in the Supreme Court library; during the afternoon I participated in a moot court organized by Harriet Pilpel and Cyril Means for Margie Pitts Hames and me, and held in the National Lawyers' Club. Many of the attorneys who had filed *amicus* briefs were present at this session to help plan strategy. Frank Susman, a well-known St. Louis attorney who was handling a challenge of the Missouri anti-abortion laws, and Joe Nellis, the attorney who defended Dr. Vuitch, also participated. Harriet commented that Fred Graham of *The New York Times* had suggested some members of the Court felt little sympathy with a pregnant woman but could sympathize with the doctor; she wondered whether we should stress the medical aspects more. The group went over the questions that the justices had asked and the points Margie and I had made during the first arguments, and discussed new questions that might arise this time.

We considered what I should do if a justice tried to back me into a comer and get me to say things I did not want to say. The most time was spent on the subject of when life begins. We knew it would come up at the hearing. Obviously life began once billions of years ago and has been a continuum ever since. But there are various key points of development: conception, implantation, quickening, viability, and birth, for example. The Court seemed uncomfortable with my prior argument that birth was the peg at which *legal rights* should attach, and that "when life begins" is an individual leap of faith that no one can prove; people tend to say "I believe." But we could find no substantial legal peg for maintaining that rights began prior to birth. Although we were not entirely satisfied with our conclusion, most at the session felt it was best for me to stick to the point as I had been making it: Legal rights attach at birth.

The next morning I woke early and reviewed before Ron and I met Linda and Margie Pitts Hames for breakfast and the walk to the Court building. (During reargument, as many noticed, my hair was in a bun, not down as I had worn it before; people have asked whether that represented "grand strategy." The truth is that Ron inadvertently decided the issue. While I was doing last-minute preparation, he showered and shaved. When he finished, I raced to take a bath, leaned over the tub, twirled the knob to turn on the water—and was drenched with a stream of water from the shower. Ron had left the shower pull up. That was in the days before I traveled with a hair dryer. I wore my hair up because it was *wet*.)

Ron and I walked along the now familiar sidewalk to the Supreme Court, through the crowd, and up the steps. Inside, the physical grandeur of the courtroom still inspired a sense of awe in me, but this time there was no electricity to the hearing. I was expecting frequent interruptions and questions from the justices, but there were few. When the justices did speak, it seemed it was primarily to ask if they had heard a certain word correctly or to finish my sentences. Their lack of response made me nervous, whereas the intensity of the first hearing had calmed me.

At one point I was restating the bases for our challenge to the Texas law. Several minutes passed before I was interrupted by Justice White. "Is it critical to your case that the fetus not be a person [within the meaning of] the due-process clause? Would you lose your case if [we held] the fetus was a person?"

"Then you would have a balancing of interests," I answered. In law, there are situations where two concerns that merit consideration are involved and one must, after fully examining each concern, decide which deserves the greater weight and therefore will be the dominant one.

White countered, "You . . . have, anyway, don't you? You are going to be balancing the rights of the mother against the rights of the fetus."

I said that I did not believe we would be balancing [the mother's] constitutional rights against the statutory rights of [the fetus]. White immediately pounced and asked my opinion as to whether a state interest could ever outweigh a constitutional law. Before I could even answer he continued, "So all the talk of compelling State interest is beside the point. It can never be compelling enough."

I replied: "If the State could show that the fetus was a person under the Fourteenth Amendment, or under some other amendment, or part of the Constitution, then you would have the situation of trying—you would have a State compelling interest which, in some instances, can outweigh a fundamental right. This is not the case in this particular situation."

From Justice Blackmun I heard, "Do you make any distinction between the first and ninth month of gestation?" I answered that the Texas statute did not. He then asked if I placed a "particular weight" on either the issue of vagueness or the Ninth Amendment. I said that I didn't, that we relied on both.

"Last June," Justice Brennan said, "this Court decided the capital punishment cases. Do you feel there is any inconsistency in this Court's decision in those cases outlawing [capital punishment as presently administered], and your position [approving abortion] at the other end of [the life] span?"

I suggested that if it had been established that the fetus were a person, it might be different, but that that determination had not been made.

"Your case depends primarily, then, on our holding that the fetus is not a person with constitutional rights."

"It is based on the State's failure to have a compelling interest in regulating the woman's rights in this area," I said.

Justice Stewart asked, "If it were established that the fetus were a life, you would have a difficult case, wouldn't you?" I had to admit that was true if such were established, but reiterated that the fetus had never been given legal rights or treated as a person for legal purposes.

I concluded by answering a question related to the recognition in civil law that a fetus had some rights in proprietary matters. I said that this did not bar a ruling that the fetus had no rights in the area we were discussing.

Robert Flowers, assistant attorney general of Texas, argued for the State. Unlike Jay Floyd at the first argument, Flowers skipped introductory comments and went straight to the business at hand. His opening remarks were clear: "It is the position of the State of Texas that upon conception we have a human being, a person within the concept of the Constitution of the United States and that of Texas, also."

Justice Stewart fired back, "Now how should that question be decided? Is it a legal question, a constitutional question, a medical question . . . what is it?"

The assistant attorney general floundered. "It could be best decided by a Legislature in view of the fact that [it] can bring before [itself] the medical testimony [of] the actual people who do the research."

"So then it's basically a medical decision?"

Flowers backpedaled some more. "From a constitutional standpoint, no sir. I think it's fairly and squarely before this Court."

Stewart then asked, "Do you know of any case anywhere that [has] held that an unborn fetus is a person within the meaning of the Fourteenth Amendment?"

"No," Flowers responded, "we can only go back to what the framers of our Constitution had in mind."

Stewart proceeded to give Flowers a brief history lesson on the Fourteenth Amendment. (It was proposed in 1866, ratified in 1868, and the framers of the Constitution were not at all involved.) Stewart asked Flowers if the Fourteenth Amendment defined "person" as somebody who was born. Flowers hesitated: "I'm not sure." Stewart again: "All persons born or naturalized in the United States." Another justice said, "That's not the definition of a 'person' . . . that's the definition of a 'citizen.'"

Flowers continued, "Your Honor, it is our position that the definition of a person is so basic . . . so fundamental that the framers of the Constitution had not even set out to define it."

Justice Blackmun then asked, "Is it [true or not] that the medical profession itself is not in agreement as to when life begins?"

"I think that is true, sir . . . [but] on the twentieth day, practically all the [faculties] are there that you and I have." I almost came out of my chair when he said that, and looked for some justice to challenge that obviously untrue statement. None did.

Instead Blackmun pursued the hypothetical situation that would result if the fetus were a person; he asked whether the State would have great trouble allowing an abortion in any circumstance. Flowers said it would. Blackmun then asked, 'To save the life of a mother or her health or anything else?" Flowers explained there would be a "balancing" of the two lives.

"What would you choose?" Blackmun asked. "Would you choose to kill the innocent one or what?"

Flowers responded that the Texas statute allowed a choice to protect the mother.

Blackmun asked, "Could Texas say, if it confronts the situation for the benefit of the health of the wife, that [someone else such as] the husband has to die? Could they kill him?"

"I wouldn't think so, sir," was Flowers's answer. The questions continued, one justice asking whether abortion was "the only operation that a doctor can possibly commit that will bring on a criminal penalty." Flowers said yes.

Anytime the justices would corner Flowers, he would come back with a sweeping statement, such as: "The concept of a fetus being within the concept of a person, within the framework of the US Constitution and the Texas Constitution, is an extremely fundamental thing."

Stewart responded, "Of course, if you're right about that, you can sit down; you've won your case."

Flowers agreed. But Justice White commented: "You've lost your case, then, if the fetus or embryo is not a person; is that it?"

Flowers admitted that was true, but later said, "This Court has not been blind to the rights of the unborn child in the past," and detailed cases he said had recognized the rights of the child. Further, he maintained, the "Court has been diligent in protecting the rights of the minority. And gentlemen, we say that this is a minority, a silent minority, the true silent minority. Who is speaking for these children? Where is the counsel for these unborn children, whose life is being taken? Where is the safeguard of the right to trial by jury?"

"If you are right that the fetus is a person," Stewart said, "it would seem that any law allowing abortions would be grossly unconstitutional."

Justice Rehnquist asked: "Does the fact that some laws allow abortion in some cases indicate that the weight of history is against the concept of life from the moment of conception?"

"Yes, I suppose it would," Flowers responded.

I had been following the argument closely so that in my rebuttal I could dispute things Flowers had asserted. Flowers's remarks had made it clear that professionals do not agree on "when life begins." It was up to me in my closing remarks to turn that fact into an advantage for our side.

The original Hippocratic oath—which forbids doctors to perform abortions—was the focus of part of my rebuttal. I pointed out it was adopted at a time when abortions were very dangerous, and the intent of the oath was to protect life. The question followed, 'What does life mean in this particular context?' I continued:

> The purpose of [the Hippocratic oath] was to prevent the citizen from becoming a dependent or ward of the State, and

also to ensure that its citizens would be available for service in the military.

[As applied to the anti-abortion laws], the rationale works just the opposite. Here a woman, because of her pregnancy, is often not a productive member of society. She cannot work, she cannot hold a job, she's not eligible for welfare, she cannot get unemployment compensation. And furthermore, in fact, the pregnancy may produce a child who will become a ward of the State.

I managed, between questions, to emphasize a few key points before my time was up:

We are not here to advocate abortion. We do not ask this Court to rule that abortion is good or desirable in any particular situation.

We are here to advocate that the decision as to whether or not a particular woman will continue to carry or will terminate a pregnancy is a decision that should be made by that individual, that in fact she has a constitutional right to make that decision for herself, and that the State has shown no interest in [or sufficient legal status to allow] interfering with that decision.

The reargument of *Doe v. Bolton* followed. I left the courtroom with the sense that the justices had already decided the cases—but were not yet willing to tell us their decision. When I got back to Austin, people asked me to predict the outcome; I told them I was unwilling to guess. I was hopeful of victory but afraid to take anything for granted.

ELECTION DAY, Tuesday, November 7, was gloomy and rainy. On the ballot for Travis County State Representative, Place 2, were my name as the Democratic candidate and Dwight Wheeler's as the Republican candidate. The major number of voters in

Travis County reside in Austin Soon after the polls closed, I was predicted the winner; almost everybody had assumed as much. When it was all said and done, 84,373 votes were cast for me, 34,970 for Wheeler. When the legislature convened in January 1973, I would become the first woman ever elected from Travis County to the Texas House of Representatives. Victory night was sweet, and the house was once again filled with volunteers and others offering congratulations.

The pace slackened only slightly after the election. I had thank-you notes to write for campaign assistance and contributions and a victory party for key volunteers to plan. I was besieged with requests to give speeches and to meet with people interested in legislative issues that would be considered in the coming session. I had to organize my office staff for the Capitol office and complete pending matters for my law office clients.

I have heard it said that one can get addicted to one's own adrenaline. Nineteen seventy-two had contained so many adrenaline highs that in contrast the end-of-year holidays were a great letdown. I still did not know the result of the Supreme Court's consideration of *Roe v. Wade*, although I expected a decision soon. And the Democrats had again lost the White House to Richard Nixon. What were becoming the annual holiday blues set in once more.

Ron and I had drifted still further apart, and he seemed to be in a bad mood as the year ended. Part of the developing distance between us was attributable to the tension of living and working and having my campaign headquarters all in the same building. I was the focus of the campaign volunteers, and they were sometimes guarded with him—something all political spouses experience. There was little privacy for us as a couple, and Ron sometimes felt like an outsider in his own home. We were both lawyers, but I was known for arguing a Supreme Court case. We had both run for political office, but I had won. The combination of those factors, added to the depressing national political scene, was debilitating.

My mood brightened at the prospect of becoming an official member of the Texas House. It was a victory I relished. If we lost in the Supreme Court, at least we would have a new chance to win in the legislature. "Just in case," I prepared legislation to introduce in the 1973 session to repeal the Texas anti-abortion statutes. I'd always heard that where there was a will there was a way. If so, somehow, someday—whether in the courts or through legislative action, whether this coming year or the next—we would free women from the horrors of illegal abortion.

The young lawyers in the abortion battle

Attorneys Linda Coffee, above, and Sarah Weddington, right, are confident of an eventual victory over Texas' abortion law.

By MARTHA LIEBRUM
Post Reporter

Woman's world

The Houston Post
Tuesday, June 23, 1970

Dear Abby discusses bad housekeeping on page 2

The day after our first victory in Dallas in 1970, the *Houston Post* ran these pictures of Linda Coffee (*left*) and me (*right*) on the front page of its "Woman's World" section. The lower corner of the page indicated what was inside: "Dear Abby discusses bad housekeeping." © THE *HOUSTON POST*

ELECT SARAH WEDDINGTON

STATE REPRESENTATIVE
PLACE 2

Sarah Weddington is a candidate who will seek to represent YOU. She is especially interested in serving you in the areas of:

    ※ Conservation
    ※ Consumer Protection
    ※ Equal Rights for Women and Men

Sarah will work in the House for You

Vote Democratic Primary May 6, 1972

An example of my 1972 campaign literature. We put these all over Austin, including in ladies' rooms.

Sarah, who is the daughter of a Methodist minister, graduated Magna Cum Laude from McMurry College in 1965 and graduated from U.T. Law School in 1967.

She served on the American Bar Association committee which wrote the Code of Professional Responsibility which governs Texas lawyers.

Prior to opening a law office in Austin with her husband, she was Assistant City Attorney for Fort Worth. She has argued before the U.S. Supreme Court and has been active in cases involving the rights of women.

Ron and me at the Texas Capitol on Inauguration Day, early January 1973. It was a far cry from my days upstairs as a clerk/typist. Still no word from Washington.

Here I am surrounded by my campaign helpers (*left to right*) Ann Richards (later Governor of Texas), Carol Castlebury, Patty McKool, Dorothy Wimberly, Linda Anderson, Susan Roberts, Caryl Yontz, and Betsy Kusin.

**GREAT
NEWS!**

The Burger Court, 1973.

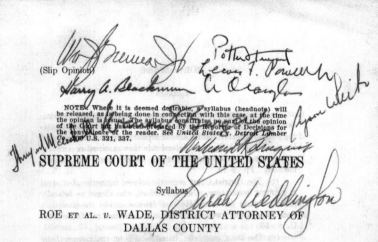

(Slip Opinion)

NOTE. Where it is deemed desirable, a syllabus (headnote) will be released, as is being done in connection with this case, at the time the opinion is issued. The syllabus constitutes no part of the opinion of the Court but has been prepared by the Reporter of Decisions for the convenience of the reader. See *United States v. Detroit Lumber Co.,* 200 U.S. 321, 337.

SUPREME COURT OF THE UNITED STATES

Syllabus

ROE ET AL. *v.* WADE, DISTRICT ATTORNEY OF DALLAS COUNTY

APPEAL FROM THE UNITED STATES DISTRICT COURT FOR THE NORTHERN DISTRICT OF TEXAS

No. 70–18.   Argued December 13, 1971—Reargued October 11, 1972—Decided January 22, 1973

A pregnant single woman (Roe) brought a class action challenging the constitutionality of the Texas criminal abortion laws, which proscribe procuring or attempting an abortion except on medical advice for the purpose of saving the mother's life. A licensed physician (Hallford), who had two state abortion prosecutions pending against him, was permitted to intervene. A childless married couple (the Does), the wife not being pregnant, separately attacked the laws, basing alleged injury on the future possibilities of contraceptive failure, pregnancy, unpreparedness for parenthood, and impairment of the wife's health. A three-judge District Court, which consolidated the actions, held that Roe and Hallford, and members of their classes, had standing to sue and presented justiciable controversies. Ruling that declaratory, though not injunctive, relief was warranted, the court declared the abortion statutes void as vague and overbroadly infringing those plaintiffs' Ninth and Fourteenth Amendment rights. The court ruled the Does' complaint not justiciable. Appellants directly appealed to this Court on the injunctive rulings, and appellee cross-appealed from the District Court's grant of declaratory relief to Roe and Hallford. *Held:*

1. While 28 U. S. C. § 1253 authorizes no direct appeal to this Court from the grant or denial of declaratory relief alone, review is not foreclosed when the case is properly before the Court on appeal from specific denial of injunctive relief and the arguments as to both injunctive and declaratory relief are necessarily identical. P. 8.

2. Roe has standing to sue; the Does and Hallford do not. Pp. 9–14.

I

A serious moment to wonder what the future for women will be after the Supreme Court's decision in *Roe*. Taken in my Austin law office.

Off to DC to work with President Jimmy Carter. Working as the top lawyer to the Department of Agriculture gave me opportunities to enjoy the out-of-doors. Here I am with members of the US Forest Service in Montana, after six days on horseback in the Big Bear Wilderness.

A tense meeting at the White House about issues of special interest to women. (*Left to right*) Vice President Walter Mondale, President Carter, presidential staffers Midge Costanza, Margaret McKenna, Jane Frank, and me.

President Carter signing the extension of the deadline for the passage of the ERA. Important people there to witness this included Maryland Congresswoman Gladys Spellman, me as Assistant to the President of the United States, President of NOW Eleanor Smeal, DNC Chair John White, New York Congresswoman Elizabeth Holtzman, and Michigan Congresswoman Martha Griffiths.

I was part of a coalition trying to defeat the nomination of Clarence Thomas to be a US Supreme Court Justice. Here's a photo of the poster I brought to the Thomas hearings which said: "Would you be more careful if it was you that got pregnant?" My poster wasn't universally appreciated, but I thought it made an important point.

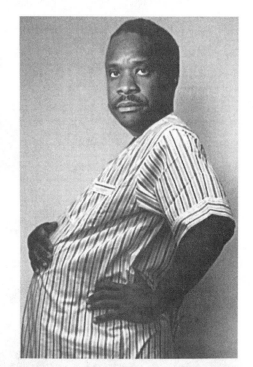

A lineup of witnesses against confirmation at the Clarence Thomas hearings. I am at the far left, with Kate Michelman of NARAL, Faye Wattleton of Planned Parenthood, and former Vermont governor Madeleine Kunin. (REUTERS/BETTMAN)

(*Above*) At the LBJ Ranch, with three former First Ladies, (left to right) Lady Bird Johnson, me, Rosalynn Carter, and Betty Ford. Republican Ford had always been a great friend of our cause.

To Sarah Weddington, trailblazer, advocate, leader, friend, with admiration and affection, Hillary

I have known Obama Secretary of State Clinton since the mid-seventies. I campaigned for her when she ran for US Senator from New York. Each of us has received the top honor awarded by the National Federation of Planned Parenthood.

Writer Molly Ivins with Liz Carpenter, press secretary to Lady Bird Johnson, and me. Each of us was diagnosed with breast cancer at about the same time. We were good friends, all living in Austin, and spoke at many events together for efforts against breast cancer.

In recent years many state legislatures have passed laws making access to abortion more difficult. These Doonesbury cartoons focus on legislation happening in Texas.

7 . VICTORY

The new year started at a breakneck pace. On Tuesday, January 9, I was sworn in as a member of the Texas House of Representatives. There were 76 newly elected among the 150 House members; five of that total were women. I was determined to do an extraordinarily fine job, as I considered my presence there an opportunity to open the door for many other women. It is said we stand taller because we stand on the shoulders of others. I wanted to ensure that women in Texas would stand taller because of the example and work of the women sworn in that day.

On January 19, I filed my first legislative package, the proposed changes to the Texas abortion law. Included were a bill to authorize pregnant females aged sixteen or older to consent to abortion, a bill providing that only a woman's consent (and not that of her husband) was needed for her own sterilization, and a bill allowing doctors to give contraceptives to women under eighteen without parental involvement.

The next day, a Saturday, Ron and I watched on television the inauguration of Richard Nixon to his second term as president. We groused and discussed again the rumor that Nixon had not wanted the "Nixon Court" deciding the abortion cases while he was running for reelection; we wondered how long it would be before the Supreme Court announced its decision.

MONDAY, JANUARY 22, was wet and wintry, the kind of day I wished I could stay in bed and read a book. Nonetheless, I went to the Capitol early to get organized for the week and catch up on correspondence. Ruth Bowers came by my office to visit over coffee before she set out to deliver pro-choice literature to all the legislators. Shortly after nine a.m. in Austin, at our law office at home, Martha Davis took a call from a *New York Times* reporter. "May I speak to Mrs. Weddington?" he asked. Martha explained I was at the Capitol. "Does she have a comment about *Roe v. Wade*?" "Is there some particular reason she could have a comment about it today?" Martha wondered. "Yes. The decision was announced in Washington this morning at ten a.m.," the reporter replied. "How was it decided?" Martha queried. "She won it, 7-2," was the reporter's answer. At the same time Patty McKool, who was answering my Capitol office phones, received a call from an NBC *Today* show reporter asking for comments.

Indeed, that morning at ten a.m. Eastern Standard Time. the Supreme Court had announced that by a vote of seven to two the Texas anti-abortion statutes had been ruled unconstitutional as violating the constitutional right of privacy. The plaintiffs in *Doe v. Bolton* had also won most of their points, but the importance of that opinion was overshadowed by the breadth of the *Roe* decision. Supreme Court decisions set the supreme law of the land; the decisions in *Roe* and *Doe* affected the laws of every state that had provisions similar to those of Texas and Georgia. Abortion was no longer illegal.

Pandemonium broke out. The phones erupted with press calls, congratulatory calls, calls requesting information about the decision. There was mass confusion and commotion. We were transferring calls and I was running back and forth between my Capitol office and our law office at home. Ron and Martha were managing the chaos in the law office, despite the fact that his favorite uncle had just died and he had a trial scheduled a few days later. Ruth Bowers pitched in to handle the people streaming through the Capitol: neighboring office staffs coming to see what the noise was all about, supporters joining in the celebration, and press photographers clamoring for pictures. Apparently people remembered how much I love fresh flowers: I have a mental image of bouquets filling up the reception area, of flowers everywhere. Because of the maelstrom that day, through the years I had come to remember having been at home when I first heard the decision. But recent interviews with others have clarified for me that I first heard the news at the Capitol.

Linda got the news on the radio while driving to work. When she arrived at her office, a senior partner told her that news about *Roe* would soon be preempted by other news: Lyndon Johnson had died. Linda called to tell me that, and to share the excitement of victory. Our conversation started on a somber note because of that famous Texan's death, but it picked up as our thoughts turned to the Supreme Court's action. We could not get over the fact that we, two young women lawyers not long out of law school, had contributed to winning a crucial Supreme Court decision. It was a decision that freed women from the fear of unwanted pregnancy, a decision that freed doctors to practice medicine according to their best training, a decision we felt would result in fewer unwanted children. As we talked, however, we kept returning to questions about the content of the decision and therefore its impact, questions we couldn't answer until we knew more about the Court's specific words.

In the midst of the excitement, we were hungry for details to answer our own questions and those being asked by the many callers. What had the Court said, exactly? Who had voted for us? Against us? Linda had someone in Washington she could call for help, and so did I. It became a race to see who could obtain expanded information more expeditiously. I got through to a lawyer friend, asked her to go to the Supreme Court and obtain a copy of the opinion, and then call me back and read me the significant portions. Meanwhile, Linda, Ron, and I pumped reporters for information.

I TRIED BUT was unable to reach Jane Roe. I finally gave up, thinking that since she remained anonymous she would not get caught off-guard by press calls. I assumed she had heard or would see press reports, since by then the news of the decision was being mentioned during every newscast.

John and Mary Doe had already heard when I got through to them; they had already been speaking with friends and relatives about the news. Dr. Hallford, we imagined, must be very happy now that the two indictments against him would be dropped. Dr. Hodgson certainly was. She was driving through pouring rain on her way to Sanibel, Florida, for a vacation when the announcement came on the radio. She stopped at the next roadside phone to call home for more details and to rejoice that her medical license was now safe.

At *The Rag* office in Austin, normally intense, hardworking writers were dancing. Judy Smith was amazed. "We never thought we would accomplish the level of decision that came back. We were so naïve." The wonderful part, she thought, was that women would never again know the agony she had seen others go through. She saw the decision not as something Austin volunteers had done, but as something broader: "All this energy from people all over the country had gone into it, and things were changed. That day was a celebration of effort."

Barbara Hines, then in law school in Boston, was bragging to other students about the effort she had been part of in Austin. She told them about the garage sale, when Judy and Bea had first asked me to research whether or not the referral project volunteers could be prosecuted for telling women the "good places to go." For the first time it seemed to her that anything was possible. Diane Dodson was in DC looking for a law job and happened to be with a group of law students when she heard the news. When she started telling them the history of *Roe* and her role, they insisted on dropping everything to go buy beers and celebrate. Their celebration turned into a huge informal gathering that lasted for hours.

Caryl Yontz, who was working for me at the Capitol, was helping me phone people who had been involved in the case— Ginny Whitehill, and the doctors who had given us affidavits, among others—to share the news and again thank them for their assistance. Caryl reported that Ginny was shocked; she had prayed for a five-to-four decision, and was overwhelmed that it was seven to two. Later Caryl yelled a phoned-in suggestion that January 22 be declared a national holiday for women.

I called Mother and Daddy, who were pastoring in Lubbock. The announcement probably meant more to Mother, since she had been in the Supreme Court with me. She was pleased by what I had accomplished. Daddy's reaction was more analytical: he was glad I had won, of course, since I'd been working so long and diligently on the case. He was glad that we had won by a strong majority, so the issue was really decided and was no longer a question. He was pleased that the principles that he personally held and which I had represented had been approved by the Supreme Court. And he was glad that women would no longer be in back alleys but rather in safe surroundings under the watchful eyes of trained professionals.

The Reverend Bob Breihan, still a leader of the Clergy Consultation Service in Austin, that morning accompanied his sixteen-year-old daughter, Laurie, to see Dr. Fred Hansen, who had often testified for the pro-choice side at hearings in the Texas legislature. When he introduced her, Breihan told Hansen: "I want you to know that she has the support of her father and mother anytime she wants to come in and talk to you about any issue in regard to her functioning as a woman, and you have our support to give her advice or participate in any procedure you deem important." Breihan then mentioned the news about the *Roe* decision. Dr. Hansen was so astonished that he could not concentrate on the appointment.

Jimmye Kimmey, who had organized the *amicus* effort, and the New York lawyers Harriet Pilpel and Cyril Means who had helped prepare the case, were having mixed reactions, celebratory yet still cautious. Jimmye, who heard the news in her office at the Association for the Study of Abortion, remembers thinking, "I can't let myself be too ecstatic until I read the opinion and see what the justices really said." Still, in her words, it was "the moment we had all been aiming for. To have it happen was glorious." She remembers speaking to Harriet, who commented: "The decision scaled the whole mountain. We expected to get there, but not on the first try."

MY FRIEND IN WASHINGTON called back to describe the opinion to me; I had gotten other details from reporters who called. I began to do press interviews but was still circumspect in what I said; I wanted to *read* the opinion. My official statement was brief:

> I am pleased because of the impact this decision will have on the lives of many women who in the past have suffered because of the current Texas law. I am especially pleased that the decision is a solid seven-to-two decision and that it was based on the right of privacy. I feel very humble to be able to represent the class of women affected by this decision and hope their lives will be better for it.

Around noon on January 23, 1973 I received the Supreme Court telegram (One thing that reminds me of how long ago the *Roe* decision was handed down is telegrams. Telegrams no longer exist and attorneys no longer receive telegrams informing them of how the Supreme Court ruled in their case. Moreover, no one has to wait for opinions to be airmailed. They have direct access to opinions online minutes after decisions are announced.): "Judgment Roe against Wade today affirmed in part and reversed in part. Judgment Doe against Bolton modified and affirmed. Opinions airmailed." I wished I could have a copy more rapidly than that. Among other things, I wondered what had been reversed.

Texas governor Dolph Briscoe responded quickly and tersely to the decision: "I am today asking the attorney general for his evaluation of this ruling and for the alternatives open to Texas as a result of the Supreme Court's decision." Lieutenant Governor Bill Hobby said, "It is my opinion that the best solution is one in which the state is neutral on the subject of abortion. I believe the medical profession of Texas will respond to the decision and will treat abortion as a medical matter in a responsible way."

There were spontaneous celebrations for the Court's decision around the country. Reactions from many recognized women leaders flashed across news wires. People often tell me that they remember vividly where they were when they heard about two events: the death of President John F. Kennedy and the decision in *Roe v. Wade*. That decision represented a change of immense proportions in the lives and futures of American women.

It wasn't until the end of the workday that Ron, Martha Davis, and I—the entire law office staff—could take a few minutes to savor the win. We shared the reactions of those we had called and those who had called us. Ron noted that the decision had been announced the first Monday after Nixon was inaugurated for his second term; that seemed to us to support the rumors that the

Court had held up announcing its decision in part out of consideration for Nixon. Of course, Martha insisted it was her typing and keeping us organized that fall that carried the day.

That night was one of the few times I canceled existing plans and celebrated with Ron. We talked and talked, about the years we had been together, and about the impact of the case—good and bad—on our relationship. And we talked about how we could start a new phase of our lives.

I could hardly believe that at twenty-seven years of age I had won an important Supreme Court case. This was, I felt, an opportunity to broaden my focus to other areas—rape-law reform, parental custody matters, the needs of children and the poor, health care, working conditions, the environment, and a long list of other concerns. I could move on. After all, I had never meant for the abortion issue to be my focus forever.

Ron and I agreed that the Court's decision was an opportunity for all women. The battle was never "for abortion"—abortion was not what we wanted to encourage. The battle was for the basic right of women to make their own decisions. There was a basic question underlying the specific issue of abortion: Who is to control and define the lives of women? And our answer was: Not the government!

Ron and I discussed our belief that the Court's decision in *Roe* was a declaration for human liberty, and was faithful to the values of the nation's founders. They had created a country where the government would not be allowed to control their most private lives—not their speech, not their religion, not their domestic habits. We felt we had been true to that tradition. The "system," it seemed, did in fact work. I had always been taught to work within the system. When others had scoffed, I just kept plodding along that path—and in the end we had won a prize bigger than we ever dreamed. Our victory solidified my faith in law, the court process, and the wisdom of our nation's founders.

The system they had created was resilient, and had proved its ability to adapt to changing times.

SOME PEOPLE LEARNED about the decision after newspapers with front-page stories about it hit the stands. Jane Roe was quoted in *The Boston Globe* of May 15, 1989, as saying:

> [My roommate] was taking a shower while I was reading about the verdict in the living room. When she came out, I said, "What do you think of this Jane Roe?" She said, "I think she's great." I said, "Would you like to meet her?" She said, "Yeah." I stood up and said, "Hello, my name is Norma."

Nick Danforth was in New York; *Roe* hadn't been on his mind much, since "the Institute had pretty much folded, I hadn't been paid for months, and I was broke." He had even begun to resign himself to our losing at the Court. He thought the chances of victory were slim, although he considered the effort one well worth making. When he passed a newsstand and saw a headline proclaiming our victory, he burst into tears. "I just stood over that bale of papers, reading and rereading that beautiful headline, crying like a baby. Tears of joy. The vendor came over to open the stack of papers and asked if I was all right. 'Fine'—I smiled— 'never better.'"

Ron and I also read about the case in the newspapers the next morning. We were up early—we had slept very little—to buy copies of every major newspaper from around the country available in Austin. The banner headlines concerned Johnson's death, but each paper had a prominent front-page story about the Supreme Court decision. The more I read about it, the more excited I became. It was a clear, strong victory. The justices who voted for the *Roe* opinion were Blackmun—who also wrote the opinion—Brennan, Burger, Douglas, Marshall, Powell, and Stewart. Justices White and Rehnquist wrote dissents.

Because of his connection to the Mayo Clinic, I was not all that surprised by Blackmun's vote. Douglas's vote I had expected; Marshall's and Brennan's pleased but did not surprise me. Stewart and Powell had been big question marks in my mind. As for Chief Justice Burger, I wondered what the inside story was on how we won his vote. I had never anticipated getting Rehnquist's; and I wondered, since White was the other dissenter, whether the rumors about the Whites' troubles in having children were true. If so, that might well explain why he could not imagine that a woman would seek an abortion when his wife had wanted so desperately and had gone through so much to have children. The justices are not supposed to decide on the basis of their own life experience, but they are human and their decisions must be affected to some degree by such events.

An Associated Press story referred to Justice Blackmun's comment that "the state could cause a pregnant woman considerable harm by not allowing her to have an abortion." How I agreed with that!

Sometimes when I read comments attributed to me, I couldn't recognize them. But most of the quotations I read that day reflected my thoughts accurately. *The Houston Post* quoted me as "feeling glad for the women of Texas, who now will have access to abortion services." It also noted my statement that "I would much prefer [that] we did not have the abortion problem, that instead pregnancies be prevented," and my vow "to lead the legislative battle to liberalize the flow of contraceptive information to minors."

One of the few stories that captured my real feelings on the day we won, however, didn't appear until a few weeks later, in the *Milwaukee Journal*: "Sarah Weddington looked uncomfortable as the women pressed close to her, offering their thanks. 'If I hadn't done it, someone else would have,' she explained to them." Indeed, I saw *Roe* as part of a much larger effort by many attorneys. I was the one who, through a series of quirks, stood before the Court to represent all of us. Had a different string of events occurred, another case might have been the one to make history.

Ron and I also read observations from those who were distressed by the Court's decision; obviously, not everyone was as pleased as we were about the news. Around the country the antis too had been burning up the telephone wires—they were talking about how they could overturn the decision, or avoid or blunt its impact. I have always wondered if some of the anti-abortion folk thought the fact that United States and Texas flags flew at half-staff on that January 22, and for a total of thirty days, as they did because of President Johnson's death, was doubly appropriate because of the depth of their disagreement with the decision.

THE COPY OF the *Roe* opinion sent by the Court arrived a few days after the decision. It was a thrill to hold the document Blackmun wrote for the Court. I skimmed it first for the main points:

— A direct appeal was proper because of the specific denial of injunctive relief regarding a statute declared unconstitutional by a three-judge federal court.
— Roe had standing to sue; the Does and Dr. Hallford did not. (Geesh, I thought, we went backward on that part. At least the lower court had recognized Hallford's standing. But it didn't matter; the outcome freed Hallford anyway.)
— The natural termination of Roe's pregnancy did not cancel her status as an appropriate plaintiff. Under strict mootness principles, hers would be a situation "capable of repetition, yet evading review."
— The Texas statute violated the due-process clause of the Fourteenth Amendment, which protects from state action the right to privacy, including a woman's qualified right to terminate pregnancy.

— The state, however, had legitimate interest in protecting both the pregnant woman's health and the potentiality of human life.

I settled back with my feet up to read the majority opinion in detail and savor its words. First the Court noted the sensitive nature of the subject:

> We forthwith acknowledge our awareness of the sensitive and emotional nature of the abortion controversy, of the vigorous opposing views, even among physicians, and of the deep and seemingly absolute convictions that the subject inspires. One's philosophy, one's experiences, one's exposure to the raw edges of human existence, one's religious training, one's attitudes toward life and family and their values, and the moral standards one establishes and seeks to observe, are all likely to influence and to color one's thinking and conclusions about abortion.

Blackmun then reviewed the Texas statute, the facts about the plaintiffs, and procedurally how the case had arrived at the Supreme Court. He examined the State's claims that the case was moot since Jane Roe was not pregnant when it reached the Supreme Court:

> But when, as here, pregnancy is a significant fact in the litigation, the normal 266-day human gestation period is so short that the pregnancy will come to term before the usual appellate process is complete. If that termination makes a case moot, pregnancy litigation seldom will survive much beyond the trial stage, and appellate review will be effectively denied. Our law should not be that rigid. Pregnancy often comes more than once to the same woman, and in the general population; if man is to survive, it will always be with

us. Pregnancy provides a classic justification for a conclusion of nonmootness. It truly could be "capable of repetition, yet evading review."

Won that one, I thought. So the end of her pregnancy had not made the issue moot.

Blackmun then reviewed the history of abortion, including ancient attitudes, the Hippocratic oath, common law, English statutory law, American law, and the history of the position of the American Medical Association, the American Public Health Association, and the American Bar Association. There was, after all, I thought, a reason for including so much historical material in our brief and Supplementary Appendix, and for the extensive *amicus* effort.

Blackmun reexamined the reasons advanced to explain historically the enactment of criminal abortion laws and to justify their existence. First, he noted, "it has been argued occasionally that these laws were the product of a Victorian social concern to discourage illicit sexual conduct." But the State had not advanced that argument. A second reason concerned abortion as medical procedure. However, Blackmun pointed out, abortion was no longer the very dangerous procedure it once was; appellants and various *amici*, he said, "refer to medical data indicating that abortion in early pregnancy . . . is now relatively safe." A third reason, he said, was "the State's interest—some phrase it in terms of duty—in protecting prenatal life." But here Blackmun commented that those challenging the anti-abortion statutes had "sharply disputed" that such was a reason for the statutes' being passed, and he noted a lack of any legislative history to support that argument. I had not been reading the extensive footnotes at the bottom of each page closely, but sure enough, when I did I found several referring to Cyril Means's writings; I knew he would be pleased.

The opinion got even better from my perspective when Blackmun began to write of privacy:

The Constitution does not explicitly mention any right of privacy. In a line of decisions, however, going back as far as [1891], the Court has recognized that a right of personal privacy, or a guarantee of certain areas or zones of privacy, does exist under the Constitution. In varying contexts the Court or individual justices have indeed found at least the roots of that right in the First Amendment . . . in the Fourth and Fifth Amendments . . .in the penumbras of the Bill of Rights . . . in the Ninth Amendment . . . or in the concept of liberty guaranteed by the first section of the Fourteenth Amendment. These decisions make it clear that only personal rights that can be deemed "fundamental" or "implicit in the concept of ordered liberty" . . . are included in this guarantee of personal privacy. They also make it clear that the right has some extension to activities relating to marriage . . . procreation . . . contraception . . . family relationships . . . and child rearing and education.

This right of privacy, whether it be founded in the Fourteenth Amendment's concept of personal liberty and restrictions upon state action, as we feel it is, or, as the District Court determined, in the Ninth Amendment's reservation of rights to the people, is broad enough to encompass a woman's decision whether or not to terminate her pregnancy. The detriment that the State would impose upon the pregnant woman by denying this choice is altogether apparent.

I wanted to stand and cheer!

But then came some not so good news. Blackmun noted that I had argued that the woman's right is absolute, and indicated that "with this we do not agree." Some state regulations in areas protected by the right to privacy would be appropriate, Blackmun wrote, for reasons of safeguarding health, maintaining medical standards, and protecting what he called "potential life." "At some point in pregnancy," the opinion said, "these respective interests become sufficiently compelling to sustain regulation of the factors that govern the abortion decision." One sentence firmly stated the Court's disagreement with "the claim asserted by some *amici* that one has an unlimited right to do with one's body as one pleases."

It is true that no constitutional right is absolute. For example, the right of free speech is limited by libel laws. The implied right to travel can be limited in the interest of national security. What I feared, even in that moment of victory, was that the Court's words might encourage the opposition to look for ways to restrict a woman's choice regarding abortion and to make access to it more time-consuming, more expensive, and more difficult.

The Court did say that "regulation limiting these rights may be justified only by a 'compelling state interest'" and that "legislative enactments must be narrowly drawn to express only the legitimate state interests at stake." It seemed to be limiting the signal it was giving to the states. But still I worried that the justices were underestimating the ingenuity and dogged determination of the opposition.

Next in the opinion was a lengthy section about the interest the state had advocated, that of preserving "unborn life" and explaining that the state had not treated the fetus as a person in legal ways.

> [Texas] and certain *amici* argue that the fetus is a "person" within the language and meaning of the Fourteenth Amendment. In support of this they outline at length and in detail the well-known facts of fetal development. If this suggestion of personhood is established, the appellant's case, of course, collapses, for the fetus' right to life is then guaranteed specifically by the Amendment. On the other hand, the appellee conceded on reargument that no case could be cited that

holds a fetus is a person within the meaning of the Four-teenth Amendment.

The Constitution does not define "person" in so many words. Section I of the Fourteenth Amendment makes three references to "person." The first, in defining "citizens," speaks of "persons born or naturalized in the United States." The word also appears both in the Due Process Clause and in the Equal Protection Clause. "Person" is used in other places in the Constitution: in the listing of qualifications for repre-sentatives and senators . . . in the Apportionment Clause . . . in the Migration and Importation provision . . . in the Emolu-ment Clause . . . in the Electors provisions . . . in the provi-sion outlining qualifications for the office of President . . . and in the Fifth, Twelfth, and Twenty-second Amendments, as well as in sections 2 and 3 of the Fourteenth Amendment. But in nearly all these instances, the use of the word is such that it has application only postnatally. None indicates, with any assurance, that it has any possible prenatal application.

All this, together with our observation . . . that throughout the major portion of the 19th century prevailing legal abor-tion practices were far freer than they are today, persuades us that the word "person," as used in the Fourteenth Amend-ment, does not include the unborn.

I remembered that night Ron had stayed up for hours writ-ing, as I typed, the section in our brief on the beginning of legal rights. The Court apparently considered it important. Blackmun went on to write:

Texas urges that, apart from the Fourteenth Amendment, life begins at conception and is present throughout pregnancy, and that, therefore, the State has a compelling interest in protecting that life from and after conception. We need not resolve the difficult question of when life begins. When those trained in the respective disciplines of medicine, philosophy, and theology are unable to arrive at any consensus, the judiciary, at this point in the development of man's knowledge, is not in a position to speculate as to the answer.

It should be sufficient to note briefly the wide divergence of thinking on this most sensitive and difficult question. There has always been strong support for the view that life does not begin until live birth. This was the held belief of the Stoics. It appears to be the predominant, though not unanimous, attitude of the Jewish faith. It may be taken to represent also the position of a large segment of the Protestant community. Organized groups that have taken a formal position on the abortion issue have generally regarded abortion as a matter for the conscience of the individual and her family.

Blackmun outlined concepts about "when life begins" that had held sway in various groups throughout history. He noted that the Roman Catholic Church had come to its current position that life begins at conception relatively recently but that it was one shared by many non-Catholics as well. However, he wrote, "substantial problems for precise definition of this view are posed . . . by new embryological data that purport to indicate that conception is a 'process' over time, rather than an event, and by new medical techniques such as menstrual extraction, the 'morning-after' pill, implantation of embryos, artificial insemination, and even artificial wombs."

To end his comments about "when life begins," Blackmun pointed out that areas of the law, other than arguably criminal abortion laws, have "been reluctant to endorse any theory that life, as we recognize it, begins before live birth or to accord legal rights to the unborn except in narrowly defined situations and except when the rights are contingent upon live birth." Blackmun almost quoted from Ron's arguments when he wrote that tort law did not involve prenatal injuries and that rights of inheritance were contingent upon a live birth. He concluded simply: "In short, the unborn have never been recognized in the law as persons in the whole sense."

I checked off the significant points: There is a constitutional right of privacy; pregnancy is fundamental; the State had no compelling reason to prohibit abortion to the extent the anti-abortion laws had provided. The Texas laws were unconstitutional.

The Court could have stopped there, but it added what is called dictum. This advisory language is not strictly part of the opinion; it suggests what the Court's response would be to issues not specifically before it. In the dictum the Court revealed what it considered appropriate state regulations of abortion. Although the opinion said the Court did not agree that "by adopting one theory of life, Texas may override the rights of the pregnant woman that are at stake," the Court maintained that the State did have important interests in preserving and protecting the health of the pregnant woman and "still *another* important and legitimate interest in protecting the potentiality of human life." I read that part again, and again I cringed.

The Court went on to outline a scheme for state regulation and procedures a state might implement if it chose to act. These suggestions were based on a trimester approach to pregnancy:

(a) For the stage prior to approximately the end of the first trimester, the abortion decision and its effectuation must be left to the medical judgment of the pregnant woman's attending physician.

(b) For the stage subsequent to approximately the end of the first trimester, the State, in promoting its interest in the health of the mother, may, if it chooses, regulate the abortion procedure in ways that are reasonably related to maternal health.

(c) For the stage subsequent to viability the State, in promoting its interest in the potentiality of human life, may, if it chooses, regulate, and even proscribe, abortion except where it is necessary, in appropriate medical judgment, for the preservation of the life or health of the woman.

I considered what I had just read. Never in any of our briefs had we suggested anything about a trimester approach to pregnancy. Never in any of the State's briefs or in the *amicus* briefs was there anything like that. Nothing like that had been spoken of directly in oral argument.

Almost never do attorneys find a concept for the first time in the opinion in their own case. But here exactly that had happened. I wondered where the concept had come from. In 1981, Woodward and Armstrong's *The Brethren* related that Blackmun had spent time during the summer of 1972 in the library of his former client, the Mayo Clinic, doing research for the opinion he was drafting for *Roe*. He learned from doctors that they often divided pregnancy into three-month stages, or trimesters. Woodward and Armstrong argue out of that evolved the trimester approach of the opinion. In contrast to what *The Brethren* says, Blackmun has told others that the approach was his independent creation.

The comment that "the abortion decision . . . must be left to . . . the pregnant woman's attending physician" would also raise hackles among feminists. It seemed to take the decision from the woman and give it to her doctor. We hoped abortion would become a part of routine medical care, generally provided by a woman's regular gynecologist or obstetrician or the doctor she went to for other reasons. Of course she would seek medical advice in the event of pregnancy, but we always meant for the basic decision to remain hers.

I skimmed Chief Justice Burger's concurring opinion (an opinion agreeing with the conclusion of the Court but stating something not in the majority opinion), which noted that he was "somewhat troubled that the Court has taken notice of various scientific and medical data in reaching its conclusion." He was obviously referring to the nonlegal information we had included in our brief, in the Supplementary Appendix, and in the *amicus* briefs. But he did not think the Court had exceeded the scope of judicial notice accepted in other contexts. "Judicial notice" refers to matters so commonly known and accepted that justices are allowed to consider them without introduction of evidence during the Court proceeding to prove those facts. I interpreted Burger's words as a warning to other attorneys that he would carefully scrutinize any nonlegal matters referred to but not proven by evidence.

Burger wrote further that "in oral argument, counsel for the State of Texas informed the Court that early abortive procedures were routinely permitted in certain exceptional cases, such as nonconsensual pregnancies resulting from rape and incest. In the face of a rigid and narrow statute, such as that of Texas, no one in these circumstances should be placed in a posture of dependence on a prosecutorial policy or prosecutorial discretion." He seemed to be disapproving of the assistant attorney general's intimation that women really could get an abortion in cases of rape and incest, even though the statute clearly said that such was not legal. Burger concluded: "Plainly, the Court today rejects any claim that the Constitution requires abortion on demand." Certainly the phrase "abortion on demand" was not in any of our briefs; it was instead the kind of thing the opposition was always saying. I wondered which of their briefs he had picked that up from. Perhaps Burger was quoting from the State's oral argument; I made a mental note to place more importance on what was said in oral argument.

Justice Douglas' concurring opinion amplified what he considered the meaning of the term "liberty" as used in the Fourteenth Amendment. It included "the autonomous control over the development and expression of one's intellect, interests, tastes, and personality"; "freedom of choice in the basic decisions of one's life respecting marriage, divorce, procreation, contraception, and the education and upbringing of children"; and "freedom to care for one's health and person, freedom from bodily restraint or compulsion, freedom to talk, stroll or loaf." He noted at one point that statutes against abortion "struck the balance between the woman and the State's interests wholly in favor of the latter," and indicated he disagreed. In essence, he said, those who oppose abortion place the entire value on the fetus and none on the woman; they seem to look right through her, as if she were invisible, and see only the fetus. I made mental note to use that concept when I spoke about the case.

Douglas quoted from "Religion, Morality and Abortion: A Constitutional Appraisal," a 1969 law review article by a former justice, Tom Clark:

> To say that life is present at conception is to give recognition to the potential, rather than the actual. The unfertilized egg has life, and if fertilized, it takes on human proportions. But the law deals in reality, not obscurity—the known rather than the unknown. When sperm meets egg, life may eventually form, but quite often it does not. The law does not deal in speculation. The phenomenon of life takes time to develop, and until it is actually present, it cannot be destroyed. Its interruption prior to formation would hardly be homicide, and as we have seen, society does not regard it as such. The rites of Baptism are not performed and death certificates are not required when a miscarriage occurs. No prosecutor has ever returned a murder indictment charging the taking of the life of a fetus. This would not be the case if the fetus constituted human life.

Douglas concluded his opinion with comments about the Georgia case; I was anxious to read that opinion after *Roe*.

But the next was Justice Stewart's concurring opinion, which hinted that the Court should not have discussed the trimester approach, since "such legislation is not before us." My bet was that he had touched a sore point and that many other critics would be making the same statement even more forcefully.

Justice White had written a dissent, which Rehnquist joined. Rehnquist had also written his own dissent. White's tone was utterly different from that of the majority opinion:

> At the heart of the controversy in these cases are those recurring pregnancies that pose no danger whatsoever to the life or health of the mother but are nevertheless unwanted for any one or more of a variety of reasons—convenience, family planning, economics, dislike of children, the embarrassment of illegitimacy, etc. The common claim before us is that for any one of such reasons, or for no reason at all, and without asserting or claiming any threat to life or health, any woman is entitled to an abortion at her request if she is able to find a medical advisor willing to undertake the procedure.

Wow, I thought, he is really antagonized by this issue! That impression was even stronger when I read his next sentences:

> The Court for the most part sustains this position: During the period prior to the time the fetus becomes viable, the Constitution of the United States values the convenience, whim or caprice of the putative mother more than the life or potential life of the fetus. . . .
>
> With all due respect, I dissent. I find nothing in the language or history of the Constitution to support the Court's judgment. The Court simply fashions and announces a new constitutional right for pregnant mothers and, with scarcely any reason or authority for its action, invests that right with sufficient substance to override most existing state abortion statutes.

The upshot is that the people and the legislatures of the 50 states are constitutionally disentitled to weigh the relative importance of the continued existence and development of the fetus on the one hand against a spectrum of possible impacts on the mother on the other hand. As an exercise of raw judicial power, the Court perhaps has authority to do what it does today; but in my view its judgment is an improvident and extravagant exercise of the power of judicial review which the Constitution extends to this Court.

The Court apparently values the convenience of the pregnant mother more than the continued existence and development of the life or potential life which she carries. Whether or not I might agree with that marshalling of values, I can in no event join the Court's judgment because I find no constitutional warrant for imposing such an order of priorities on the people and legislatures of the States. In a sensitive area such as this, involving as it does issues over which reasonable men may easily and heatedly differ, I cannot accept the Court's exercise of its clear power of choice by interposing a constitutional barrier to state efforts to protect human life and by investing mothers and doctors with the constitutionally protected right to exterminate it. The issue, for the most part, should be left with the people and to the political processes the people have devised to govern their affairs.

The pages were almost singed by the heat of his words. I had not anticipated the intensity of his reaction; White had voted with the majority in *Griswold*, and because of that I thought of him as a maybe. His was a short dissent, but a passionate one. I was glad only one other judge had been willing to sign it.

Justice Rehnquist's dissent took a different tack. He first pointed out that the Court was saying that a state could impose very few restrictions in the first trimester. But he then raised the question of whether Jane Roe had been in the first trimester when the suit was filed. "We know only that plaintiff Roe at the time of filing her complaint was a pregnant woman; for aught that appears in this record, she may have been in her last trimester of pregnancy as of the date the complaint was filed." That was the first hint that a justice was curious about how far along she was when we filed the suit. Linda and I had not focused on the issue of what stage of pregnancy our plaintiff was in. After all, you can't be just a little bit pregnant. Either way you are or you aren't. Rehnquist was saying, in essence: Maybe the state could prohibit abortion for Jane Roe except to save her life at the stage of pregnancy she was in.

But he went on to say that even if the plaintiff were one capable of litigating the issue, he would still reach an opposite conclusion. His next words were to be repeated many times in the future by anti-abortionists. "A transaction resulting in an operation such as this [abortion] is not 'private' in the ordinary usage of that word." Even now, the opposition is always saying that abortion is not private because the doctor and the "unborn child" are there, that is, the woman is not alone. The *Griswold* case stands for the principle that there is a right of privacy to use contraception; but I've never heard of anyone using contraception "in private" if by that one means alone.

Rehnquist said the Court should have used a test of whether the state legislation had a *rational* relation to a valid state objective, not whether the state had a *compelling reason to regulate*, as the majority had ruled. The first test would make it much easier for the state to win. Rehnquist did mention one circumstance in which the state would be going too far: "If the Texas statute were to prohibit an abortion even when the mother's life is in jeopardy, I have little doubt that such a statute would lack a rational relation to a valid state objective."

Rehnquist maintained further that "the fact that a majority of the States, reflecting after all the majority sentiment in those States, have had restrictions on abortions for at least a century is a strong indication, it seems to me, that the asserted right to an abortion is not 'so rooted in the traditions and conscience of our people as to be ranked as fundamental.'" The very existence of the modern debate on abortion, Rehnquist asserted, was evidence that the right to abortion was not universally accepted.

But, I thought, laws often reflect the sentiments of just those who are most active. The majority of people don't vote and don't get involved in public issues. Rehnquist mentioned recent years when states had anti-abortion statutes, but what about the many years before, when the national and state constitutions were written, during which abortion was legal? Even when the anti-abortion laws were passed, the fetus was still not treated as a legal person. When I read his phrase "right to an abortion," I wanted to say, "No, no, it's a right to make one's own choices."

He ended in the usual way—"I respectfully dissent." I was thinking not of those words as I closed the opinions, but rather of the fact that Rehnquist was the newest and youngest justice. We would have to deal with him for a long time. That was too bad. Still, he was clearly in a minority on the Court.

I picked up the opinion on *Doe v. Bolton*, the Georgia case. Blackmun first set out the differences between the Texas and Georgia statutes. Then the Court basically relied on its opinion in *Roe*, but it also said explicitly that certain of what I called hurdles or roadblocks were invalid: namely, the requirement that abortions be performed in hospitals meeting standards set by the Joint Commission on Accreditation of Hospitals, approval by a hospital abortion committee, confirmation by two independent physicians, and residence.

I SAT BACK to review the opinions mentally. I had been taken off-guard by the trimester approach, by the inclusion in the opinion of something that had not been included during the briefing and arguing of the Texas and Georgia cases. I could guess only that Blackmun, knowing that he needed a majority of justices to vote for his opinions, and that some might have been reluctant to do so if the decision prohibited all state regulation until birth, wrote what the justices had perhaps talked about in conference. I wondered whether he sensed that anti-abortion activists would immediately begin efforts to pass state regulations, and was thus trying to avoid endless future litigation by giving some signals about what the Court would consider within and outside state authority. Maybe he saw the dictum, although not usually included in a decision, as economizing the Court's future time and consideration.

It was clear the two dissenters felt strongly about their positions; and I knew that the opinions contained passages that each side would disagree with. For example, the Court had qualified a woman's ability to make the abortion decision; it had said the state *could* regulate. I knew the opposition would use that to try and put a camel through a keyhole. There was language about a woman's being "in consultation with her doctor" that, some would worry, might result in undue power in the hands of professionals. And what would happen to the trimester approach if and when medical science made advances? Sure enough since the *Roe* decision opponents of abortion have passed many laws to make access to abortion services more and more difficult.

The language "in consultation with her doctor" made me think about the "Rule of 120," a medical custom that doctors routinely followed even though it was never required by law. Many women sought sterilization as a method of birth control because few safe and reliable contraceptives were available. But doctors usually refused to perform sterilization unless a woman's age multiplied by her number of children equaled at least 120 (a woman of thirty couldn't get sterilized until she had four children, a woman of forty needed to have three children, and so forth). I worried that if the medical community came up with similar rules of thumb to apply to abortion, even after we had won our case, medical services might not be as uniformly available as had been our goal.

But that day as I read, I rejoiced that the decision was seven to two, that it was strong and clear, and that it established a fundamental right of privacy extending to the abortion issue. An important court doctrine is *stare decisis*: it is a tradition in which present courts respect the decisions of the past. One of the most important functions of lawyers is to predict how a court will decide a specific issue; their tool for doing that is the body of past decisions. *Roe* would now become part of our respected body of law and established case law; it was reasonable to expect future courts to respect its words and provisions.

I KNEW THAT if you won a Supreme Court case you could request a signed group photograph of the justices. I requested and received mine, an image of nine men, some sitting, some standing, before a heavy velvet curtain. It is signed by each of the justices. The photograph hangs in my office near my two goose-quill pens, the symbols of having argued *Roe* twice. Occasionally someone looking at my wall of memorabilia will ask, "Do you get a photo if you lose?" and I can say, "I do not know. I have never lost a case in the Supreme Court."

But I quickly add, "Thank goodness I was able to win the only one I argued."

Today a photo of the Supreme Court would be different because it would include women, three of them; Justice Ruth Bader Ginsburg, Justice Sonia Sotomayor and Justice Elena Kagan, who joined the Court in 1993, 2009 and 2010 respectively. In 1973, there were *no* women on the Court.

Roe v. Wade became the law of the land and a national icon; the Court took no further action on pending cases. The rulings affected the laws in forty-four states, thirty-one of them with statutes similar to Georgia's. There were follow-up actions in many state legislatures and courts after the *Roe* and *Doe* decisions. In many of those states the laws were declared unconstitutional by state or federal courts or by opinion of the state attorney general. Some state legislatures immediately passed new statutes; other legislatures—as in Texas—did not pass any new regulations until years later. The pattern across the nation regarding abortion regulation was extremely varied.

On April 20, 1992, *The Washington Post* ran a story about the decision, derived in part from a speech Justice Blackmun gave in Paris in 1979. Blackmun admitted to being a reluctant author of the opinion; he had "accepted the assignment without enthusiasm." Evidently after the Court discussed the cases, the vote was "indecisive." Burger gave mixed signals about his position but assigned the case to Blackmun, despite Court tradition that the senior justice on the majority side would make that decision if the chief justice was not among those voters. Blackmun believed he had received the assignment because of his interest in medicine (he had toyed with the idea of becoming a doctor) and his decade of experience as resident counsel at the Mayo Clinic.

Blackmun drafted a memorandum on the abortion cases "leaning toward the results that eventually were forthcoming." He also called on the Court to put off the matter until Powell and Rehnquist were confirmed to fill the two Court vacancies. Douglas objected; Blackmun thought he was worried that the additions and the passage of time might change the result, and perhaps even Blackmun's thinking. But Blackmun prevailed, and set the case for reargument. He also began to prepare the opinion laboriously and agonizingly.

"That summer," the *Post* article quoted him as saying, "I spent two full weeks in the medical library of the Mayo Clinic in Rochester Minnesota. I traced down . . . the attitudes toward abortion of the American Medical Association, American Public

Health Association, and American Bar Association. I wished, furthermore, to study the history of our state abortion statutes and to ascertain the origin and acceptance of the Hippocratic Oath [which forbids doctors to perform abortion]." The opinion he wrote reflected his work and a sensitivity for deeply held opposing beliefs held by members of the American public. Blackmun said that he generally tried never to display agony in making any legal decision. But in *Roe* he purposefully did not follow that standard.

THERE WAS A short lull while advocates of choice celebrated the legal victory, and then attention quickly shifted to making the words a reality. The new priority was to ensure that women had access to contraception, abortion, and basic health services. Unless that happened, our victory would be hollow. In fact, even while I was finishing the court battle, the anticipation that we might win caused others to begin working on plans for providing safe, legal, affordable abortion services to women.

The first abortions were performed in doctors' offices. In Austin, the first legal abortion was done the day of the decision. Dr. Fred Hansen, who had become personally aware of the need for safe abortions when two of his patients died from illegal, back-alley abortions, had earlier ordered the necessary equipment, and it arrived fortuitously that morning. On the afternoon of January 22, he had a call from a member of the UT nursing faculty who was leaving for New York to have an abortion. He told her she could cancel her reservations and come to his office instead.

Quickly there were a handful of offices in Texas where, for $140 or so, a woman could obtain a legal abortion—she could even bring a friend to keep her company. Bobby Nelson, one of the law students who had helped with our research, went with a friend who was having an abortion and later wrote in *The Rag*:

"What a difference the [Court] . . . made with this rare human legal decision." She continued:

> Two important thoughts are with me: first, we must understand that the Supreme Court was responding not just to technical and impressive briefs or strong oral arguments on the rights of women. They were responding to the rallying of women across the nation—a rejection of women as reproductive machines and an acceptance for women as individuals capable of choice.
>
> Secondly, we must understand that the battle has only just begun. An abortion still costs $140, more than many pregnant women can afford; few doctors have the modern equipment; most will still require the consent of a husband.
>
> But we can begin with the token [knowledge] that it makes an immediate difference in the lives of many women. Now we can redirect our energies to other issues.

Expanding access to abortion did not go smoothly. Although a few doctors had the necessary equipment, most did not. For those who didn't, the only place to perform an abortion was in a hospital. Yet hospitals were very hesitant to open their operating rooms until they were sure they would not be in legal jeopardy. A week after the decision, the executive director of an Austin hospital, St. David's, was quoted in *The Daily Texan*, the UT at Austin student newspaper, as saying, "We must be certain we are protected from a legal standpoint . . . Texas does not have a law pertaining to abortion. This clears the doctors but leaves some question about the hospitals." Dr. Joseph Quander, head of the obstetrics-gynecology service at Brackenridge, a public hospital in Austin, said he was awaiting opinions from both Attorney General John Hill and City Attorney Don Butler. Quander acknowledged one major ongoing problem: "It's still going to be a problem for poor people to obtain abortions. It's going to be a situation where money in the hand will make it easy."

Frustrated over the slow pace of services in Texas, some people decided to speed things up. Ruth Bowers had been optimistic before the decision and urged that preparations be started for offering services. Dr. Alan Guttmacher, in San Antonio to give a speech and to see his protégé Dr. Paul Weinberg, commented that abortion clinics were needed; doctors' offices would never be able to meet the demands.

Ruth gave $10,000 of Sears, Roebuck stock, and San Antonio Planned Parenthood, encouraged by its executive director, Myron Chrisman, decided to start a clinic. A place had been rented, but it was not completely set up when the decision was announced. Ruth bought furniture and, with two members of her household staff, got the location ready to open. The clinic eventually became independent of Planned Parenthood and was named Reproductive Health Services.

Most of the names of the doctors who bravely stepped forward are known only to their patients. In San Antonio they included Brandon Chenault and Foster Moore. Chenault experienced what many doctors went through: the management of the office building where he had his private practice said he would be evicted if he persisted in doing procedures in his office. Chenault responded by becoming a cooperating physician for the Planned Parenthood clinic, and continued his routine practice at his private office. Dr. Weinberg, a professor at the San Antonio medical school, contributed by instituting a program that trained medical students to perform abortions safely.

Access to abortion was not just a local problem. On March 26, 1973, the executive director of NARAL issued a statement:

A "wait and see" attitude prevailed as the health establishment looked to . . . state attorney general's office[s] and/ or state courts for "clarification," and to . . .state health department[s] for guidelines. Catholic hospitals announced a refusal to perform abortions; non-Catholic hospitals, reluctant to adopt new abortion policies but afraid of damage suits if they refused to do abortions, hedged and hid behind procedural delays. With the exception of Florida, the South continues to show strong resistance and little, if any, movement. Elsewhere some hospitals are beginning to perform first-trimester, in-hospital abortions, with few reportedly ambulatory procedures. A decline in demand by out-of-state women in New York, Wisconsin, and Kansas clinics indicates that early abortions are becoming more available nationwide . . . Most hospital abortions are occurring in larger cities. Very little is happening in smaller towns.

The clinic picture is disappointing. Clinics have opened in Atlanta, St. Louis, San Francisco, Miami, Detroit, Columbus, Chicago, Boston, Milwaukee, Philadelphia, Pittsburgh and Erie, (in Erie at $260). Others are planned for Des Moines, Kansas, Houston, San Antonio and Fort Worth. But elsewhere bureaucratic red tape and state laws (such as [those] requiring a certificate of need for setting up or adding to health facilities) are impeding the establishment of clinics. So is the difficulty of locating physicians willing to staff them.

Roe and *Doe* had obviously changed the legal battles being fought, but those battles—and our victory—would be insignificant if the decisions did not result in pregnant women having access to safe medical care. We had won Round 1, the Supreme Court decision. It was quickly apparent that Round 2 would be a battle to make abortion services available to women.

8 . Storm Clouds Gathering

Before the *Roe* victory, momentum and dedication rode with those who thought abortion should be legal. It was as if we were on the high end of a seesaw. We believed that basic changes in the roles and status of women were possible, and we saw them happen first through *Roe* and then, as we expanded our efforts, through the passage of positive legal legislation affecting women. We said, "Let's get Texas to ratify the national Equal Rights Amendment" and accomplished that during a special session of the Texas legislature during the summer of 1972. "Let's put an ERA into our Texas Constitution," and that was accomplished by public vote in November 1972. "Let's pass a state law so pregnant teachers can return to work instead of being fired," and we did that: later federal law was changed to require that leave during pregnancy be afforded to women working for larger employers. "Let's be sure women have equal credit rights," and we passed the Texas Equal Credit Act. After the Supreme Court's decision, however, the record of successes around reproductive rights gradually dissipated; those who had been active dispersed and chose a variety of other matters to work on.

The day *Roe* was decided, in fact, the positioning of the forces for and against choice began to reverse. Anti-abortionists experienced a new surge of energy—energy which has not flagged to this day. The seesaw began to move, with the side opposed to abortion rising in commitment, funding, legislative victories, and ability to limit access to abortion procedures. I felt—and still feel—a chill when I think of the years since the Court decision.

The movie *Arachnophobia* reminds me of this period. It begins with a blissful scene of the members of a perfect two-child family joyfully going about their daily activities after moving to a tranquil rural setting, oblivious to the fact that in their nearby barn a spider of great destructive potential is beginning to multiply. As the movie spins its tale, the dangerous spiders, growing in numbers and venom, jeopardize the lives of the family members and others. In the end, however, the nearby town is saved. While we were blissfully celebrating our victory in *Roe*, the anti-abortion forces began to proliferate and increase in strength, which continued until they were able to undermine the Supreme Court decision in a variety of ways.

The goal of the anti-abortion forces was, of course, to make abortion illegal once again. They labeled January 22, the date of the Court's decision, "Black Monday," and they march in Washington on each anniversary. They declared war on the availability of abortion, and brainstormed and developed ways to deaden the impact of *Roe* and/or defeat the decision itself. They began a grass-roots campaign to involve their previously complacent supporters. Their political strategies ran the gamut of actions, whatever they could devise at the local, state, and national level, and would eventually help in electing three presidents who shared their cause. Even in the 2012 presidential election the sides were sharply drawn with a pro-choice candidate, Barack Obama, on one side and an anti-choice candidate, Mitt Romney, on the other.

Immediately after the Court's decision, opponents worked to have Texas and Georgia ask for a rehearing. The newly elected Texas attorney general, John Hill, requested such a rehearing, and the attorneys general of Virginia and Connecticut filed *amicus* briefs supporting him. On February 26, 1973, however, the Court denied the petition. It considered the matter ended.

But for the opposition it had not ended. The *Roe* decision itself was attacked, as was the notion of a right of privacy. Some said it was not mentioned in the Constitution and so did not exist. Others argued that while such a right did exist in US law, it was not broad enough to cover abortion. Still others maintained that the Court's dictum and the trimester approach indicated that it was taking over the power of the state legislatures.

The Court was said to have erred in the relative weight it gave the woman and the fetus. Some opponents of the decision claimed that they, unlike the Court, knew when life began: at conception. Others picked up on an idea from the dissent, namely, that a woman had a choice—about whether or not to get pregnant. Once conceived, no baby would choose to die, others said. The most vigorous critics said abortion was murder.

Months after the Court announced its decision, the first extensive legal work to criticize it was published in the *Yale Law Journal*. "The Wages of Crying Wolf: A Comment on *Roe v. Wade*," written by John Hart Ely, became a legal rallying cry for some who opposed *Roe*; it is cited—and criticized—to this day.

Any Supreme Court decision can be criticized, but I thought the Court had written a clear, strong opinion setting out the right of privacy. The dictum was written in recognition of the fact that opponents of abortion might try to pass limiting legislation; I assume the justices wanted to guide them as to what the Court would accept, and thereby also reduce future abortion-related litigation before the Court.

I do not believe the opposition got its fuel from perceived

legal flaws in *Roe*. The legal and constitutional arguments were calm and cool compared with the shock tactics adopted by anti-abortionists. They began using words and images in new ways, emphasizing the graphic depictions of what they claimed was the developing fetus, even playing tapes of what was said to be the heartbeat of a fetus. Experts questioned the accuracy and validity of this "evidence," but reason could not erase the impact of those tactics. Anti-abortion speakers and writers also used language masterfully. As they fine-tuned their rhetoric, they replaced the scientific terms "zygote," "embryo," and "fetus" with "baby." They encouraged frequent use of words such as "killing" and "murder." Their ultimate aim was to undercut public support for the availability of abortion.

And yet, as Marian Faux says in *Crusaders: Voices from the Abortion Front*, "Despite their best efforts to engage the attention of the American public, anti-abortion activists . . . in the immediate post-*Roe* era were unable to establish themselves as a mainstream force. In fact, most people viewed them as fringe radicals, even though the leadership consisted of respectable and often well-funded groups with ties to the Catholic Church. Occasional outbursts of violence against abortion clinics, which escalated in the late 1970s, did little to enhance their image." Pro-choice groups such as the NARAL worried about the tactics of the opposition; according to one NARAL mailing, "Rational arguments have limited impact against the opposition's emotional frenzy. It is time to meet shock with shock." But advocates of choice never came up with symbols as powerful as the opposition's.

WITHIN TEN MONTHS of *Roe*, the attack on abortion availability was heating up. Some anti-abortionists were promoting a strategy of preventing doctors from performing abortions. Thus, even if abortion were legal, as a practical matter it would not be available. Some opponents looked for opportunities to file criminal charges against doctors in an attempt to frighten them away from performing abortions. Others resorted to acts of violence. Among the first doctors to feel the effects was Kenneth Edelin, a respected figure who was later elected chair of the board of the Planned Parenthood Federation of America. Edelin, a dedicated doctor working with the poor of Boston, performed an abortion on a teenager in October 1973 at a Boston hospital. He was charged and convicted of manslaughter, as it was a late-term abortion, but eventually his conviction was overturned. Criminal accusations were also leveled against a doctor at a medical center in Nassau County, New York. In 1982 a doctor who performed abortions was kidnapped along with his wife. Only after the FBI was called in to investigate were they released.

One of the traditional lessons of activism is that it is important to give followers specific actions to perform. The opponents of abortion followed this lesson energetically: adherents wrote letters, engaged in traditional protest activities such as picketing and applying economic pressure, and registered and organized voters to elect anti-choice candidates. As the opposition mobilized further, it sought new support and funding from prior allies, among them the Roman Catholic Church. On November 20, 1975, the US Catholic Conference of Bishops unanimously adopted the "Pastoral Plan for Pro-Life Activities." An eight-page, single-spaced typed explanatory document, it called for "a systematic organization and allocation of the Church's resources of people, institutions and finances" and for unity with non-Catholic foes of abortion, with the goal of ending abortion. Like many, I was shocked at the lengths to which the bishops proposed to go to impose their beliefs on non-Catholics. The impact of the Pastoral Plan seemed to me to disregard the principle of separation of church and state.

The plan was in essence a policy initiative directed toward

the legislative, judicial, and administrative branches of government to ensure effective legal protection for the "right to life." It entailed a public information effort to inform, clarify, and deepen understanding of the basic issues and to promote "pro-life attitudes," and a pastoral effort addressed to the specific needs of women with problems related to pregnancy and to those who had had or had taken part in abortions. The plan also detailed a grass-roots political organization as the most effective means to communicate the pastoral position:

> It is absolutely necessary to encourage the development in each congressional district of an identifiable, tightly knit and well-organized pro-life unit. This unit can be described as a public interest group or a citizens' lobby. No matter what it is called: a) its task is essentially political, that is, to organize people to help persuade the elected representatives; and b) its range of action is limited, that is, it is focused on passing a constitutional amendment . . . this type of activity can be generated and coordinated by a small, dedicated and politically alert group. It will need some financial support, but its greatest need is the commitment of other groups who realize the importance of its purposes.

Simultaneously, a new effort against abortion involving evangelical Protestants and the right wing of the Republican Party was being developed. A new group of activists, including Richard Viguerie, a computer-mail genius; Paul Weyrich, an issues and strategy expert; Howard Phillips, a grass-roots political whiz kid; and Terry Dolan, a fund-raiser with a special instinct for the jugular, began to organize. Many of the people they reached out to opposed abortion or saw the political value of doing so.

"It was Weyrich," writes Michele McKeegan in *Abortion Politics*, "who understood the political importance of the abortion issue. From the outset, no candidate got his backing without first declaring opposition to abortion. This was the first time conservatives had made abortion a litmus test." Weyrich was opposed to abortion even to save a woman's life, McKeegan reports. She says he insisted that "if you have to choose between new life and existing life, you should choose new life. The person who has had an opportunity to live at least has been given that gift by God and should make way for new life on earth."

While the Catholic and evangelical Protestant hierarchies were never able to enlist vast numbers of their members, there were still many of those faiths who did rally to the call for action. As the coalition of Catholics and evangelical Protestants was solidifying, Congress became the focus of new lines of attack. The abortion opponents had as their first goal a constitutional amendment to prohibit abortion; the second was to pass legislation to inhibit access to abortion.

Meanwhile, I continued to be involved in the abortion issue, but not to the extent I had been previously. I now had personal matters to deal with and an expanded legislative agenda to push. I did not want *Roe* to turn out to be a hollow victory, however; I wanted to maintain the integrity not only of the decision but also of its principles. Initially I joined others in thinking that the basic question had been settled: abortion was and would continue to be legal. In a few years, I thought, the decision would be accepted, abortion would become a part of routine medical practice, and the opposition would go away. Until that time, we just needed to protect what we had won.

AS THE FIRST ANNIVERSARY of the *Roe* decision neared, the Court continued to receive a steady flow of mail about it. According to *The Douglas Letters*, Justice Douglas wrote his colleagues Brennan and Blackmun on January 22, 1974, saying: "On this anniversary week of our decision on abortion, I am getting about 50 letters a day. I'll be happy to share them with you if you feel neglected."

To mark *Roe*'s first anniversary, NARAL (National Abortion Rights Action League), the only national group whose goal had been to nullify restrictive abortion laws, held a ecumenical service at St. Mark's Church on Capitol Hill. During 1973 I had been an active member of NARAL and a frequent speaker at its meetings; early the next year I became a member of the national board of directors, and in December 1974 was elected president. Clearly we would have to be constantly vigilant to prevent passage of the anti-abortion amendment being proposed to the Constitution, and we had a tough fight ahead to protect access to abortion. We moved the main office from New York to Washington to symbolize our focus on the nation's capital, and Karen Mulhauser, an expert strategist who worked with me for the rest of my tenure as NARAL president, became executive director. We kept the initials of the organization but adopted a new name, the National Abortion Rights Action League.

Presiding over the board meetings and directing the activities of the small but passionate staff, I had a role in key events. I wanted NARAL to be the leader in the political struggle. As the board expanded the lobbying program and public relations efforts, NARAL soon became the primary source of information on abortion for members of Congress and the public. I testified in congressional hearings on anti-abortion bills, cooperated in fundraisers for state NARAL affiliates and Planned Parenthood chapters, and worked against candidates and measures that would undermine *Roe*.

The NARAL board concentrated special efforts on organizing at local and state levels; the stronger the state affiliates were, we thought, the stronger the national organization would be. Anti-abortionists were increasing their grass-roots organizing efforts, and we had to exceed their efforts. We also needed local supporters to regularly contact their local, state, and national elected officials.

The newly animated opposition kept us constantly busy, and we often felt under siege. A variety of constitutional amendments to prohibit abortion were introduced every congressional session. Sometimes I thought each anti-abortion member of Congress was determined to throw a bill in the hopper just to be able to say to constituents, "Look—see what I'm trying to do?" Some said that life began at implantation and abortion should be allowed only to save the life of the woman; others said that life began at conception and abortion should never be allowed; still others said the word "person" as used in the Fifth and Fourteenth Amendments applied to the unborn; and others passed the authority for a decision back to the states. Bills often included language declaring that a fetus was a "human being" from its first moments and was thus entitled to due process and equal protection under the law.

One of a long series of hearings was held in 1975 before Indiana Senator Birch Bayh's Subcommittee on Constitutional Amendments, after Senator Jesse Helms of North Carolina submitted yet another Human Life Amendment. This provision sought to establish that life began at conception and should be protected from that time on. By then there had been so many congressional committee and subcommittee hearings involving various aspects of the abortion issue that witnesses recognized each other and knew generally the comments others would make. During the hearings, Dennis Horan, a longtime legal opponent, testified that as a result of the *Roe* decision a constitutional amendment would be required to give fetuses full constitutional protection; another law professor testified that the amendment was necessary to give standing in court not only to the unborn child but to potential fathers as well.

Senator Robert Packwood of Oregon and a number of other pro-choice voices, including Harriet Pilpel, who appeared on behalf of national Planned Parenthood, testified against Helms's amendment. I joined them in my capacity as co-counsel of *Roe*, president of NARAL, and as an elected official. I stated that abortion should be legal and should be constitutionally protected, and made a point pertaining to electability, since several members of Congress feared that if they voted against the proposals of the abortion opponents, they would not be reelected. I shared with the committee members the fact that I was identified as an advocate of choice, yet I had twice, in 1972 and 1974, been elected to the Texas House of Representatives. My purpose was to give the senators courage, to show them that they could vote against the amendment and still be reelected.

As the hearings continued in the Senate, we were also organizing a letter-writing campaign and lobbying members of the House of Representatives, asking them to vote pro-choice. Representative Don Edwards of California was leading the strategy in the House. Once again the Human Life Amendment went nowhere. As was generally true for these constitutional amendments, there was plenty of motion and commotion, but very little of it really mattered in the long run. The House would pass something but the Senate wouldn't, or vice versa.

The individual skirmishes over particular bills may have been for the most part inconsequential, but their overall impact was important. There was always a battle in progress. The opponents of abortion introduced bills to limit access to abortion funding. They proposed anti-abortion riders to bills totally unrelated to abortion. Sometimes they were really serious about passing a measure; in other instances they knew they didn't have the votes to win, but they wanted to force members to vote and to have their votes recorded against unrelated, often desirable legislation; abortion opponents could then pound them with those same negative votes during the next election. We would stop a bad bill in one congressional committee only to find a new one pending in another committee.

Likewise, we would keep something bad from happening in Congress and turn around to find something bad happening in a state legislature. The antis had adopted the tactic of proposing bills in state legislatures to restrict access to abortion in any way possible. Among the bills, some of which were passed, were those requiring that a minor have parental consent and a married woman her husband's consent. Lawsuits were filed and fought over those measures and over the legal responsibilities of hospitals to provide services.

There were occasional highlights to my NARAL leadership, for instance participating in an ABC television special on abortion moderated by David Frost. But generally our energy and contributions sagged, and we seemed only to plod forward. We were forever trying to increase NARAL membership, raise the funds necessary to keep the organization afloat, respond to press requests, and maintain and build our public support. But it was hard not to give the impression we were simply crying wolf. When we talked about the importance of organizing and pro-choice voting, people tended to think, "Now, really. I'm so busy. And after all, *Roe v. Wade* decided the matter." We missed the energy of our pre-*Roe* crusade. The opposition was fighting a battle of attrition, keeping the pressure on in so many different arenas hoping that eventually our resources would collapse, and in fact that was happening.

We continued to rack up wins as far as the proposed constitutional amendments were concerned, but we began to lose on matters of access. The opposition mustered the votes and passed measures that denied government funding for almost all Medicaid recipients, even though the government would then provide prenatal and delivery services at greater cost to those same women. Anti-abortionists lobbied and passed measures to cut off insurance funding for abortion for federal employees, and made it almost impossible for people in the military and their dependents to obtain abortions. Even when we could collect the votes to defeat one of their anti-funding measures, the opponents of abortion would roar right back with another.

We were, however, encouraged by a Supreme Court ruling in 1976. On July 1, in *Planned Parenthood of Central Missouri v. Danforth*—a case argued for Planned Parenthood by pro-choice attorney Frank Susman—the Supreme Court decided by a vote of six to three that a state could not empower a husband to veto his wife's decision to have an abortion, and struck a variety of other provisions. It also ruled five to four that parents of unwed minor girls could not be given the absolute right to a veto on their daughters' decisions to have an abortion, but this was not *absolute*. (In 1979, in *Bellotti v. Baird*—in which Roy Lucas represented the pro-choice position of Bill Baird—the Court implied that states could require parental consent so long as an alternative procedure, such as letting the minor seek a judge's approval instead, was included in the law.)

I was particularly worried about the future of minors' access to services. The Court's decision in *Danforth* would have a significant impact; approximately one-third of all abortions in the country each year were sought by teenagers. If they were denied access to legal, safe termination of pregnancy, many would be forced to bear unwanted children (and perhaps endanger their own health and that of their children), to give up their education or job security, and to risk parental censure. Moreover, the requirement for parental consent might discriminate unduly against poor and minority teenagers, who could not afford to travel to places where abortions for minors were more readily permitted.

IRONICALLY, as the nation celebrated its bicentennial year and the principles of freedom, the Republican presidential process was dominated by the emerging New Right coalition, which aimed to limit freedom of choice for women. The incumbent president in 1976 was a Republican, but the far right did not like Gerald Ford. In addition, under the specter of Watergate, the Republican Party was perceived by many voters to be a party of corruption and deceit.

In the first presidential race since *Roe*, Jimmy Carter and Gerald Ford both opposed a constitutional amendment to ban abortion. But support for such an amendment became the bottom-line demand of anti-abortionists, and the Republican Party joined in. Before 1976 the Republican platform made no mention of abortion; in that election year, the party convention voted to support "the efforts of those who seek enactment of a constitutional amendment to restore protection of the right to life for unborn children." The Democratic platform called such a constitutional amendment "undesirable."

In November, I celebrated both Carter's victory for the US Presidency and my election to a third term in the Texas House. I read the election as a tremendous win. I thought the entire women's agenda would move forward while Carter was in the White House. We had chosen a president who supported the principles of *Roe v. Wade* and who opposed a constitutional amendment against abortion. Also, Carter had talked about the importance of appointing greater numbers of women to important posts, and he favored a variety of other policies I supported.

It never occurred to me during my jubilation about election day that I would be one of the women summoned to Washington. John White, a Texas friend and prior state commissioner of agriculture with whom I had worked closely on several pieces of successful state legislation, was appointed by Carter to be the number-two person at the US Department of Agriculture. White called me in 1977 and said, "Sarah, I want you to consider moving to Washington and accepting a presidential appointment as general counsel of USDA." "Thanks, John," I told him, "but I've always said I'd stay in Texas." "Well, at least talk to some of your friends and see what they say," he urged. I did. Their advice: "Washington is a place with no country-and-western music, no barbecue, no Mexican food. It's not civilized."

But the more I considered his suggestion, the more I was inclined to accept. I felt I had accomplished a great deal as a Texas legislator, but I was ready for new challenges. Nothing really tied me to Texas now. I began to think of that wider world I had always wanted to explore and the bigger levers of power in Washington, levers that I thought could be used to advance the position of women.

I WAS NO LONGER married. I cannot help but believe my public successes were a major factor in the failure of my marriage. Ron supported me in almost everything I did, but I sensed that it was grating to him—he was, after all, as smart as I was and had lived more fully—not to be receiving equal public attention. And I was busy—maybe too busy.

However, our years together were good ones, and the positive points still outweigh the negative. Ron was one of the few men in those days willing to accept a bright, strong woman who did not make him the primary focus of her attention. While I was with him my interests expanded, and I grew as a person. When I needed help with *Roe*, he was there. When I ran for office, he was there.

We arranged our own divorce, which was amicably completed on September 5, 1974. Since we had no children and only limited financial resources, we didn't have the reasons to fight that make many divorces vicious. In fact, we practiced law in the same building for a year after the divorce, and we still have dinner together once a year or so. For that I am grateful. I am not sorry I married, and I continue to believe divorce was the best option for us.

My experience as a member of the Texas legislature, the central focus of my energy since 1973, gave me a feeling of aliveness: I was always involved with critical issues, and sponsored or cosponsored many successful bills. Eddie Bernice Johnson, soon to be a member of Congress from Dallas, and I passed a bill prohibiting school districts from firing pregnant teachers. Never again would education classes have to discuss whether one had a moral obligation to tell a principal about pregnancy. We passed an equal credit bill, and I got a credit card in my name without Ron's signature, although I was still married at the time. I helped get an amendment through to the Family Code that gave fathers and mothers equal consideration in custody disputes. I cosponsored a bill to revise the rape statutes with Kay Bailey Hutchison, a law school classmate who was then a member of the Texas House of Representatives and later became a US Senator representing Texas. Each session we successfully defended the Texas Equal Legal Rights Amendment in our state constitution and the state's ratification of the national Equal Rights Amendment with the help of volunteers like Barbara Vackar Cooke and Cissy Woomer Ellis. I felt that I had made a positive difference.

By now, a team was in place in Texas that could continue resisting the anti-abortion legislation that was introduced every session. In 1973 I had recruited Peggy Romberg to lead the citizen effort that complemented our legislative work. Peggy was trained, capable, and devoted. Her group, Texas Citizens for Parenthood by Choice, was an outgrowth of Ginny Whitehill's prior efforts; later it became a Texas chapter of NARAL called TARAL, which is now known as NARAL Pro-Choice Texas. In the past we had generally been able to stop bills from coming out of legislative committee by coordinating the presence of committee members so there was never a quorum at any single time, although each member was in the room at one time or another.

There was not a vote, and no one "got cut up" or was vulnerable to political attack. Typically we prevented bills that were voted out of committee from being considered by the House of Representatives by scheduling the vote on them behind so many other matters that they simply never came up. Bills might be "on the calendar" to be voted on, but late in the session there is often a logjam and even pending bills just stay there and die when the session runs out.

Peggy and I often commented about how much we preferred to try to defeat legislation than to pass it. Lieutenant Governor Bill Hobby was a friend to choice; we knew he wouldn't let anything through the Senate. Every session I was reminded of the importance of electing pro-choice candidates to key positions like his.

From 1975 into 1977 my legislative office ran at maximum efficiency. Ann Richards was my administrative assistant before she launched her own political career, first as Travis County commissioner, then as state treasurer, and then in 1991 as governor. The notepads she had printed up said it all: "Ann Richards—Problem Lady." I learned a great deal from her, including not to be so serious. I was trained to work hard, study hard, and try to do good; I was always a very serious person. Ann once told journalist Molly Ivins, "It is not that Sarah has no sense of humor. It is just that you have to say to her, 'Sarah, this is a joke,' and then she will laugh." Laughter helped me get through the tough personal times and some legislative losses in those years.

One of the benefits of being a Texas legislator then was Tuesday nights at Austin's celebrated country-and-western dance hall "The Broken Spoke." Only those associated with the Texas Legislature and their guests were admitted. James White, the owner, was always there to be sure women were treated well, and the overwhelming majority of men there—some of the fabulous boot-scootin' dancers—made Tuesday evenings "a nice slice of heaven." The country bands were wonderful and I got to dance every dance!

I hated to leave my best Texas friends, among them legislators and others at the Capitol with whom I had enjoyed the out-of-doors. There are few things finer than driving on old ranch roads in a beat-up pickup, admiring the deer and looking at the cows, singing vigorously (even if sometimes off-key) in accompaniment to country-and-western music on the radio. My friends and I would often gather on weekends at the ranch of House parliamentarian and former House member Bob Johnson and his sons. We spent our time working: stringing barbed wire fences, worming goats, working with the Santa Gertrudis cattle (the men humored me by naming the large red cows for women leaders; the biggest, at more than 1,800 pounds, was called Susan B., for Susan B. Anthony), and doing the other chores around the place. I also rode horseback across pastures and enjoyed the easy camaraderie of campfire talks. Through it all I learned about the legislative process, about how to work comfortably with the "good old boys" and how to win respect for my values and commitments. I would miss my friends if I went to Washington, but they urged me not to let such a marvelous opportunity slip by.

Serving in the Texas House gave me a tremendous education about the state and its people. But I had never considered it a "forever" job when I ran, and to anyone involved in American politics, Washington is mecca. I said yes to the USDA job, resigned my volunteer NARAL post, and made plans to resign my House seat after the 1977 session. But before the session ended, Peggy Romberg and I once again found ourselves leading the charge in response to a bill that aimed to restrict abortion and make performing an illegal abortion punishable by up to twenty years in prison. This time our opponents managed to get the bill out of committee and to the floor of the House. We were desperately trying to stop its passage.

My last major speech in the Texas legislature was an attempt to defeat that measure. I had offered a variety of amendments to weaken the bill, generally without success. When the final vote was called, after hours of debate and maneuvering, I rose to ask my associates in the House to vote no. My voice cracked as I talked about how terrible it would be if we were to return to the days before *Roe v. Wade.* I received resounding applause, but when the vote was taken I lost overwhelmingly. House members were relying on Hobby and the Senate to kill the bill; if it passed, they thought, it could do no real harm because of the Supreme Court's *Roe* decision. There was no incentive for them to stand up to the antis, who had become more vocal and more determined in the years since *Roe.* Again and again they said to me, "But Sarah, what we do doesn't make any difference. After all, the Supreme Court won't let these restrictions be enforced." We could win through parliamentary maneuvering, but this time we lost virtually every up-or-down vote. *The Lubbock Avalanche-Journal* headline the next day read, "Legislature Lurches Emotionally into Last Stage." The Senate killed the bill, but I had a premonition of danger and wondered whether the same scenario would be played out all over the country.

As I packed to move, I lingered over my collection of materials about abortion. I hoped I would never again need the box of photographs of women who had died because of an illegal abortion, and I gave them to someone who wanted them. I had so many files of information and clippings that I couldn't move them all; some I threw away, some I gave away, some I kept. Now I wish I had kept every one of those files and photographs.

The year I left Texas, 1977, was the year the Association for the Study of Abortion in New York disbanded. The organization had determined the focus now should be on services rather than education, although its members pledged to continue to protect the constitutional right of privacy that made the work of clinics legal and therefore possible. In hindsight, ASA's action was also precipitate.

MY WORK AT USDA was a challenge. I liked the people I worked with, and I cared about the tasks that crossed my desk. It was enjoyable to explore Washington and historical sites in surrounding states. I felt as if I were breathing history, and I had a sense of continuing the traditions established by the nation's founders and of contributing to decisions that would have far more impact than those I had participated in previously in the state legislative system.

And I got to work with the US Forest Service. Congress had passed legislation establishing a system of wild and scenic rivers and wilderness areas and I was supervising the pertinent legal work regarding Forest Service land. It gave me the enviable opportunity to go with Forest Service professionals and a few natural resources USDA attorneys on a horseback and camping trip into the Big Bear Wilderness in Montana to view sites where there were legal problems. I will never forget when, after we had been on the trail for six days, riding from shortly after sunup to shortly before dusk each day, the weather turned nasty. It was afternoon, bitingly cold; we had been rained on since dawn. All seven of us were silent, trying as best we could not to freeze and watching the footwork of our horses on the rain-slippery rocks. It may have seemed a miserable, even an insane moment, but I thought about how glad I was to be there. I prized the quiet, the grandeur of those woods, and the companionship of the forest rangers—who had provoked raucous laughter around evening campfires with their stories, and who, moreover, taught me a great deal about the wilderness and the need for its preservation.

I had campaigned for the Democratic slate in 1976, of course, but I did not meet Jimmy Carter until 1977, at the White House. I was one of some seventy-five women holding top administration positions invited to a meeting with him and Vice-President Walter Mondale in the Roosevelt Room. On the agenda were various topics about which we felt strongly and wanted our opinions heard. My designated role was to disagree with Carter's policy on abortion funding. While the president was personally opposed to abortion but in favor of *Roe*, he was against federal funding of abortion, even for women on Medicaid or otherwise dependent on federal medical services. Most of the women who served in his administration felt that the government should be neutral: women for whom the government provided prenatal and delivery care should also be allowed the option of abortion. A woman should be allowed to choose, not be coerced into continuing a pregnancy because the government would fund only her prenatal care and delivery.

The meeting was tense; the tone of many who attended, defiant. Carol Tucker Foreman, then an assistant secretary at USDA and who went on to become the director of the Food Policy Institute at the Consumer Federation of America, later described Carter's face as "so tight you could see the tension." When my name was called, I stood and addressed the president. In substance I too felt defiant, but I wanted to create a more receptive atmosphere, in the hope that Carter might listen more openly to what we had to say and might soften his position. I started by looking for common ground and chose to evoke our shared small-town and religious heritage.

"My name is Sarah Ragle Weddington, and I argued *Roe v. Wade* before the Supreme Court," I told him. "I feel it is fair that you know something about me before I tell you my position. I grew up in small West Texas towns, and my father is a Methodist minister. I was elected three times to the Texas House of Representatives." Carter seemed to relax somewhat and listen to my plea to support funding of abortion for those women who were otherwise eligible for federal medical services. At that time opponents were using the phrase "abortion on demand," as if we were advocating that all women have access to government funded abortion. That was not happening, and we were not advocating for it. Carter listened but gave no response. I left the White House certain that my words had not swayed him.

I was thoroughly surprised a few months later to be invited again to the White House, this time to explore the possibility of a position working with the president. First Carter and I talked about the staff needs he had and my background and talents, but I thought it was important that we also discuss the abortion issue in general and the funding issue in particular. We came to an understanding that I, in deference to his stance, would not be active on the funding issue while working in the White House and that he would not encourage forces seeking to overturn *Roe*. I felt comfortable enough with this arrangement: I thought I could still accomplish much for women from inside the White House, and others would continue to press on the funding issue from outside.

My White House job, as special assistant and then assistant to the president, was the most exciting I have ever had. There were nine assistants to the president, among them Jody Powell and Hamilton Jordan. I had two portfolios, one dealing with women and the other setting up White House briefings for a variety of public leaders. I was responsible for finding women qualified for various federal positions and presidential appointments, and women to include in White House activities. For a Labor Day picnic, for instance, I would suggest women labor leaders who might be invited; for a business briefing, women business leaders; for the installation of a new secretary of education, women college presidents; for a scientific event, women scientists. It was exciting to see the face of government change. Women were taking their proper roles as decision makers, and White House events became less and less the predictable all-white male gatherings.

As the point person for any issue of special interest to women, I adopted a theme, which, as I explained in a memorandum to President Carter and reiterated in my office publications, was *choice*: the choice to focus on one's family and be respected and honored, not penalized, for it; the choice of combining both family and paid work outside the home; and the choice of emphasizing the professional. I often furnished copies of my memorandums prepared for President Carter to Rosalynn Carter because of her interest in women's issues and her frequent assistance in accomplishing goals. Carter appointed so many women to top positions that women serving in his administration were able to start a group, Washington Women's Network, to give women outside government access to those inside. Carter appointees began programs at the Small Business Administration and in the Farmers' Home Administration to make loans to women entrepreneurs and women professionals starting offices in rural communities. The Carter administration expanded opportunities for women in the military. When Carter entered office, for example, the Air Force considered all flying as combat, and therefore off-limits to women. We had that changed so women could fly troop transport, reconnaissance, and refueling missions. I did not like watching the Persian Gulf war in 1991, but I was encouraged to see the new roles women were playing. I felt I had contributed to the ability of women to live out their own choices. In addition, the Carter administration started the first federal program to combat domestic violence and help its victims. I was thrilled with others when President Carter signed the bill extending the deadline for ratification of the Equal Rights Amendment. My office put together a wonderful ceremony in the Cabinet room for the signing so those who had worked hardest would witness the event. It was heartbreaking that the ERA was finally not ratified. President and Mrs. Carter did everything they were asked to do by pro-ERA groups and coalitions, but state legislators apparently were more worried about what some grass-roots voters thought than what the President and First Lady had to say. Once again the forces against us were energized, and those who favored the ERA had been so successful in changing customs and laws that had limited women that it was difficult to maintain the ERA's status as a top priority for the necessary number of citizens.

WHILE MANY INSIDE and outside the Carter administration continued to push an agenda of choices for women, others were planning the demise of at least one choice: that of abortion. Immediately after the 1976 election, some in the New Right coalition sought clues in that campaign and election to their own future victories. Jimmy Carter won, most political analysts agreed, as an "outsider." He had been helped by evangelical Christians because of his strong personal commitment to his southern Baptist heritage. Richard Viguerie, a strategist for the opposition, realized that many people had voted for Carter because of his honesty and trustworthiness. Viguerie needed an issue to overcome public perception of the Republican Party as dishonest and untrustworthy: he picked abortion. One reason may have been that, thanks to the Catholic hierarchy and other major contributors, the anti-abortion movement was relatively well financed. And Viguerie saw the emerging fundamentalist movement as one whose members would be willing to support candidates on the basis of that one issue alone.

According to Michele MicKeegan's *Abortion Politics*, by 1979 the National Right to Life Committee—a spinoff from the US Catholic Conference of Bishops—boasted more than 1,800 affiliates and 11 million members, a number of whom were not

Catholic. Abortion foes by then had an established network of newsletters and phone trees, and they had proven, in the 1978 campaigns, that they knew how to raise money and stump precincts. The energy level of their volunteers was legendary.

Some evangelical Christians who had supported Carter became disillusioned at his failure to defer to their opposition to abortion, homosexual rights, and the ERA. As the 1980 election loomed, they found a presidential candidate who would give them an audience: Ronald Reagan. Perhaps Reagan, a media master, recognized the power of television and radio evangelists at a time when one out of every seven radio stations in the United States was operated by a Christian broadcaster.

On June 30, 1980, we lost our first important vote in the Supreme Court. Its decision in the case of *Harris v. McRae* said that neither the federal government nor individual states were required to pay for even medically necessary abortions sought by women on welfare. Pro-choice forces had hoped to overturn those provisions, but we struck out. The vote was five to four in favor of Justice Stewart's opinion; Burger, White, Powell, and Rehnquist joined him.

The Court found the Hyde Amendment, a provision Congress had passed that limited federal dollars for abortion, to be "rationally related to the legitimate governmental objective of protecting potential life," and stated further that the federal restrictions did not violate the due-process and equal-protection clauses of the Constitution. "Government may not place obstacles in the path of a woman's exercise of her freedom of choice," the Court said, but "it need not remove those not of its own creation, and indigency falls within the latter category." And the fact that the Hyde Amendment's restrictions might "coincide with the tenets of the Roman Catholic Church" did not constitute a violation of the First Amendment. The Court also rejected three consolidated appeals challenging an Illinois statute restricting the use of state funds for abortion; states, it said, could decide not to fund abortions.

Justice Marshall wrote an eloquent dissent, but it could not negate the fact that we had lost. Justice Brennan, who with Blackmun and Stevens also dissented, called the Hyde Amendment "nothing less than an attempt by Congress to circumvent the dictates of the Constitution and achieve indirectly what *Roe v. Wade* said it could not do directly."

I was mystified by the rationale of the legislative policy the Court had allowed. It had ruled that the states and the federal government could decide how to spend money and that they could refuse to pay for abortions, even for women eligible for government-funded prenatal and delivery care. This policy made no sense to me, first because it effectively deprived those women of their choice, and second because it upped the costs for taxpayers; abortions cost less than prenatal, delivery, and postnatal services.

But the Supreme Court ruled that the Hyde Amendment was a legal restriction. Although the *Harris* case turned out to be a harbinger of losses to come, my natural optimism allowed me to hope that at least the Court would still refuse to allow states to pass restrictions that would make abortion more difficult to obtain and therefore more expensive.

Political action went on at a rapid pace. *The Christian Science Monitor* reported in June 1980 that the Reverend Jerry Falwell's political action organization, the Moral Majority, was working with some 72,000 churches across the country to urge evangelicals to register to vote. Falwell said Reagan was the only candidate he could "swallow." One political lobby that endorsed and financially supported Reagan was Christian Voice, in Pacific Grove, California, which represented thirty-seven denominations, most of them evangelical.

The platforms of both parties in 1980 took firmer stands on

abortion. The Democrats strengthened their advocacy of a woman's right to choose. The Republicans hardened their opposition to legalized abortion and pledged "the appointment of new justices to the Supreme Court who respect traditional family values and the sanctity of all innocent human life." The American Bar Association labeled this part of the Republican platform "contrary to everything the organized bar has done to build and strengthen a qualified, free, and independent judiciary."

When he was being pushed about his opposition to Medicaid funding for abortion, Carter had made the statement, "There are many things in life that are not fair." Senator Edward Kennedy, his opponent for the presidential nomination at the Democratic National Convention, supported *Roe* and funding. Carter's forces had hell to pay at the convention; many women delegates were concerned at the attitude behind the President's unwise remark and especially aware of Kennedy's pro-funding stance.

George H. W. Bush was also running for president in 1980. He had previously been considered a friend of family planning, and as a congressman he had cosponsored legislation that created a domestic family-planning program. In the primaries he ran as a Republican pro-choice candidate. About *Roe v. Wade*, he told one reporter during the primaries, "I happen to think it was right." But when Reagan picked him as his running mate at the Republican National Convention, Bush changed his stance, and he has been opposed to abortion ever since. There is nothing like the zeal of a convert.

Carter never met formally with representatives of anti-abortion groups while he was in the White House. Their growing strength was evident during the 1980 campaign, but his answer to requests for meetings, perhaps not the most politically expedient, continued to be no. He stuck by his support of *Roe v. Wade*.

Carter's loss in the election and the resulting change in Washington represent one of the hardest periods of my life. It was bad enough to lose the White House, but in addition the Democrats lost the Senate and many pro-choice Democratic and Republican senators would not be returning. People from the Reagan transition team came to visit those with offices in the White House—everyone except me—as we finished our last business, emptied files and desks, and otherwise prepared to move out. None of them indicated any interest in the women's issues I had been working on or in the information I had accumulated. I finally took what I thought was most significant and gave it to Elizabeth Dole, a prominent Republican woman in a key position on the Reagan transition team. She was cordial but said she doubted any use would be made of it.

It was extremely difficult for me to watch the Reagan and anti-abortion camps take over. The *Roe* victory was an integral part of my values and my self-concept. I had traveled across the country giving speeches about the accomplishments of the Carter administration, especially regarding women, about Carter's support for *Roe*, and about the frightening prospect of a different president who would have the power to make Supreme Court appointments and thereby change the vote on the abortion issue. The path was being paved for forces dedicated to overturning *Roe*.

Several years later I did an interview with three former First Ladies, Lady Bird Johnson, Betty Ford, and Rosalynn Carter, for a *Good Housekeeping* piece, "Women and the Constitution." While traveling back to Dallas after a weekend at the Johnson ranch, Mrs. Ford and I talked about how hard it was to leave the White House. "Yes, Sarah," she said, "and no matter who follows you, you know they didn't deserve to be there." Rosalynn Carter, who was listening to our conversation, perked up and said, "Betty, you are so right!" I guess all First Families and their staffs feel that way. I know I did.

ON JANUARY 22, 1981, I watched television coverage of the annual anti-abortion march from the White House to the Capitol for the first time. The marchers were demanding a constitutional amendment to prohibit abortion. Because of my role in *Roe*, DC friends had often teased me about encouraging "all those people who tie up traffic and make life miserable" to come to DC, but I had never paid any attention to them before. Pro-choice forces around the nation were sponsoring a variety of events on the same day, but none of them received the press coverage accorded the approximately 50,000 abortion foes who joined the march that day.

Representatives of the marchers had met with President Reagan, administration officials, and congressional leaders earlier in the day. The coalition of the conservative wing of the Republican Party and organized opponents of abortion—the Religious Right—had participated in the election of a president, and they were there to claim their reward: the president's help in banning abortion. That year a newly formed anti-abortion caucus in Congress claimed more than two hundred votes in the House and forty-one in the Senate.

As I watched the marchers, I was on edge—my emotions the complete opposite of those I had experienced on the same date in 1973. We now had a president whose avowed purpose was overturning *Roe v. Wade*. Reagan let it be known that a judge's position on abortion was a litmus test for admission to the federal bench, especially the Supreme Court; no one would be selected without being opposed to *Roe*. Carter had never had a Supreme Court vacancy to fill. I hoped Reagan would have the same fate.

During Reagan's first year in office, Justice Potter Stewart resigned. Stewart had voted for *Roe*, but had authored the *Harris* decision upholding the Hyde Amendment. Reagan appointed Sandra Day O'Connor, fulfilling a campaign promise to put a woman on the Court. O'Connor, a former Arizona legislator, had opposed an Arizona Senate anti-abortion bill. As a result, anti-abortion activists were more opposed to her than were advocates of choice. But Reagan appointed her, so we were cautious, even though the idea of a woman on the Supreme Court was a plus. In our minds she was "half," not obviously on the other side but also not certainly on our side. O'Connor was confirmed by the US Senate on September 21, 1981.

On May 24, 1982, the Supreme Court agreed to rule on the constitutionality of the array of obstacles that state and local governments were placing in the path of access to legal abortion. Questions included whether states could require a twenty-four-hour waiting period between a woman's signing an abortion consent form and having an abortion performed, what information the doctor would be legally required to tell her, and whether second-trimester abortions would have to be performed in hospitals, which were far more expensive than clinics.

The lead case was *Akron v. Akron Center for Reproductive Health*; there were two companion cases, one of them *Planned Parenthood of Kansas City v. Ashcroft*. That summer the Justice Department filed a twenty-two-page brief, reportedly cleared by presidential aides James Baker and Edwin Meese, urging the Court to expand the authority of state and local governments to restrict abortions by limiting the power of the courts to second-guess state and local legislative decisions. Although it did not directly ask the Court to overturn *Roe*, the Justice Department argued that elected officials should be permitted to regulate abortions, even in the first trimester in certain instances. This marked the first time the Justice Department had filed a brief for an abortion case in which no federal law was being challenged and in which the government was not a party.

Although the Justice Department denied that the brief was politically motivated, Associate Deputy Attorney General Bruce Fein telephoned New Right leader Paul Weyrich to announce the filing just before Weyrich and Jerry Falwell were scheduled to hold a Washington press briefing. Falwell declared that it was "good to have the federal government on the side of the unborn." Dan Donehey, a spokesman for the National Right to Life Committee, was equally pleased: "We have been saying for ten years that a court shouldn't be legislating. This is the product of a pro-life administration."

NARAL countered with a new "Silent No More" program of speak-outs, a letter writing campaign, and other activities featuring personal testimonials of women who knew the horrors of illegal abortion and of the rightness of safe, legal abortion.

On June 15, 1983, the pro-choice position emerged partially victorious. By a vote of six to three in *Akron*, the Court made it absolutely clear that a state could not impose any significant restriction on first-trimester abortions and that during the second trimester it could regulate only if there was a "reasonable medical basis" for doing so. The Court struck down the hospital requirement in *Ashcroft*, saying that, since *Roe*, clinics had been the primary abortion providers and therefore were more experienced and safer than hospitals. Although the dictum in *Roe* said states could require that second-trimester abortions be performed in hospitals, dictum is not precedent; the Court looked instead at the facts that supported or failed to support the requirement ten years after *Roe*. As a result of the decisions, laws in twenty-two states requiring hospitalization for all second-trimester abortions became invalid. The Court also struck the regulations requiring the twenty-four-hour waiting period.

One major disappointment was that the youngest judge on the Court, and the only woman, O'Connor, had written the dissent. She was joined by Rehnquist and White. Her opinion contended that the state's interests in maternal health and protecting potential human life were "present throughout pregnancy" and that states should be able to regulate first-trimester abortions to ensure that they were performed as safely as possible.

She commented that the trimester framework adopted in *Roe* and modified in the *Akron* decision was "on a collision course with itself. As the medical risks of various abortion procedures decrease, the point at which the state may regulate for reasons of maternal health is moved further forward to actual childbirth." At the same time, she said, "as medical science becomes better able to provide for the separate existence of the fetus, the point of viability is moved further back toward conception."

Pro-choice groups were disappointed by O'Connor's first official words in an abortion case, but we were not unduly surprised. In fact, we had generally expected to win the cases: the Court had decided in our favor in every abortion case since *Roe*, except those about funding. Anti-abortion groups were highly critical of the Court decisions and avowed to increase their efforts to obtain a constitutional amendment outlawing abortion. They must have been pleased by O'Connor's dissent, however.

Reagan continued to use the White House as a bully pulpit against abortion, frequently and vocally, throughout 1983. In a radio address on January 22, he said he would continue to back legislation to end what he called "abortion on demand." He sent a letter to anti-choice groups saying, "We have waited for ten years for Congress to rectify the tragedy of *Roe v. Wade*. The time for action is now. I assure you that in the 98th Congress I will support any appropriate legislation that will restrict abortion." Speaking to a convention of Christian broadcasters in late January, he vowed to renew his efforts to ban abortion. In March, before the National Association of Evangelicals, he urged federal legislation to restrict abortion.

Opponents of abortion within the Reagan administration used their bureaucratic positions to undermine abortion rights. Donald Devine, who had been named head of the Office of Personnel Management, set out to block reimbursement for abortion under the health insurance plan covering 10 million federal employees, retirees, and dependents. His initial efforts in 1981 were stopped by a US district judge, but two years later Congress went along, cutting reimbursement except for lifesaving abortions. Devine sought to exclude Planned Parenthood and other organizations that dispensed information about abortion from the Combined Federal Campaign, through which military and civilian employees could donate money to an approved list of charities. Only by numerous lawsuits was Planned Parenthood able to remain in the program.

At the Centers for Disease Control, Reagan appointee Dr. James Mason sought to suppress information about abortion. In *Roe* we had used CDC data showing that legal abortion was seven to ten times safer than childbirth. In 1977, when Congress cut off Medicaid funding for abortion, a CDC physician predicted that several deaths would occur as a consequence, and later documented that they had. The physician was transferred to another division. A 1981 CDC task force writing guidelines preventing the transmission of AIDS from mother to child was not allowed to mention abortion as an option.

I had talked about the importance of the presidency when campaigning for Carter in 1980, but now I must admit I had not truly appreciated the difference the president could make. Reagan made a difference by cutting off money to programs he opposed and putting people in charge of programs who were actively opposed to the programs' purposes as laid down by Congress. However, many who voted for Regan expected him to *do something* immediately that would end abortion availability. Their expectations were not met.

AS 1984 AND ANOTHER presidential election year arrived, both sides of the abortion debate knew that the critical issue for the next several years was who would vote on Supreme Court decisions. The antis were training their sights on the Court. Five of the justices who voted for *Roe*—Brenner, Burger, Powell, Marshall and Blackmun—were more than seventy-five years old. Justice Stevens, who joined the Court after *Roe* but had supported it, was a bit younger. Whoever was elected president, everyone knew, would likely be making several appointments.

Reagan kept up a steady drumbeat of anti-abortion statements during the election year. He declared the eleventh anniversary of the *Roe* decision "National Sanctity of Human Life Day" and held a highly publicized White House meeting with anti-abortion leaders. He pledged "stronger support in the future than they had seen in the past" and also promised to make his position against abortion part of the State of the Union address. He kept his promise on January 25. A few days later, Reagan's speech to a National Religious Broadcasters convention in Washington included six paragraphs against abortion. Afterward the Reverend Jerry Falwell told the convention it was "significant" that Reagan had chosen to address the 4,000 evangelical Christians attending the conventon shortly after announcing his reelection bid, and he reminded them that the key reason to work for Reagan was the expected vacancies on the Supreme Court. He expressed hope that in Reagan's next five years in office there would be at least two more appointments to the Supreme Court who could swing the balance to produce a five-four decision against legalized abortions. Reagan used the same refrain of banning abortion on March 6 in an address to the National Association of Evangelicals. Later the same month, participants at a Chicago seminar entitled "Reversing *Roe v. Wade* Through the Courts," hosted by the anti-choice group Americans United for Life, reported Reagan's comment that "one sure way eventually to overcome *Roe* is by improving the Supreme Court."

The pro-choice side, perhaps, needed to hear these declarations as much as the opposition did. As syndicated columnist Ellen Goodman wrote in February: "All in all, it's just as well that the man in the White House has taken up his old preaching role against abortion again. It's a good reminder for those pro-choice people who had gotten a bit complacent. The man who bears the title of president gets to dispense the title of justice. In 1984, the cut of the campaign cloth may turn into judicial robes."

NARAL, aware of the critical nature of the election, made Reagan's defeat its number-one priority at its DC meeting in June. "He is the most staunchly anti-choice president in the country's history," said Executive Director Nanette Falkenberg. "If he is reelected, President Reagan may well have the opportunity to appoint at least two new justices to the Supreme Court . . . enough to overturn *Roe v. Wade*, and thus make abortion illegal. Moreover, the emotionally charged tenor of his anti-choice statements has fueled an increase of despicable acts . . . [ranging] from harassment of women entering clinics to firebombing of these facilities."

Indeed, there had been recent acts of violence. When anti-abortionists became frustrated with the lack of progress in the Supreme Court and Congress, some of them went to the streets. They went beyond threatening tactics and harassment and picketing, and began to bomb and burn clinics. From 1977 to 1981, sixty-nine violent or aggressive incidents were reported. But the violence would become even worse within a few years as the antis lost legal battles.

On July 4, 1984, a bomb went off at the headquarters of the National Abortion Federation, the only national organization of professional abortion-service providers. By November, there would be a total of nineteen reported bombing and arson incidents against abortion clinics and related offices in that year. Abortion had not become illegal, but access was being hampered as clinics were attacked.

At the Democratic National Convention that summer, the platform that was adopted included a plank calling for "reproductive freedom" and the right of choice. Adding to the excitement among pro-choice Democrats was the selection of Walter Mondale and Geraldine Ferraro as the party's standard-bearers. I had enjoyed working with Mondale in the Carter White House and was particularly fond of his wife, Joan. And I took personal pride in his selection of Ferraro as his running mate. In 1980, I had urged that a diversity of people be selected for key positions in the Carter-Mondale campaign. Soon afterward Carter asked me if I had a suggestion for a woman to be vice-chair of the campaign. Various people I talked to consistently rated Ferraro high on competence and dedication, so I recommended her, and she was appointed. She had a perfect voting record on the issue of choice and had been a leader for pro-choice forces for years.

The Republican Party platform hearings and the outcome of its national convention in August were dismal for advocates of choice, but several courageous Republicans tried to reverse the flood of anti-abortion sentiment in their party. Mary Dent Crisp, a former co-chair of the Republican National Committee and the chair of the NARAL Political Action Committee, testified at a Republican platform hearing that "the majority of Republicans, like the majority of Americans, feel that abortion is an intimate, personal and very private decision that needs no bureaucratic meddling." President Reagan, she said, was all for "getting government off our backs and out of our lives, yet he would have the government become an unwanted partner in the most basic right of women." Crisp's words might as well have been shouted into the wind. The Republican Party platform included support for a constitutional amendment banning abortion and reaffirmed, through thinly veiled words, that federal judges should be appointed on the basis of their anti-choice positions:

The unborn child has a fundamental individual right to life which cannot be infringed. We therefore reaffirm our support for a human life amendment to the Constitution, and we endorse legislation to make clear that the 14th Amendment's protections apply to unborn children. We oppose the use of public revenues for abortion and will eliminate funding for organizations which advocate or support abortion . . . . We applaud President Reagan's fine record of judicial appointments, and we reaffirm our support for the appointment of judges at all levels of the judiciary who support traditional family values and the sanctity of innocent human life.

The abortion issue was on the ballot in Colorado and Washington that year, in the form of a measure to deny state funding of abortion unless it was necessary to save the life of the woman. Although federal funds were no longer available to provide abortion even for the poorest women, some states had chosen to continue those services. In states where the antis found they could not get the legislature to discontinue funding, they were now trying to get the voters to stop it.

Even with Ferraro on the Democratic ticket, Mondale's chances of winning seemed minimal. Still, the election results, an overwhelming Reagan-Bush victory, were a disappointment. In addition, there were not the victories for pro-choice forces that 1982 had seen. In that year the House of Representatives had gained twenty-five pro-choice votes, and not a single US senator targeted by the anti-abortionists had lost. But now, just two years later, we barely held our own in Congress. The bright spot of an otherwise dismal post-election morning was that Colorado and Washington voters had defeated anti-abortion referendums.

The violent acts of some anti-abortionists was an ongoing problem. On October 10, 1985, security was tightened at the Supreme Court after Justice Blackmun received a death threat. The day before, an anti-abortion protester had disrupted court proceedings; anyone who has ever attended a Supreme Court hearing knows one doesn't even whisper, *much less* interrupt the Court. On December 4, the FBI released figures on terrorism, but these did not include data on abortion clinic bombings, as they were supposedly not attributable to organized groups. On Christmas Day, three clinics were bombed in Pensacola, Florida, and on New Year's Day, 1986, a Washington, DC, clinic was bombed. The Christmas bomber, who was later arrested, said his actions had been "a Christmas present for Jesus."

Six months later, on June 11, 1986, we did win a big case, *Thornburgh v. American College of Obstetricians and Gynecologists*, which had originated in Pennsylvania. The Supreme Court said states could not prescribe what a doctor should tell a pregnant patient and denied other state restrictions. But the vote was five to four, with Burger, White, Rehnquist, and O'Connor in the opposition. Now we were down to a one-vote margin. Only as long as our five justices stayed could we still win.

Chief Justice Burger resigned in June, shortly after the *Thornburgh* decision was announced. Reagan appointed Rehnquist to take over as Chief Justice. The chief justice has influence beyond his vote. It is he who decides which justice will write certain opinions and he who presides at meetings of the Court. Rehnquist could use the power and prestige of that position to work against *Roe*. Reagan then appointed Antonin Scalia, a Catholic with nine children, to the bench. As Reagan had made the choice, none of us looked upon Scalia as a potential friend.

However, even with Scalia's appointment, we were still up five votes to four. But for how much longer? What would happen if any of our champions on the Supreme Court died or resigned? Everyone knew Reagan's prerequisite: Only candidates against *Roe* need apply. A year later, in 1987, we lost our fifth vote when Justice Powell retired. After Powell's resignation and before a new justice was seated, the Court deadlocked four to four on the abortion case *Hartigan v. Zbaraz*, with Rehnquist, White, O'Connor, and Scalia voting together. The effect of the deadlock was to invalidate an Illinois law restricting access to abortions for some teenagers, but it was the vote itself that held our attention: it was a *tie*. That meant whoever took Powell's place would move the Court into the pro-*Roe* or anti-*Roe* column.

Reagan's first choice was Robert Bork, who had a proven record of statements and writings that criticized the Court's decision in *Roe* and the constitutional right of privacy. Pro-choice forces and civil rights advocates at last had a record around which they could galvanize opposition. The public could also read the writing on the wall from the Court's tie vote. The rallying cry became: "This is the vote that counts," and Bork was turned down by the Senate.

After his second choice, Douglas Ginsburg, withdrew, Reagan appointed Anthony Kennedy. Kennedy quieted the Senate's fears by saying that he did believe in a "zone of liberty, a zone of protection" for individual privacy against intrusion by the government. We were skeptical of his position, but the Senate confirmed him in February 1988.

David Savage, in a 1992 book entitled *Turning Right*, claimed that when Kennedy was nominated for the Bork vacancy, the White House knew his views on abortion, although they denied it. Savage reported that Reagan aides had checked with Kennedy's law clerks who said they believed he would vote to reverse *Roe v. Wade*.

IN THE 1988 presidential campaign, Michael Dukakis, the Democratic candidate, was pro-choice, and George H.W.Bush was not. But issues other than abortion overwhelmed the Democratic ticket, and Bush won. Once again the fallout had potential impact on *Roe*. Justices Brennan, Marshall, Blackmun, and Stevens were among the oldest members of the Court. The oldest of those, Brennan and Marshall, seemed to take a firm position that they had been appointed for a life tenure and would serve it out. During that period I was saying, only somewhat facetiously, that I was for mandatory life-support systems for the oldest members of the Supreme Court. I could not imagine how we could hold the line if either of them left, given the likelihood that an anti-*Roe* person would be appointed to replace each of them.

9 . *Rising Opposition to* Roe

When *Roe* was decided, pro-choice forces were at the top of the seesaw. By 1989 that had reversed and the opposition to abortion was at the top, as a result of being better funded, more vigilant and passionate, and of having elected presidents who agreed with them in 1980, 1984, and 1988. They were often seen in demonstrations and picketing abortion providers. Pro-choice forces were at a low point, having been unable to blunt or stop the juggernaut or to energize the majority of citizens who supported reproductive freedom.

In 1989 an abortion case, *Webster v. Reproductive Health Services,* finally made its way from Missouri, an anti-abortion hot spot, to the Supreme Court. Three years earlier the Missouri Catholic Conference and Missouri Right-to-Life had combined efforts to pass a law they hoped would give the Reagan Court an opportunity to change direction from decisions of the past. The law had two primary parts, general language about "unborn children" in the preamble and specific restrictions on abortion in the main body.

The preamble included two statements: "The life of each human being begins at conception" and "Unborn children have protectable interests in life, health, and well-being." Further, the act required that all Missouri laws be interpreted to provide "unborn children" with the same rights enjoyed by other persons, "subject to the Federal Constitution and [Supreme Court] precedents." The preamble attacked the portion of the *Roe* decision that said the State had never treated the fetus as a person and therefore had failed to prove a compelling reason to regulate abortion. Missouri was saying, "Well, to the extent we can, we will treat the fetus as a person."

However, the body of the statute did not outlaw abortion. It did not set out reasons for which abortion could or could not be performed. Rather, it restricted access to abortion (unless the procedure was necessary to save a woman's life) in three separate ways. First, the law said no abortion could be performed in a public hospital or facility, even if the woman paid all of the expenses. Second, it said no publicly employed doctor or other personnel could perform or assist in performing an abortion. And third, it said that if a woman was twenty or more weeks pregnant, certain tests for viability (the ability of a fetus to survive outside the womb) had to be performed, as consistent with a physician's professional judgment. Other Missouri law made abortion illegal after viability except in very limited circumstances.

The Supreme Court in *Harris v. McRae* had said government could decide how its money would be spent and could encourage childbirth by prohibiting dollars for abortion. Missouri thus sought to use its control of public health dollars in expanded ways to prevent access to abortion.

The last provision of the proposed Missouri law was aimed at the *Roe* dictum that abortion could be prohibited after viability except to protect the woman's life. In her 1983 *Akron* decision, Justice O'Connor had said that *Roe v. Wade* was on a collision course with medical science. Because we still thought of her as a swing vote and wanted to pull her to our side, we were especially attentive to what she said. We speculated that she might be thinking medical science would eventually push viability back to a point early in pregnancy. Our experts said that could not happen. The key to viability was lung development, and science hadn't found a way to speed that up at the time. Great pro-choice effort had gone into submitting *amicus* briefs in *Webster* to demonstrate that *Roe* was *not* on a collision course with medical science.

One brief, filed on behalf of 167 scientists and physicians, argued that the Justice Department, a number of organizations, and, most important, O'Connor were wrong about whether the point at which a fetus could live outside the womb had changed since *Roe*. The signatories argued that such an assertion was "flatly contrary to scientific evidence." In *Roe* the Court had spoken of viability as being at twenty-four to twenty-eight weeks, generally the latter. By the time of *Webster*, it was still between those two limits, but often closer to twenty-four. Some experts were saying that as medical science progressed, viability might be pushed back a week or two; others said doctors might miss by several weeks, based on whether they had judged accurately how far along a pregnancy was.

Actually, few abortions are performed after the first trimester, which has been true from 1973 on. Those in the second trimester generally involve women who fail to recognize pregnancy (such as those in menopause), women so young they don't know what to do and so try to avoid acknowledging the pregnancy, and women who learn of genetic abnormalities through testing. Very few abortions are done in the third trimester, but can be necessary for any number of reasons, including, for example, when the fetus has died in utero or if the woman's life is at stake.

Another especially important brief was filed on behalf of a hundred civil rights, women's, labor, and religious organizations—among them the National Council of Negro Women, the American Indian Health Care Association, the Asian American Legal Defense Fund, and the Mexican American Legal Defense and Education Fund—whose members feared that tampering with *Roe* would have a powerful, adverse impact on the liberty, civil rights, and health of poor women and women of color. The brief contained statistics proving that women of color "were over-represented among the women who died, were left sterile or suffered other serious medical complications" before *Roe* and concluded that such was likely to happen again if *Roe* were diluted. Similarly, it was pointed out that women of means could negotiate such hurdles as waiting periods, which could put legal abortions out of reach for poor women, and especially poor teens, because of the costs of travel and accommodations, child care, and time lost from employment.

The brief appealed further to the justices to think about the social and psychological price of compelling women to choose between illegal abortion and involuntary pregnancy, by quoting the words of Justice Marshall in an earlier case:

> An unwanted child may be disruptive and destructive to the life of any woman, but the impact is felt most by those too poor to ameliorate those effects. If funds for an abortion are unavailable, a poor woman may feel that she is forced to obtain an illegal abortion that poses serious threat to her health and even her life. . . . If she refuses to take this risk, and undergoes the pain and danger of state-financed pregnancy and childbirth, she may well give up all chances of escaping the cycle of poverty. Absent day-care facilities, she will be forced into full-time child care for years to come; she will be unable to work so that her family can break out of the welfare system or the lowest income brackets. If she already has children, another infant to feed and clothe may well stretch the budget past the breaking point. All chance to control the direction of her own life will have been lost.

Both sides of the abortion issue exerted Herculean efforts to win in the Supreme Court and with public opinion. Each sensed the critical point the Court was reaching as its composition shifted. About seventy-eight *amicus* briefs were filed in *Webster,* more than in any prior case—a record war of words. The Bush administration filed one urging the Court to take advantage of the opportunity to reverse or severely limit *Roe. USA Today* published assorted statistics on the briefs: Longest brief: 225 pages, with the names of 2,887 women who had had abortions and supported the right for others. Congressional tallies: 9 senators and 45 House members against abortion rights; 25 senators and 115 House members in favor of choice. Surprises: The National Coalition of American Nuns argued for abortion rights, noting that some non-Catholic religions did not condemn abortion.

AS THE DATE for the Supreme Court hearing of *Webster* neared, national pro-choice organizations including NARAL, Planned Parenthood, and NOW hosted a march and rally in Washington on April 9, 1989, to demonstrate the broad-based support for *Roe.* People traveled from all across the country to participate. The US Park Police estimated that 300,000 people attended; unofficial reports ranged up to 600,000. This was one of the most uplifting experiences of those otherwise dreary years.

Molly Yard, president of NOW, had asked me to be a speaker at the rally, and as I waited for my turn to speak, I was awed by the crowd, by the surrounding sea of faces. The speaker ahead of me was Byllye Avery, from the Atlanta Women's Health Project. She was such a terrific, energizing speaker that I wished I were following someone else. But my spirits soared as a cheer went up from the crowd when I was introduced and approached the mike.

"History will not record our names," I said, "but the nation will not forget that we were here. Our presence in Washington—along with [that of] those who stand beside us in spirit—is a symbol of our dedication to our unfinished work, and our determination that neither those who arrogantly attempt to rule our personal lives, nor the powers of government that seek to burden our choices, shall prevail. It is for us here to rededicate ourselves to the great task remaining before us—to proclaim the importance of personal choice and to give thanks for the freedom from terror that millions of women have enjoyed these past years."

I remember various images from that day: Tim Robbins taking care of Susan Sarandon's daughter while Sarandon spoke; one couple in their seventies proudly displaying pro-choice paraphernalia; a man in a big cowboy hat carrying a sign that read: "Cowboys for Choice"; a number of older women identifying themselves as a "Menopausal Woman Nostalgic for Choice," and younger ones calling themselves "N.Y. Yankee Fans for Choice." I was buoyed by the pageantry of young people holding up placards proclaiming: "Pro-Choice, Pro-Life, Anti-Bombs," "Stand UP for Choice," and "We Will Not Go Back." Children wore pins that said "I'm a Choice," and families carried placards announcing: "This Family Is Pro-Choice." Parents who remembered the days before *Roe* were there with young adult daughters and sons who didn't share the memories but did share a commitment to choice.

I was encouraged by the diversity of those who gathered; Texas journalist Katie Sherrod described the marchers as "a sea of bodies. Women and men and children, mothers and daughters, fathers and daughters, mothers and sons, fathers and sons, grandmothers, grandfathers, uncles, aunts, white and black and Hispanic and Asian—they marched, putting their bodies where their beliefs are."

When people asked me whether I thought a march could change the Supreme Court, I had to say no. The march was more for the purpose of energizing those who came and those who saw it. It was a political statement to the nation. And while we were marching in DC, countless others marched in cities across the country to make the front pages of their local papers. I felt again the positive emotions of the days before *Roe* when we were united, dedicated, and making progress.

I WAS BACK in Washington on April 26, this time as an observer for the *Webster* hearing. When I arrived at the Supreme Court building, the sidewalk was a spectacle of proponents from each side swirling in front of cameras and reporters, and police officers trying to maintain order and keep those with clashing opinions physically separated. Several reporters requested interviews, and from them I picked up New York and Washington gossip about what was likely to happen. Waiting for the Court to convene also gave me the chance to talk to other lawyers and pro-choice activists I had worked with for years; they felt the same anxiety and urgency I did.

I was apprehensive as the courtroom quieted and the justices took their places. William Webster, the attorney general of Missouri, was the first to present his case. Rumor had it that he was preparing to run for governor and thought he would gain politically by arguing the case himself. He did not do a good job; his comments were sloppy and vague. When, for example, Justice Stevens questioned him at length about the penalty for doctors who violated the statute prohibiting abortions in public hospitals, Webster gave nothing but evasive answers. After Webster's twenty minutes were over, I thought, Well, that presentation certainly won't swing this case for Missouri. But I also knew that a justice's conclusions are based on more than just oral argument.

Webster gave his last ten minutes to Charles Fried, special assistant to the US attorney general, who spoke on behalf of the Bush administration. His first words were, "We are not asking the Court to unravel the fabric of unenumerated and privacy rights which this Court has woven [in cases like *Griswold*]. Rather, we are asking the Court to pull this one thread."

Justice Kennedy jumped in. "Your position, Mr. Fried, then, is that *Griswold v. Connecticut* is correct and should be retained?" Fried responded, "Exactly, Your Honor." I was glad to hear the government was not trying to get the Court to reverse *Griswold*, and allow states to once again create laws against the use of contraception, but I knew it was probably because the Bush administration was aware of the outrage that would result if it were to try.

I perked up when Justice O'Connor asked about a hypothetical situation: an overpopulation problem in the United States. Would taking away the right of privacy mean the government could require women to have abortions after having a certain number of children? I was pleased that O'Connor was thinking about the flip side of *Roe*, which guaranteed that a woman could make the decision. What if the government wanted to *force* a woman to have an abortion? It could not do so as long as *Roe*'s right of privacy was in place. But would that still be true if the Court overturned *Roe*? Fried's position was that he did not think the government could require a woman to have an abortion; that would not be "preventing an operation, but violently laying hands on a woman and submitting her to an operation."

Justice Kennedy, curious about Fried's position that a woman would have a constitutional right to be protected against forced abortion if the right of privacy were taken away, challenged him to give a constitutional basis for his belief. Fried relied on the Fourth Amendment, which, he argued, included the woman's right to liberty "against a seizure."

He later concluded: "Now if the Court does not, in this case, in its prudence decide to reconsider *Roe*, I would ask at least that it say nothing here that would further entrench this decision as a secure premise for reasoning in future cases."

As I looked at the eight men and one woman, I could count four votes for *Roe* and three against. That left Kennedy and

O'Connor as the critical votes that Frank Susman, who rose to argue for the pro-choice side, had to win. Susman had helped with the preparation for the *Roe* case and since then had argued several abortion-related cases in the Supreme Court. He was certainly experienced.

Susman began his presentation by referring to Fried's comment about "pulling the thread" of *Roe*: "It has always been my personal experience that when I pull a thread, my sleeve falls off. . . . It is not a thread he is after. It is the full range of procreational rights and choices that constitute the fundamental right that has been recognized by this Court. . . . There no longer exists any bright line between the fundamental right that was established in *Griswold* and the fundamental right of abortion that was established in *Roe*." I thought Susman's response was a good one; and his analogy to pulling a thread was his comment most repeated in the press.

Justice Scalia, however, ignored Susman's response as he started the questioning. "I can see deriving a fundamental right from . . . a long tradition that this, the right to abort, has always been protected. I don't see that tradition. But I suppose you could derive a fundamental right just simply from the text of the Constitution plus the logic of the matter . . . [But] how can you derive it that way here without making a determination as to whether the fetus is a human life or not . . . ?"

Susman replied that "the basic question as to whether this is a human life or whether human life begins at conception is not something that is verifiable as a fact. It is a question verifiable only by reliance upon faith."

Scalia agreed, but then asked, "What conclusion does that lead you to? That, therefore, there must be a fundamental right on the part of the woman to destroy this thing that we don't know what it is . . . ?"

Susman: "The conclusion . . . is that when you have an issue that is so divisive and so emotional and so personal and so intimate, . . . it must be left as a fundamental right to the individual to make that choice."

I hoped Susman had scored some points with Scalia. Earlier the justice had questioned the appropriateness of discussing contraception in regard to the case. This time he said that Susman had made "the very good point that it is impossible to distinguish between abortion and contraception when you define abortion as the destruction of the first joinder of the ovum and the sperm."

As it turned out, I was the first prominent attorney down the Court's massive front steps when the hearing ended. Several reporters yelled for me to come to the plaza location where thirty or forty microphones were grouped, in a press custom called a "stakeout." I had never seen a bigger cluster of mikes—or reporters. I talked about what had happened inside, answered questions, and stepped aside for Susman, Faye Wattleton, head of the Planned Parenthood Federation of America —someone I greatly admire—and others to comment on the day's events.

I left Washington optimistic, hoping we could hold off any major loss, but I knew the vote would be close. The results would be made public by July 4, before the Court recessed for the summer. The waiting began.

In early June, ABC News was told confidentially that the Court would soon announce its *Webster* decision. I was asked to stand by on June 12 to comment on the decisions. I could not go to New York as requested, because of my summer teaching schedule at Texas Women's University in Denton, so arrangements were made for me to be at an ABC regional studio near Dallas. I had thought through the possible decisions and how I might respond to them, and I intended to emphasize the importance of the right of privacy established by *Roe*: The pregnant woman, not government or other strangers, was the appropriate person to make her abortion decision.

After everyone was in place and ready for broadcast, word was relayed that the decision would not be released that day. ABC asked me to return, and I eventually stood by on a regular basis. The decision was not announced during the week of the twelfth or the week of the nineteenth. Blackmun, the rumor was, had requested more time to complete a "bitter" dissent. That scared me. Had the changes in the makeup of the Supreme Court left us without the five votes we needed to hold the line?

As the week of June 26 began, the press got tired of writing stories that said, "Tomorrow the Supreme Court is expected to decide . . ." and then "Today the Supreme Court failed to decide . . ." On June 29 there was still no decision. I held a press conference that day at Texas Women's University, thanking the Supreme Court justices who had voted for *Roe*, justices who had been vilified, and had death wished on them by fundamentalist preachers. One, Blackmun, had had a shot fired by a never-identified source through his living room window as he sat reading nearby. I thanked those who had helped to win *Roe*, medical personnel, people who lobbied for legislative change, and those who had otherwise assisted the case.

I also shared my pride in the "freedom from that gut-gripping fear of unwanted pregnancy many knew before 1973," a freedom that women in the United States had experienced for sixteen and a half years as a result of *Roe*. Whatever the Court did, I would always have that to cherish. I recognized that the abortion issue would always be the focus of public debate and that there would always be opposition to abortion, but I stated my belief that the majority of citizens sitting in their living rooms and watching the tactics of Operation Rescue and similar groups were thinking: "I don't want those people to be in charge. I don't want them telling me what to do." Someday, perhaps, the legal and political battle could be ended with a unified stance that abortion should be an individual decision.

I commented on the "march of time and progress," including the efforts of Margaret Sanger's generation and of people in the 1960s to create services like Planned Parenthood and to make contraceptives available; of those in the 1970s who fought to make available to women not only abortion but also professional options; of those in the 1980s who sought to overturn laws that blocked access to services. "In the 1990s," I said, "those of us who have held the spotlight will peel off, and a new group will be front and center." Whatever happened, I knew that some tasks would continue to be the same: that of improving the kinds and availability of contraceptives; that of preventing unwanted pregnancies; that of being sure women had *all* choices, including the choice of carrying a pregnancy to term; and that of more adequately supporting children already among us.

I closed the press conference with the hope that we could still celebrate the existence of *Roe* after the *Webster* decision. I was making a public effort to be optimistic, but privately I felt gloomy. The Court in *Webster* might duck the issue of whether *Roe* was still the law of the land, but if Rehnquist and White were determined to overturn it, the question was how many more justices they could get to agree.

On the morning of July 3, I was once again in the regional ABC studio. By then I had dressed for the occasion on at least ten mornings. In place with my mike and earplug, I could see on the monitor the action at the Supreme Court building in Washington. The tension in the air there was palpable. Outside, hundreds of people jostled for places in front of the network cameras and shouted at each other as large numbers of police kept the peace. Inside, in the Court Public Information office, reporters crowded the desk to learn whether the copies of decisions stacked in the office included *Webster*. The line of representatives from interest groups stretched out the side door to the sidewalk. I knew that "fax trees" had been arranged so that people were ready, after grabbing a copy of the opinion, to hurry to a nearby fax machine and transmit it to a few others, who would in turn fax it to others.

Then on the monitor I saw Tim O'Brien, the ABC reporter covering the Supreme Court, rushing from the building. The first words I heard from him were: "Justice Rehnquist has written the opinion." My face froze; time seemed to stop.

I knew that *Roe v. Wade* was unlikely to be intact. Rehnquist was one of the two justices who had dissented in *Roe*, and he had voted against its principles at every opportunity. If he had written the opinion, it meant that he had finally swayed a majority on the Court to his point of view. The right of privacy which Americans had enjoyed and the choice of abortion which women had come to take for granted were succumbing to the onslaught that had been mounted against them.

While O'Brien riffled pages and scanned the words, millions of television viewers were, like me, watching and waiting for the news of the decision. O'Brien clarified that *Roe* had not been overturned, that O'Connor had once again talked about not "unduly burdening" a woman's decision about abortion, and that Blackmun had written a strong dissent. But the words "Justice Rehnquist has written the opinion" kept running through my mind.

A studio technician pointed at me and started a countdown just before I heard Barry Serafin, the ABC anchor that day, say, "Sarah Weddington is standing by now. What is your reaction to this?"

I was reluctant to say much about *Webster* because I knew so little of the specifics. I needed to read the words the justices had written. But my fears made me nostalgic about what *Roe* had meant. "I am thinking back to twenty years ago, when I started doing the research on *Roe v. Wade*," I said. "We should say thanks to the majority of the Court in 1973, because at least women have had a choice for all these years. Clearly what the Court has done is a major change in direction from *Roe v. Wade*." I felt justified in making that comment because Rehnquist had written the opinion, but added that I would need to look at the language of the opinion closely to see what it meant before I could accurately assess the damage.

Across the studio a fax machine spit out the words of the *Webster* decision: the NARAL fax tree was in action. There were five separate opinions, each long and tedious. The Court was divided and at odds. What a contrast this was to the 1973 *Roe* opinions which had been short and written in strong, simple language!

The Court had upheld each of the specific restrictions in the Missouri bill. That meant they could immediately go into effect in Missouri. Any other state that wanted to pass the same restrictions could lawfully enforce them. The Court refused to comment on the preamble language, which maintained that life begins at conception, saying it did not have the effect of law and did not prohibit abortion; rather it was advisory. The Court would wait to see how Missouri courts interpreted it. That was good news for the moment, but it did not mean the Court would never approve such language in the body of a bill in the future.

Justice Scalia's position was crystal clear. The opinion he wrote stated that the Court should overturn *Roe* immediately. He, Rehnquist, White, and Kennedy constituted four firm votes against *Roe*. O'Connor, who said it was not the day to consider the language in the preamble, may have saved *Roe* this time, but since she was the swing vote we had to depend on in the future, her hedging words made me uneasy. Her opinion mentioned not "unduly burdening a woman's decision" but did not define what she meant by "undue burden."

In his dissent, Blackmun had written: "For today at least the law of abortion stands undisturbed. For today the women of this

Nation still retain the liberty to control their destinies. But the signs are evident and very ominous, and a chill wind blows." I could feel that chill. The Court was prepared to give state legislatures increased power to regulate, and it had invited further challenges to *Roe*. This decision was a U-turn in women's rights. We were heading backward.

We lost again on June 26, 1990, when, in *Hodgson v. Minnesota*, the Supreme Court voted five to four to allow states to require that a pregnant minor inform both parents before obtaining an abortion, so long as the states gave the minor the opportunity to ask a judge to waive the notification requirement. O'Connor's was the key vote. Without the judicial bypass provision, she said, the state would have gone too far. Of slight consolation was the fact the Court did not accept the Bush administration's invitation to use the case to overturn *Roe*.

The same day, in *Ohio v. Akron Center for Reproductive Health*, the Court ruled that the states could require a physician to notify one parent of a minor of her intent to have an abortion unless the minor proved to a judge "by clear and convincing" evidence that she should not be required to do so.

Bad news piled on. On July 21, 1990, the retirement of Justice Brennan was announced. He was one of the four votes we counted on. I knew that he had been sick, and was being ordered to retire by his physician. Nevertheless, my heart sank when I heard the news. Friends of mine wanted to say to Brennan, even knowing he was eighty-four and ill, "How could you do this to us?" George H.W. Bush was likely to appoint someone to fill the vacancy who would vote against the right of privacy. And the ages of the remaining justices who supported *Roe* were not encouraging: Marshall, eighty-one; Blackmun, eighty; and Stevens, sixty-nine.

How had we arrived at this point, where we now had only three solid votes on the Court for *Roe*? What had weakened the political momentum we had established before 1973? What would my future role be?

ON JULY 23, 1990, President Bush appointed David Souter to the Court, and the confirmation process began. Souter was called the "stealth candidate," so well hidden were his views on privacy and abortion. Everyone was trying to guess his position from the few clues available. He had been on the board of trustees for a New Hampshire hospital that performed abortions. While a state judge he had written a letter saying it was not appropriate for a judge to decide, after a few minutes' hearing, whether a minor was mature enough to have an abortion. During his confirmation hearings he said there was an unenumerated constitutional right to privacy, but he did not elaborate on whether it applied only to contraception or also to abortion, and whether it applied to married or also to single people.

My longtime friend Bill Hamilton, then director of the Washington office of the Planned Parenthood Federation of America, said I was foolish even to hope Souter might be on our side. Bill pointed out that he had been recommended by John Sununu, Bush's chief of staff, who was vehemently against abortion and appointed by Bush. There was no way, according to Bill, either of those men would propose someone unless they were sure the nominee was against *Roe*.

The first abortion-related case heard by the Supreme Court after Souter took his seat was *Rust v. Sullivan*. This involved the federal government's Title X program, initiated in 1970 to provide money for basic health care and family-planning services for poor women; abortion services were excluded from the beginning. However, medical personnel were allowed to answer any questions a patient might ask, including any about abortion.

When the Reagan administration had tried to prevent employees of Title X clinics from *talking* about abortion, Congress refused to allow it, and Reagan tried a new tactic. In 1988 the Department of Health and Human Services adopted the regulations that if a pregnant woman came to a Title X clinic, staffers could tell her where to get prenatal care, and that if she asked about abortion, staffers could only say, "Abortion is not an approved method of family planning." It was the first time the government had taken a position that the use of federal funds carried with it the right to control speech. The medical community went up in arms, and the regulations were immediately challenged. Many Title X providers vowed to turn down federal dollars if necessary rather than desert proper medical-ethical standards toward clients.

During the *Rust* hearing, Souter asked the government's lawyer a question that I interpreted as a favorable sign. If a woman came to a Title X clinic and was pregnant, and had a medical condition that indicated pregnancy might injure her health, Souter wondered, could a doctor tell her that or not? The lawyer's answer was no. Souter had a look on his face that to me said: "You can't be serious about that." I thought we would win him in *Rust*, but probably lose him on a case directly about abortion. I was wrong—we lost him in *Rust*. He became the fifth and the essential vote to uphold the so-called gag rule and to allow the government, via its funding, to control professional speech.

Now that we had lost Souter, even on that case, I didn't see how we could win his vote on a direct abortion question. It was hard to believe that a majority of the Supreme Court had voted that the government's money allowed it to control professional speech—not just services, but even speech. Congress passed a bill to prevent implementation of the HHS regulations, but Bush vetoed that bill. The House then failed by twelve votes to override the veto with the necessary two-thirds majority.

ANOTHER BLOW THAT made *Roe's* future more difficult, it seemed to me was completed on October 15, 1991, with the confirmation of Clarence Thomas as a Supreme Court Justice.

I was on my way from Austin to visit friends in Brussels when, on June 27, 1991, I learned of Justice Thurgood Marshall's retirement. On my stopover in New York, my office paged me and told me the news. Before continuing to Europe I made a short press statement: "Today the women of America have lost a dear friend on the Supreme Court. What an irony that we soon will celebrate July 4 and the freedom we hold dear in America, knowing that the freedoms of women will be limited in the years to come."

My spirits were rock-bottom at this latest news. It was distressing to imagine the Court now: Rehnquist and White had voted against *Roe* in 1973 and had continued to vote against its principles ever since. Kennedy had joined them in every abortion decision since he had arrived. In his *Webster* opinion Scalia had stated he wanted to overturn *Roe* immediately. Souter had voted to uphold the gag on medical free speech in *Rust*, and I felt he was likely to vote with Rehnquist, White, Kennedy, and Scalia. With Marshall's departure, only two pro-choice voters remained, Blackmun and Stevens. O'Connor's vote I considered "half"—and that might be too generous from the pro-choice side. She had voted for almost any abortion regulation a state adopted. Only in *Hodgson* had she deemed it an undue burden for a state to require a minor to have both parents involved before an abortion, including cases where one parent had never been a part of the minor's life or in cases of abuse.

Once I arrived in Europe, over wine, fresh cheeses and breads from a neighborhood bakery, I discussed the situation with my friends and my fears and frustrations at the events unfolding. I expected Bush to appoint someone who was opposed to abortion and add one more vote to the anti-privacy side. The odds now were that sooner or later the Court would directly or indirectly overturn *Roe*. That would not outlaw abortion; it would simply make it a political issue and allow elected officials to pass laws against abortion.

When the Court adopted *Griswold* and *Roe*, it had erected a shield between citizens and the power of government to prohibit contraception and abortion. If the Court overturned *Roe*, it would dissolve at least the part of the shield that had protected women from the accumulated force and vindictiveness of those seeking to prohibit abortion, even in cases of rape or incest. Women would be vulnerable to whatever laws were passed, and their only means of protecting themselves would be to elect pro-choice officials willing to rebuff the steady pressure from the "mandatory-birthers." The abortion issue would not be over; rather, it would be transferred from the courtroom to the voting booth.

The Washington Post, reviewing Marshall's last decisions, commented on his dissent in one, *Payne v. Tennessee*, saying it was a bitter blast at what he viewed as an activist conservative majority poised to dismantle scores of precedents and abandon the Court's historical role "as the protector of the powerless. Tomorrow's victims," he commented, "may be the minorities, women, or the indigent." I was betting that he, too, was worrying about *Roe v. Wade*.

What I learned about Clarence Thomas, whom George H.W. Bush nominated for the Court on July 1, was depressing. It seemed to me Thomas lacked the credentials and stature to take Marshall's place. The American Bar Association gave Thomas only a mild, "qualified," rating. I do not believe Thomas was the best *man* for the job; I *know* he was not the best *person* for the job.

When Thomas was asked by Senators what he considered the most important Supreme Court cases of the past twenty years, he mentioned only two. One was an employment case, and the other was *Roe v. Wade*. But then he said he had never discussed *Roe*. If he had not thought about and discussed what he said was one of the two most significant cases, that alone should have disqualified him. He was a Yale law student when *Roe* was announced. Every other law student from that era that I have talked to has told me they read *Roe* and discussed it in class.

Despite his statements that he had no opinion, Thomas had written and commented about abortion. He had once claimed that the Republican position against abortion would help the party win black voters. In a 1987 speech, he had described as a "splendid example of applying natural law" an article that stated abortion was a holocaust and should be illegal. At confirmation hearing time, Thomas called his praise a "throwaway line." When questioned further by senators, he tried to run away from his clear record of hostility to the right of choice.

As chairman of the Equal Employment Opportunity Commission in 1986, Thomas had cosigned a report to President Reagan from the White House Working Group on the Family that included a section on abortion. It referred to the Court's *Roe* decision as "fatally flawed" and criticized the *Planned Parenthood v. Danforth* ruling, which reversed a Missouri law requiring spousal permission for abortion. (The "Danforth" in the case was the state's attorney general at the time, John Danforth, who was a US senator in 1991 and Thomas's primary Senate sponsor.)

Thomas's evasiveness on the issue of abortion was frustrating. He seemed to have opinions on other controversial topics. When asked about the death penalty, he responded, "It is nothing that would bother me personally." But he would not commit to an opinion on the right of choice, saying that having an opinion "could undermine—or create an impression that could undermine—my impartiality." The press pointed out that in some polls only about one percent of adults had "no opinion" on the issue of abortion.

On September 19, 1991, I joined a panel to testify against Thomas before the Senate Judiciary Committee, a panel which also included Kate Michelman, executive director of NARAL, Faye Wattleton of Planned Parenthood, and former Vermont governor Madeleine Kunin. Each of us was allotted five minutes. The week before I was to testify I talked to my students in a UT pre-law class about the Senate proceedings. Several students offered suggestions about what to include in my testimony. One student, who worked in the child-support enforcement division of the Texas attorney general's office, brought me a poster from that office, with the picture of a man who looked pregnant. The caption below asked: "Would you be more careful if it was you that got pregnant?" I found a picture of Thomas's face in an appropriate size, and my assistant deftly clipped it and superimposed the head on the poster. I took it to Washington with me.

I was the first speaker. Now I know why the other presenters asked *not* to testify first: very few senators were present when the hearings began. My initial statement was to the cameras, to presiding Senators Joseph Biden of Delaware and Strom Thurmond from South Carolina, the ranking Democrat and Republican on the committee. During the five minutes I was testifying, a few other senators wandered in. When the question and answer session ended two hours later, almost all of them were finally present.

I was the only lawyer on the panel, so we four panelists had agreed in advance that my key comments would be about Thomas's legal philosophy and opinions. I pointed out Thomas's past statements that indicated he was opposed to abortion. I reminded the senators that when previously asked about some of those statements, Thomas had said he was simply "appealing to his audience." I suggested to them that Thomas did not really mean what he was telling them, but rather that he was trying to appeal to *them* as an audience. It seemed to me that he would say anything he needed to, true or not, to win confirmation. "To vote to confirm Judge Thomas when he has responded with only evasion," I said, "would be to treat the right to choose abortion as a second-class right."

During my testimony I put the "pregnant Judge Thomas" poster against the microphone in front of me, where the camera and the senators present could see it. I said I had heard Thomas had a sense of humor and I trusted he would not mind if I used his picture to make a point. He was, obviously, someone who would never have to face the issue.

Kate Michelman shared the story of the abortion she had had when her husband left her and their three children. She had to justify her decision to a panel of doctors, and was then forced to leave the hospital, find the man who had deserted her and the children, and get his permission for the abortion.

Faye Wattleton talked about the plight of women, particularly African-American women, in the United States. She spoke of her experience as a nurse-midwife in the days before *Roe*, when abortion was illegal, and she reminded the senators of the medical horrors possible if abortion were declared illegal once again.

Madeleine Kunin made a most eloquent statement, putting into words what I was feeling. "The very fact that Judge Thomas has succeeded in not clarifying his philosophy on this issue creates a quiet fury in many women. Once again, when it comes to our issues, we find ourselves repeating the ancient cycle of helplessness that women have experienced throughout history. The sense of powerlessness is painful. It is apparent right here in this room, where women are not equally represented in the decision-making process of this country." She continued to address the senators: "We are put in the position of pleaders, asking you to ask our questions for us, to be our stand-ins, to intercede on our behalf. Once again, our question, central to our lives, the one that women all over this country are asking, is not being answered.

We have to take our chances. We have to live on hope. We have to believe that silence equals fairness when, in fact, we fear that silence equals just the opposite."

Indeed, I felt powerless that day to protect the victory of *Roe*, to spare women the heartaches that led to the fight for *Roe*, and to avoid the political struggle I saw looming ahead.

The senators did say we were the best-prepared panel they had heard. But it seemed to me they were talking a good game for the official record. They were aware of the growing political heat from women and pro-choice voters. I almost felt some were trying to emphasize their pro-choice positions in an attempt to deflect the fury we were warning of if they voted for Thomas.

Some, however, were offensive. Senator Alan Simpson of Wyoming, who I had always thought of as a friend of choice, stunned us at one point by saying that the debate "flopped around." He lectured us as a teacher would school children, and asked, "When will somebody cut the high drama that this is the end of the earth if this happens one way?"

Madeline Kunin quickly responded: "Those of us who have been entrusted with making public policy know that we have to create a rational process and a fair process. . . That removes it from some of the drama of life, but we cannot for a moment forget that the consequences of our decisions in a public arena are very dramatic and very personal for the people affected. . . . I do not think that this drama has been exaggerated."

I wanted to tell Simpson that confirming Clarence Thomas was a disservice to the future of *Roe* and the women of the country. The stakes were higher because of the number of anti-*Roe* justices already confirmed to serve on the Court. We could not adequately dramatize the impact of the abortion issue on the ability of women to participate equally in society; it was an issue worth being dramatic about. I will never forget or forgive Simpson's disregard and high-handed arrogance.

My instincts tell me that only two people know the full story of what happened between Clarence Thomas and Anita Hill—they themselves. But I believe her. I don't believe him. It was infuriating to hear senators asking again and again, "Well, why did she wait ten years?" Any woman could have answered that. First, I doubt Hill would have come forward if Thomas had been nominated for anything else. But he was nominated to be a member of the US Supreme Court, an institution that we as lawyers are taught to respect. She had a duty as a lawyer to tell what she knew about someone about to be seated on that bench, especially when what she knew contravened his public words. Second, for decades and more, women in subordinate positions have remained silent when a detrimental incident occurred involving a supervisor or someone in power. Countless women have experienced sexual harassment and never said anything publicly—or even privately—about it until ten or twenty years later, if ever. Senators seemed to be so worried about being "fair" to Thomas that they stepped aside and left Hill without champions to combat the marauding techniques of those who sought to destroy her testimony. Bush's people were apparently using every persuasive weapon in their arsenal because he was so determined to win a place on the Court for Thomas. "Capitol Hill," Ellen Goodman wrote in her syndicated column, "is a place where men can listen to Clarence Thomas's straight-faced claim that he had no opinion on abortion, and then question Anita Hill's credibility."

Everywhere I traveled around the time of the confirmation hearings, women expressed their outrage at the way Hill, and others of us who testified, had been treated. As we watched senators demeaning Hill, we felt again the emotions when we had been similarly treated. Women had come so far, accomplished so much, been involved in the political process, but when it really counted, we simply were not in the ball game.

I was in Washington State promoting Proposition 120, a referendum to put the principles of *Roe v. Wade* into the state constitution, when the Senate voted on the Thomas nomination. I watched the proceedings during a break from speaking events and press interviews, and cheered early in the voting when Texas senator Lloyd Bentsen cast a no vote; I had worked with others to lobby him. Then, however, the grim reality of the final outcome became evident.

A Seattle TV crew was recording the moment. Undoubtedly my face mirrored my misery as Thomas was confirmed to a seat on the Court.

10. Words of Choice

W hen this book was first published in 1992 the seesaw began to move once again. Americans were reacting to their feelings of vulnerability. They saw the changes that had taken place in the membership of the Supreme Court, and they worried about the future of the right of privacy. A series of events in 1991, including the Clarence Thomas hearings, made many Americans, especially women, angry and determined. I sensed renewed dedication and commitment to the pro-choice position, and a searching for ways to strengthen the protection women and their families had enjoyed for almost twenty years.

AS VOTES WERE BEING subtracted from our side of the Supreme Court scorecard, I looked for a way to contribute to the crucial effort to defend the principles of reproductive freedom without duplicating what others were already doing well. During the years I was busy winning legislative and administrative battles for women, other lawyers with full-time positions to defend reproductive rights emerged as our legal champions. Lawyers at the American Civil Liberties Union Reproductive Freedom Project, the Planned Parenthood national office, and elsewhere were doing a great job, assisted by others at the NOW Legal Defense and Education Fund, and NARAL. Pro-choice groups such as NARAL and Planned Parenthood, with knowledgeable staffers and large mailing lists, were devoted to providing information and organizing public events.

But two needs not being adequately met were those of involving younger generations in this struggle and explaining the legal aspects of the issue. As presented in public discussion and in ten-second sound bites, the issue seemed to be: Are you for or against abortion? But that was *not* the issue then and is not the issue now. The issue is: *Who* should make the decision about abortion—the government, strangers, or women?

I began to travel and speak, particularly on campuses, about *Roe v. Wade*. When people asked me where I lived, I sometimes answered, "Delta Airlines." Some weeks I seemed to eat, sleep, work, and even dress in airports and on planes. My friends teasingly called me "Paulette:" In the tradition of Paul Revere, I was riding through the sky to warn citizens, "Beware! The Supreme Court is changing. Beware!"

Those travels and speeches had various results. An unexpected one was being named the best college lecturer in 1990 by the National Association for Campus Activities. This book, in fact, was another outgrowth of those trips. I realized that if I gave a speech every night for the rest of my life, I couldn't reach as many people as I could through a book. And traveling was already getting old back then. I wouldn't mind a hectic speech schedule if I could be 'beamed up" and then immediately "beamed down." But it is hard to fly anywhere directly from Austin, so hard we say that to get to heaven or hell, you first have to go through Dallas or Atlanta.

This book answers the questions people across the country ask me most frequently when I lecture: How did you get involved in *Roe v. Wade*? What was it like to try a case in the Supreme Court, especially when you were so young? What are the legal principles of *Roe*? Why is *Roe*'s strength being reduced? What can we do to stop that? A book is also a means to share the valuable insights I have gained from people who have lingered, talked, and posed questions after my speeches. I am absolutely convinced that the majority of Americans want abortion to be legal. Many who have qualms about abortion from a personal perspective (and it is much easier to have qualms when there is no actual pregnancy involved and no actual decision to be made) still say, "But I don't want the government making that decision. And I don't want to make it for others."

Many who share my beliefs are pro-choice, not pro-abortion. The best analogy I've found is divorce. When someone announces wedding plans, the response is never, "That's terrific. Maybe someday you can get a divorce." Most people try hard to avoid divorce, yet many have been through one. We are not for divorce, but we no longer make divorce illegal. We know that making divorce illegal would only cause different and more difficult problems.

Similarly, abortion must be a legal choice. It is an appropriate choice in various circumstances. Many advocates of choice want to ensure that women have all options—including that of carrying a pregnancy to term and keeping the child or placing it for adoption. But it would be better to prevent pregnancy altogether in most circumstances. I agree with C. Everett Koop, a Reagan appointee, who was Surgeon General from 1982 to 1989, and who said we need to discuss methods of contraception. (I also appreciated his pointing out that he was the nation's doctor, not its spiritual advisor.) To my mind, the best way to prevent abortion is to prevent pregnancy, and the best way to prevent pregnancy is to use contraceptives, although since none are failure-proof there will always be some unwanted pregnancies. Yet some anti-abortion leaders oppose the use of contraceptives and stand in the way of sex education implemented by local school boards. Abstinence until marriage has long been the official teaching of most religions and parents. Nevertheless countless young people discover sex. According to a 2012 study US teens are two and a half times as likely to give birth as teens in Canada, around four times as likely as teens in Germany or Norway, and almost ten times as likely as teens in Switzerland. Among more developed countries, Russia has the next highest teen birth rate after the United States, but an American teenage girl is still around 25 percent more likely to give birth than her counterpart in Russia.

In 2012, the antis came back with a vengeance, proposing to cut contraceptives from health insurance reimbursement, and to end funding for Planned Parenthood's non-abortion services like mammograms, breast cancer screening, and general well-women care, and contraception. As of this writing, they haven't succeeded, but the battle is more intense than it's been in years, and they have had many success in making services more difficult to access

The Supreme Court has never empowered the states to brand millions of Americans as criminals for making and acting on a decision that the same Court had assured Americans was theirs to make. But opponents of abortion have been trying to pass laws against abortion in virtually every state for forty years. The country has become a patchwork of abortion laws: abortion is legal in all states, but heavily regulated in many. In 2012 there were no abortion clinics in 87 percent of all counties in the US. Once again women in states where abortion is prohibited in many instances and where there is no nearby abortion clinic have to travel to obtain safe, legal services. Those with money will be able to do so. Those who are younger, less sophisticated, or poorer will once again end up in back alleys and emergency rooms, or have babies against their will, and the horror stories of the past will begin again. I have yet to be in a state where women *feel* safe.

Pro-choice forces are pursuing plans to rewrite this script. Abortion is being transformed from a courtroom to a ballot-box issue even as pro-choice legal eagles continue their efforts in the Supreme Court and in many other courts around the country. Our immediate task is to push our side of the seesaw up, through increased education and motivation. I still speak all over the country and recently taped a segment for the PBS/AOL series, "Makers: Women Who Make America" about the women whose work has altered "virtually every aspect of American culture" (makers. com/weddington-0). Perhaps the invitations come because I am history; sometimes I feel like *ancient* history. Today's college students of traditional age were born long after I started researching the abortion issue, and few people younger than I remember what things were like before *Roe*.

The fact that legal and safe abortion is an option and is often taken for granted is both a plus and a minus. It is a plus in that Americans have never given up a constitutional right once they've had it, and I do not believe American women will give up the freedom to make their own decisions and turn decision-making power over to state legislators. Young women today have a far stronger sense of self and their right to make decisions for themselves than my generation did at that age. I am counting on that same strength to activate them now. If someone tells them, "Once you are pregnant you become a prisoner of state policy and the state will tell you what to do," I cannot picture them meekly saying, "Well, okay."

On the other hand, the fact that many do not remember the horrors of illegal abortion sometimes makes the job of motivating young people harder. In addition, everyone is busy with school, job, family, and other daily activities. Basic social change, I sometimes say, is often created by those who can stay up past midnight. I used to be able to, but it's harder now. My students at the University of Texas seem *never* to go to bed before midnight. They have the enthusiasm and some of the idealism that made so many victories possible for us in the seventies.

Pro-choice people are generally "live and let live" people; we aren't trying to convince those on the other side to agree with us. We are simply trying to keep them from forcing their beliefs on us. Those opposed to abortion have had an organizational advantage for many years. They used churches as their meeting and information centers. We have had churches on our side too, but they were not always as forceful and we had a harder time reaching our people. At the same time technology has changed that dynamic in exciting ways: we can now reach millions of pro-choice people through social media.

My experiences these past years tell me abortion is not purely a conservative-versus-liberal or a Democrat-versus-Republican issue. Barry Goldwater, Sr., the former Arizona senator and Republican presidential candidate, whom no one ever accused of being liberal, said that the true conservative position is that abortion is not the government's business. It seems that within twenty-five minutes of my arrival in a new town, except some traditionally liberal enclave like Ann Arbor or Reno, someone says in a low voice, "Now, this is a very *conservative* area." My response is, 'Well then, people here ought to be for choice and for keeping government from making private decisions."

Certainly the Democratic and Republican parties do have opposite platforms on abortion. And it has become harder than ever for pro-choice Republicans to have an impact on their party, but pro-choice Republicans still exist and still show up at party events to voice their opinion. As we know, not all Democrats favor choice.

To me, the public controversy over abortion is primarily a religious conflict. Religious faith is of course important, but it is upsetting when religion is invoked as the source of authority for imposing a set of ideas on people who do not share them. When people tell me they are opposed to abortion, they inevitably cite their religious affiliation or an interpretation of biblical scriptures that do not directly relate to abortion. However, there is a strong pro-choice movement among religious individuals: In a 2011 Public Religion Research Institute poll, majorities of all major religious groups with the exception of white evangelical Protestants said abortion should be legal in all or most cases. Religious groups who believe in maintaining abortion as an appropriate option include several major Jewish groups, Unitarians, Methodists, and Presbyterians. Divisions of those groups have often filed *amicus* briefs supporting the principles of *Roe* in abortion-related cases pending before the US Supreme Court.

Certainly the Roman Catholic hierarchy and various fundamentalist Protestant leaders continue to organize against legal abortion, and they have made no secret of their activities. They have a right to their own beliefs, but we whose beliefs differ have a right to oppose them and their efforts to use the might of their religious organizations to force their beliefs on us.

There is no scripture that contains the word "abortion." There is an Old Testament passage that says if a pregnant woman is injured and miscarries, for the loss of the fetus a fine will be paid to the husband but for injuries to the woman, the penalty is more severe, an eye for an eye, and a tooth for a tooth. However, there are many scriptures not specifically about abortion quoted by each side. The antis refer to passages about being "known" while still in the womb, and the pro-choice folks refer to those about becoming a human being upon receiving "the breath of life."

Yes, we do have laws that coincide with various biblical passages, but we do not enforce them because they come from the Bible, and we don't enforce other biblical commandments at all.

The Bible says to observe the Sabbath and keep it holy, but we allow observance days other than Sunday, and we no longer punish people who play (or work) rather than praying on the Sabbath. The Bible says to honor one's parents, but we don't punish people who have a negative attitude. Some people believe it is against God's will to rely on doctors, but we don't close down hospitals. Some say no Christian should use contraceptives, but their sale and use are no longer illegal, as they once were in Connecticut, Massachusetts, and other states.

True, we do impose moral standards when the vast number of people agree on the same standards. Although the commandment says "Thou shalt not kill" and states no exceptions, we allow capital punishment and killing in war. Since abortion is not a matter of overwhelming public agreement, we should leave the decision about abortion up to each individual to decide. Even if there were majority support for making abortion illegal, the Constitution was meant to protect an individual's liberties against even the majority.

At a speech to a group of nurses in Dallas, one commented during the question-and-answer session, "I am going to try to prevent any person who favors abortion from ever being invited to speak to us again. After all, we Christians . . ." She went on to indicate that anyone who disagreed with her *could not* be a Christian. I resented that remark, and there are many Christians who would disagree with her. Our citizens include many who are not Christians, whether they are of another faith or no faith at all. This nation has prospered in part because people of many faiths have been able to live peaceably together. We have succeeded because we have separated church and state. I worry that some people are getting perilously close to abandoning those principles. After another speech of mine, a man in the audience commented about how amazed he and other Europeans were at what was occurring in the United States. "In Europe we had religious wars for 800 years," he said. "We know better than to do that again."

Justice Stevens said that there is no secular reason to outlaw abortion and theology is an improper reason to do so. I believe he is right on both counts. Outlawing abortion would not end illegal abortion; rather, it would reinstitute the horrors that existed before *Roe*.

THERE ARE MANY positive steps we should be taking, including doing more for pregnant women who want to carry pregnancies to term and doing more for those children who are here, not forcing women to have children they say they cannot care for. Yes, there are thousands of couples who want to adopt but cannot find a child who fits their specifications. Surely we are not going to force women to give birth so others can adopt. There are already many children who need homes, but who are older or who have physical or psychological difficulties. As we have emphasized the right of women to make choices, more pregnant women, including teenagers, have chosen to keep their own children rather than place them for adoption as they often used to.

Unfortunately, even though most citizens want to keep abortion legal, our political system frequently does not reflect the will of the majority. Many citizens don't vote; According to the US Census Bureau, in 2008, 36 percent of eligible voters did not vote in the Presidential election. Politics can be swayed by a dedicated minority whose votes are focused on a single issue. That's how opponents of abortion have won some political fights. The majority of voters, satisfied with the status quo, were not involved on a daily basis in fighting for pro-choice principles, while people who disagreed with current law were very motivated to vote and to work to change our laws.

The level of passion that abortion evokes in some who oppose it, particularly those who participate in the assault waves against clinics and women seeking services, has puzzled me. Why are they so passionate about forcing women to go through every pregnancy? Do they think that if a woman is sexual, then pregnancy is her "punishment" and she must not be allowed to avoid it? In February 2012, a prominent backer of Rick Santorum, a Senator who was running for the Republican nomination for President, told the world that, "Back in my day, they used Bayer Aspirin for contraceptives. The gals put it between their knees and it wasn't that costly." He said this to back up Senator Santorum's previous statements that he did not believe in birth control.

One member of Congress has said opponents of choice seem to believe that "life begins at conception and ends at birth." While a few anti-abortionists have supported efforts to help pregnant women as a group, they have not been visible leading the charge for better health benefits for poor pregnant women or for more extensive prenatal care programs or programs to make the lives of children better once they are born. The same zealots are not in the halls of state legislatures and Congress pushing for funding to care for these children.

Is it that some people who have not been successful in worldly terms find self-esteem in being able to look down on others? In the past and still today, there were those who say, "I'm white and you're black. Therefore I'm better than you are," or "I'm male and you're female. Therefore I'm better than you are." In general, that is no longer acceptable. Maybe the new language is, "I'm moral and you're immoral. Therefore I am better than you are." I don't see love and concern in the eyes of those who picket outside abortion clinics. I see hatred, condescension, and a feeling of moral superiority.

Many believe that these are often people who feel powerless. They think their way of life is threatened, and they seek to gain or regain control by trying to control women and their decisions. Others characterize the antis as people who dislike most recent societal changes, and their anti-abortion efforts symbolize to them a return to "the way it was before." That's exactly what frightens many women: they don't want to go back to "the way it was before."

Charlotte Taft, whose Dallas clinic was often picketed, once said, "They are addicted to religion and to belonging. For a lot of them their main sense of belonging comes from religion." In contrast, many young people today are to be admired for being more deliberate and realistic in deciding when to marry and when to have children. I hear many college students saying, "I'm going to postpone marriage until I get established in a career," and "I'm not going to have children until I'm in a position to give them the financial support and the love and care that I think children need." To me, those statements represent a far more admirable and moral position than those of people who say, "It's up to me to tell every woman who becomes pregnant what she must do."

OUR OPPONENTS TRADITIONALLY maintained that a person exists at conception. But that is consistent with neither biology nor our legal history. Once egg and sperm have joined, even if you magnify the product eight hundred times, its length is still less than an inch. Up to 75 percent of all fertilized eggs are spontaneously aborted and do not result in a live birth. Biology, according to a *Webster* brief filed by 167 scientists and physicians (including eleven Nobel laureates and five National Medal of Science winners), says life began billions of years ago and has been a continuum ever since, marked by important moments such as conception, implantation, quickening, viability, and birth. Biologists speak of a zygote, an embryo, a fetus, and, at birth, a baby. Biology can describe the facts of fetal development, but it does not mandate the conclusions to be drawn from those facts.

Like me, many do not believe that the joining of egg and

sperm should cancel out any consideration for the woman or her life, family, and dreams. What about her? What about the dignity of women? Women have abortions for many reasons, including economic ones. Women head a majority of American families below the poverty level. Having more children generally means a woman has less chance to provide well for the children she already has. Women often work because they must support themselves or others. Fifty-eight percent of women are in the labor force; 23 percent of women are single, 16 percent divorced, 12 percent widowed, and 3 percent separated. The highest unemployment rate among married women is for those whose husbands earn less than $15,000 annually.

Just as biology does not equate "fetus" with "baby," law has not customarily treated the fetus as a person. The arguments Ron and I made in 1970 are still true. The word "person" appears in a number of contexts in the Constitution, but never in a way that would apply before birth. The Constitution states that "all persons born or naturalized in the United States . . . are citizens." The US Census does not count pregnant women twice. Tax deductions for children are allowed when they are born, not when they are conceived. Rights of inheritance are contingent on being born alive. Even when abortion was a crime, it was never the crime of murder. We record birthdays, not conception days. Birth is still the determining legal event.

But describing fetal development in an exaggerated way to persuade others to reach their conclusions continues to be a favorite technique of those opposed to abortion. They look at the moment of conception, see a "person" in those forty-six chromosomes, and decide that "person" is more important than any consideration of the woman. She is invisible to them other than as a carrying case for the fetus. Yet she is a fully developed person with full legal rights—or at least someone I believe *should* have full legal rights, including the ones anti-abortionists would take away. A majority of Americans look at the fertilized ovum and do not see what anti-abortionists see.

Likewise, opponents describe abortion procedures in an outrageously gruesome manner, often dwelling on techniques used only in extraordinary circumstances. I have read descriptions of childbirth and of the physical changes a woman experiences during pregnancy written in the style of anti-abortionists and they are terrifying. There is no medical procedure that can't be described in a way to make people shudder. If I used the technique of the opponents to describe a tonsillectomy, I would say: "The menacing doctor grips a cold steel instrument and pries open the mouth, exposing a column of pink flesh. The doctor then takes an instrument resembling an ice pick and chips away at the offending mound of tissue until the body reacts in pain. Satisfied with his work, the doctor takes a pliers-like tool and thrusts it into the pink column, and with a cold glint in his eye grabs the bloody mass and jerks it away from the exposed flesh. He carelessly tosses the human tissue aside and goes on to his next victim." Getting one's tonsils removed is a safe, legal procedure, but I'm not sure how many people would want to go through it if they had to read an account like that. In the end, people do not really *want* to go through any medical procedure. They do so in order to secure the benefits that will follow.

I AM OFTEN ASKED what the legal implications are of a law that says life begins at conception. I don't know the answer. That has never been the basis of our laws. Some lawyers, however, are looking ahead and playing the "what if" game. What would be the consequences of adopting a legal standard that starts legal rights at conception?

First, some contraceptives might be outlawed. While most opponents of abortion do not say they want to make contraceptives illegal, some do. Most abortion opponents avoid talking about contraception although there is a recent trend of conflating abortion and contraception in order to defeat reproductive health funding. Opponents will drop the word "abortion" into their arguments against government spending/subsidies for screening for sexually transmitted infections or contraceptive coverage, even though none of the funding will go to abortion. However, there are a few extreme right-wing Tea Party politicians who are happy to use contraceptives as a political wedge. During the 2012 Republican primaries, Rick Santorum said that states should be able to ban contraception.

Second, a criminal penalty might be imposed on a woman who has an abortion. It is claimed by some that women were not prosecuted before *Roe v. Wade*. But in 1958, before the reform movement, eighteen states had penalties for any woman who survived an illegal abortion. As late as 1972, it was illegal in fifteen states to aid or counsel a woman who had an abortion. A good many states considered the woman who had an abortion a criminal. Back then, a doctor who performed an abortion in Connecticut was subject to as many as five years in prison, while the woman could receive as many as two. Frequently women were refused emergency medical care until law enforcement authorities were called and the women were "persuaded" to help prosecute whoever had performed the abortion. Those laws, adopted in the mid 1800s, were based on the risk of infection and a concern for the woman's health, not on a concept of when life began.

Obviously mifepristone, the abortion pill, would be illegal. The benefit of mifepristone in terminating pregnancy is that it does not involve surgery; there is no risk of perforation or infection, and the drug could be dispensed in places other than abortion clinics. The fact that most abortions are now done in clinics has allowed opponents to target clinics in a way that would not be possible if a woman received the necessary treatment from her regular doctor. I worry that if states again make abortion illegal, mifepristone would become a back-alley drug. It needs to be used under a doctor's supervision, although it would be safer than methods often used before 1973.

What about in vitro fertilization? It is the hope for thousands today who want children, but the Catholic Church is officially opposed to the procedure because it involves taking an egg and sperm and combining them in a petri dish. The Church's position is that life has begun in that dish and in vitro fertilization is "playing with life."

What would happen when there is a conflict between the appropriate medical treatment for the benefit of the woman and the health of the fetus? Certain medications for epilepsy, diabetes, and stomach ulcers, for example, help the woman but might harm the fetus. Because cancer is generally speeded up by pregnancy, most doctors advise cancer patients not to go through pregnancy; women with multiple sclerosis are generally advised to avoid pregnancy. Would consideration for the woman's health be set aside, and abortion not be allowed?

Might a woman be forced to have a cesarean procedure against her will? Such situations have already been litigated. In June 1987, twenty-seven-year-old Angela Carder, six months pregnant, was expected to die within days because of inoperable lung cancer. Without notice to her family, George Washington University Medical Center in Washington, DC, apparently out of fear of legal liability if it did nothing to save the fetus, asked a local judge whether a cesarean should be performed. Angela's personal doctors advised that the fetus was probably too underdeveloped to be viable and a cesarean would only shorten Angela's life. She was heavily medicated and could not express her own wishes. Her family believed that under the circumstances she would not want the surgery. The court said, "Take her to surgery." The fetus died within two hours, Angela lived another two days. In December 1990, the DC Court of Appeals overturned the lower court's ruling. In an out-of-court settlement, the medical center gave Angela's parents an undisclosed sum of money and the center changed its policy for such situations in the future. About fourteen women in this country have been ordered by a court to go through that kind of medical treatment even though some of them actually gave birth without a cesarean before the order could be carried out. Might treatment injurious to the woman be ordered to benefit the fetus?

What if a woman is discovered to be carrying what is already a dead fetus? Surely she should have the right to an abortion. Or what about the woman who is carrying an anencephalic fetus, one with such limited brain development that it will die soon after birth? Why should she have to carry the pregnancy to term? Shouldn't she have the right to obtain an abortion?

What about an employer who refuses to hire women who might become pregnant? The Supreme Court in *United Auto Workers v. Johnson Control* reversed a lower court's decision that a company could refuse to hire a woman when, if she were pregnant and on the job, there could be damage to the fetus, but the high court based its opinion on specific federal law that prohibits discrimination in employment regarding pregnancy. One of the dissenting judges in the lower court said there were 20 million industrial jobs that could be closed to women if that kind of policy were adopted.

What about the responsibility of a woman (who, some opponents of abortion would say, is guilty of being sexual and therefore must accept the consequence) to the fetus (who, opponents say, is innocent)? If she were to go skiing, fall down, and miscarry, would she be guilty of negligent homicide? Would waiters and waitresses be forbidden to serve her a glass of wine? Would convenience stores not be allowed to sell her cigarettes? What about a pregnant woman who has small children and contracts German measles from one? Is she a criminal because she has possibly caused damage to the fetus?

Pregnant women have been jailed to keep them from having access to drugs. Everybody agrees that if a woman is pregnant and she is going to carry the pregnancy to term, she ought to conduct herself in a way that gives the fetus the best chance of beginning life healthy and wholesome. But does one brand her a criminal if she doesn't, and how far does one go in penalizing her?

There is some evidence that a man's use of drugs or heavy drinking before conception can cause problems and affect the sperm and ultimately the fetus. Should society hold him responsible for that? If so, how?

What will happen to the medical research and the medical benefits that come from the use of fetal tissue? It has great potential for treating Alzheimer's disease and Parkinson's disease. It has saved the life of a baby born to the wife of a fundamentalist Baptist preacher opposed to abortion. Yet anti-abortionists usually claim that medical use of fetal tissue should not be allowed, as it might cause more abortions. That seems like saying that if you allow people to pledge their organs for transplants if they are in a fatal accident, it will increase the number of accidents. Medical standards specify that a woman who has an abortion may not designate a specific use for the fetal tissue, but she may give permission for a doctor or scientists to decide its use in order to better the lives of others. Recent administrations have been mixed in their use of federal dollars for medical research involving human fetal tissue. President George H.W. Bush vetoed an attempt to lift the ban on fetal tissue research, but in 1993, Bill Clinton did lift the moratorium. President George W. Bush's first veto rejected Congress's bid to lift funding restrictions on embryonic stem cell research, but then, early in his presidency, Obama moved to lift those funding restrictions.

Opponents often understate the human cost of illegal abortion. I once heard someone say, "The year before *Roe v. Wade* only thirty-nine women died from illegal abortions in this country." When I related that to a group of nurses in Colorado, one of them said, "Why, I saw more women than that die as the result of illegal abortions in Chicago alone the year before *Roe v. Wade!*" Fewer illegal abortions may have been recorded in 1972: by then abortion was legal in several states. Also, doctors in emergency rooms generally did not list abortion as the cause of death, but listed instead the consequences of illegal and self-induced abortion—sepsis, or infection; cardiac arrest; or other conditions. Had a doctor written abortion as the cause of death for a Catholic woman, she would not have been allowed a religious burial.

ANOTHER QUESTION I am often asked is: "How can you live with yourself, knowing *Roe* was based on a lie?" *Roe v. Wade* was *not* based on a lie. There is confusion, it is true, as a result of comments by Jane Roe.

In 1970, when Jane Roe asked Linda Coffee and me whether it would help her case if she had been raped, we said no. That was not a legal reason for abortion under Texas law. In addition, when she said there were no witnesses and no police report had been filed, we decided not to put anything in our court papers that we could not prove. We left out any mention of how she got pregnant, because we weren't sure of the real story and our goal was broader than helping victims of rape. In court papers, in oral argument, in the decision, there was never anything about how she got pregnant. After the case was decided, *Good Housekeeping* sent a reporter to do a story on the young women who had won the case; he also interviewed Jane Roe. When I read the article, in June 1973, I was startled by many of the details, including those of a dramatic rape. I assumed he must have spent hours with Jane Roe and had drawn from her more information than Linda and I had from our meeting and phone conversations with her. Only Jane Roe knew what the true story was. Even if I had known the truth, I would have felt bound by attorney-client privilege to remain silent.

A few years later someone sent me a book by Barbara Milbauer, *The Law Giveth*, which quoted Jane Roe telling an even more extensive rape saga. I wondered if the author was suspicious of her dramatic description, which included that the rape occurred in rural Georgia in 1969, and that "one of the men was white, another was black, and a third was possibly part black and part Mexican." During the summer of 1987, columnist Carl Rowan did a series of interviews for a PBS special on important constitutional cases. During an interview with Jane Roe he asked, "What about the rape?" Her response was "I lied." Later she said the pregnancy was the "unplanned result of a casual affair."

I thanked my lucky stars that Linda and I had excluded any mention of how she got pregnant. Neither her lie nor her admission could hurt the case from a legal point of view. I do wish she had told us about the content of the interview with Carl Rowan before we learned about it in newspaper headlines. Three days before Reagan's nomination of Robert Bork for a Supreme Court seat was to go before the Senate, with pro-choice forces working around the clock to beat his nomination, headlines announced varieties of the following theme: 'Jane Roe, Winning Plaintiff in *Roe v. Wade*, Now Says She Lied." Reporters were calling NARAL, Planned Parenthood, NOW, and other groups, whose staffs were caught off-guard and did not know what to say. If Linda and I had known in advance, we could have alerted them and suggested a reply.

A few days later a reporter who identified himself as being from the Christian Broadcasting Network called me and said he was going to do an exposé of *Roe v. Wade*. "On what basis?" I asked. I remember a sinister voice saying, "Because Jane Roe lied." I told him to go look at the court documents, the transcript, the Court's opinion—I told him to look at anything about the case, and he would find no reference to how she got pregnant until *after* the case was decided. He later called back to say he had done that and, sure enough, the rape was not in there. He offered an apology, which I appreciated, and asked why she had lied *after* the decision. That is a question I cannot answer.

Unfortunately some opponents of abortion are quick to comment: "See, women will lie about rape if they think it will help them get an abortion, just like Jane Roe did." I can only repeat the truth of what happened and say that I think by far the bigger problem is that most women do not report rapes that actually occur.

Rape and pregnancy were again in national headlines in the fall of 2012. US representative Todd Akin who was running for US Senate in Missouri was asked by a reporter whether or not abortion should be legal if the woman had been raped. He said he had been told by doctors that if a woman were legitimately raped, "her body has ways to shut that whole thing down," and she wouldn't get pregnant. Medical authorities did not back him up and many Republicans refused to support him from that moment forward.

Many times antis also observe, "Well, if every woman would carry her pregnancy to term, she would end up loving it like Jane Roe." That line is the result of interviews Jane Roe did in 1989 and a story in the *National Enquirer* that she had asked for help to find the child she had put up for adoption in 1970, so she could tell the child she loved it. I can't imagine exposing a child to that kind of publicity and don't know the truth of the *Enquirer* article.

At the time of *Roe v. Wade,* Jane Roe favored the principle that women should be able to decide what to do in the event of a pregnancy. However, twenty-five years after Linda and I filed the *Roe v. Wade* case, Jane Roe "changed sides" and said that she opposed abortion being legal. From a legal perspective her change didn't hurt the case. Of course people were curious about it. Jane Roe began traveling with an anti-abortion leader named Flip Benham to fundamentalist churches where Jane Roe would talk a little bit, then Benham would talk at length and pass a collection plate asking for contributions to support their work. After a year or so they parted ways and Roe began working with another of the most intense anti-abortion leaders in this country and the head of Priests for Life, Father Frank Pavone. They also stopped working together eventually, and I read a newspaper clipping that Roe had started her own ministry. I certainly can't explain what was behind her change. We haven't talked since she used the public's interest in her to focus attention on the anti-abortion position.

Occasionally people are curious about what I thought of the NBC movie *Roe v. Wade*, the result of Jane Roe's hiring a Dallas attorney to "sell her story" without telling Linda or me. I was surprised, and when approached by a Hollywood television producer, I was not very enthusiastic. The producer, however, explained that I was a "public person", that my Supreme Court argument was public, that my speeches were public, and that a person could represent my role without my permission. However, they preferred to have my cooperation in connection with the movie. Eventually Linda, Ron, and I agreed to cooperate in order to safeguard the accuracy of the movie as far as the legal aspects of the case. Linda and I wrote into our contract that we would not be responsible for any information about Jane Roe. By then Roe was being quoted in some publications as making statements directly contradictory to those she was quoted as saying elsewhere. Reporters obviously were not checking anything she said, even against stories others had written. Since neither Linda nor I knew what was and what wasn't true about Jane Roe, we decided to say nothing except what we were sure of: she had been pregnant and she had wanted an abortion.

The movie, at any rate, is a docudrama, not a documentary. For a lawyer, it is hard to see "made-up" things on the screen. There is a scene where Ron and I are having a fight over the amount of time I am spending on the case. We never had that fight. I called the producer about it, and his response was, "Well, your life has not had enough drama." So they added some. In another scene, Linda Coffee tells me she just can't go on with the case. That never happened in reality, and its inclusion in the movie made Linda furious. The writer also had a problem with Jane Roe's involvement, or lack thereof, in the case: it was so minimal that it was hard to tie together Jane Roe's situation and the work on the case.

Amy Madigan portrayed me in the movie. She is a talented actress, but it was strange to see someone "play me" who did not talk like me and certainly did not look like me. Not long after *Roe v. Wade* was broadcast I flew to a college town to give a speech. At the airport, no one waiting at the gate seemed to be looking for me. Finally, when a young woman and I were the only two people left, she said, "Are you Sarah Weddington?" I said I was. "You don't look like Sarah Weddington," she said. I realized that she was waiting for Amy Madigan. I had become the impostor; Madigan had become the "real" Sarah Weddington.

I understand people's curiosity about Jane Roe. After all, often the plaintiff is a vital part of the case. Few people realize, however, that was not the situation with *Roe*. The fact that she was pregnant was important, but the case was a class action on behalf of all women who were or might be pregnant in the future. It was fought for all women. Jane Roe's inconsistencies may hurt the public perception of the case, but they cannot hurt the case as a legal document, or the principles it represents.

A few years ago Jane Roe got an anti-choice lawyer to file a suit asking that *Roe v. Wade* be overturned on the grounds that more information about the fetus was known and that she had changed her position. The courts turned down that suit on the basis that it was filed far too long after the *Roe v. Wade* decision was announced.

PEOPLE OFTEN WONDER whether there are new pro-choice arguments that might win in the future. Frankly, as the Court changes, it's hard to tell.

However, many attorneys are looking anew at the First Amendment principle of separation of church and state. Linda and I mentioned that, but we didn't have the evidence of organized religious involvement that we have now. Others are emphasizing the issue of gender-based discrimination. Linda and I mentioned that also, but again did not emphasize it because of a lack of precedent before 1971 when we were working to win the district court decision. The gender-based discrimination argument stresses the fact that only women can get pregnant, and to force a woman to carry her pregnancy to term against her will violates her right to due process of law. Perhaps some of the new efforts will eventually bear fruit, but I believe the privacy argument continues to carry the most weight.

Abortion is also an issue elsewhere in the world. An estimated 70,000 women worldwide die each year from unsafe abortions. The United Nations Population Fund (UNFPA) estimates that every minute of every day, forty women undergo unsafe abortions. A 2012 study by the Guttmacher Institute and UNFPA reported that 215 million women in developing countries do not have access to modern contraceptives. In the late 1990s and early 2000s, there was a substantial steady decline in the global abortion rate; however, this has plateaued in recent years. Nearly half of all abortions in the world are unsafe, and most unsafe abortions happen in the developing world. Recent cross-country comparative studies also confirm that restrictive laws do not lead to lower abortion rates, but rather to increased incidence of maternal illness and deaths resulting from unsafe abortions. A new study, Making Abortion Services Accessible in the Wake of Legal Reform, examines the implementation and impact of legal reforms in six settings—Cambodia, Colombia, Ethiopia, Mexico City, Nepal and South Africa—and finds that expanding access to legal abortion does not in itself guarantee a decrease in unsafe procedures. The findings indicate that increasing safe abortion services following legal reform requires sustained commitment and dedicated human and financial resources. In 2009, a hard fought two-decade-long battle was won in Nepal: the Supreme Court there ordered the government to enact a comprehensive abortion law, ensuring safe and affordable abortions and providing subsidies for low-income women.

IF SOMEONE HAD TOLD me in 1969 that I would still be talking about abortion forty years later, I would have thought that preposterous. Yet when people ask me if I'm tired of talking about the subject, I sincerely say, "No." I care too much about the case and its future not to continue to work for the legality and availability of abortions. Of course, none of those involved with the beginning of *Roe*, including me, had any idea of the power of what we were unleashing or what we would ultimately accomplish. Even if I had known in 1969 the impact *Roe* would have on my life—both the good and the bad—I would have gone forward. But it is clear that my life would have been very different if I had refused the request for help. The abortion question has opened doors for me, but it has closed others.

There have been missed professional opportunities. The first was in 1969, just before Christmas. Ed Wright, the exceptional Little Rock trial lawyer who headed the American Bar Association committee that Professor John Sutton and I worked with, had become president-elect of the ABA. I admired him tremendously, and I still pattern my professional relationship to others on his example. Wright asked me to be his special assistant, his right hand, at the ABA. At any other moment I would have leaped mountains for that opportunity. But the offer meant moving to Chicago and bowing out of the abortion case. With a heavy heart I said no, and then spent the Christmas holidays in the library researching for *Roe*.

After leaving the Carter White House, I interviewed with several law firms. They were complimentary of my record, my skills as a lawyer, and my hardworking nature, but each asked questions like, "You wouldn't do anything controversial, would you?" They were afraid my ongoing public involvement in the abortion issue would cause them to lose clients. I said I planned to continue my involvement; once again I received no job offers, and eventually I opened my own office.

Some people take the position I should not be invited to speak—on any subject, not just abortion—because I am pro-choice. Others are afraid to invite me to speak for fear of picketers and controversy. Keppler Associates, my speakers' bureau, tells me: "You don't know how many times we get your name right up to the final selection for a corporate or association meeting speaker on leadership—we know you are good, the sponsors admit you are great—but they select someone else, someone who doesn't have a controversial side that might cause complaints."

Although colleges and universities are sometimes pressured by anti-abortionists not to invite me, or to a cancel a speech, I have never had an institution withdraw an invitation once issued. Schools pride themselves as bastions of free speech, and the students, who are often the ones making the decisions about speakers, are especially interested in a legal analysis of the abortion issue. I do sometimes arrive to find that the college has received threats of protestors or an effort "to close the building down," and is nervous about my safety. I used to categorize speeches according to the number of uniformed and/or plainclothes officers present. Wheeling, West Virginia, topped the list: ten uniformed and seven plainclothes officers. Only once, at Elgin Community College in Illinois, have protestors tried to block the exits; the students handled the situation beautifully and the moment passed. Some schools decide to check me into a hotel under a false name. It really makes no difference to me, but it has created some problems when family members or business associates call the hotel where I am to stay and are told that there is no Sarah Weddington registered there.

I have received my share of letters saying, "I wish your mother had aborted you," and worse. And I still haven't grown accustomed to seeing my name on picketer's signs. On one occasion I flew to Houston to speak at a Planned Parenthood event, and was met by two women volunteers. A group of anti-abortion men apparently had discovered my arrival time, and as we left the airport, a van started tailing us. When we slowed, the van slowed; when we left the expressway, the van followed. Then the van pulled in front of us, and one man held up a sign: "Baby Killer." When we arrived at the hotel, security guards spoiled whatever other plans the men might have had.

My involvement has had a cost in terms of time. Since my divorce, I have never slowed down long enough to find another man willing to put up with my schedule. I have decided Harriet Pilpel, the former Planned Parenthood attorney who was so helpful on *Roe v. Wade*, is my role model in that regard; she remarried in her seventies. When I reach my seventies I should be ready to settle down. And I have never had children. I recently talked to a New Mexico woman in her mid-twenties who is determined to have children and has allotted a certain number of years to finding a husband; and if that does not work out, a certain number to finding a father for her children; and if neither of those plans works out, she will go to California for in vitro fertilization. I respect her longing for a child; however, I am now too old.

EXPERTS SAY THE final stage of grief is hope; that's the stage I'm in now. In traveling and talking to others, I have learned there are thousands who are looking at the abortion issue anew, who are determined to defend the principles of *Roe* , and who are willing to devote time and resources to another stage of the battle.

People are responding to new issues. In February 2012, when the Susan G. Komen Foundation decided to withdraw its funding to help poor women get mammograms through Planned Parenthood—believed to be because Planned Parenthood clinics provide abortions—its effort created a backlash. Donations fueled by outrage at this decision poured into Planned Parenthood allowing the organization to reach low-income women who previously were not aware that they offered this service. The bad publicity Komen received forced it to backtrack. And, according to Planned Parenthood, the number of active, pro-choice supporters who newly committed to standing up for women's health care increased by 1.2 million nationwide after the Komen story broke. Yet, at the same time, a 2012 Gallup poll reported only 41 percent of Americans identify as pro-choice, a significant decrease from the 1995 figure of 56 percent.

Older women are getting into—or back into—the fight. When I was in a small college town to speak and was staying at the college guest house, the retired woman who ran it leaned over to me while we were watching the news and said, "Are you the abortion lady?" I didn't know what was coming next but I said yes. And she said, "Well, listen, honey. I watch those men on TV trying to tell women what to do, and I sit here and say to them, 'Get your hands off my body, buster.'" I am heartened by the spirit of the women who do remember the days before *Roe*. At a rodeo I was attending, a vigorous older woman was going up and down the aisles selling popcorn. As she came to where I was sitting with friends, she stopped and said, "I know who you are. I'm pro-choice all the way. Keep up the good work!"

A little later a woman sitting nearby approached me when her twentyish daughter, her son-in-law, and their friends went for food. She confided to me the story of her daughter, who had been going through a rough period in her life a few years ago when she had an abortion. She was now married, with a daughter, and things were working out fine. The woman told me how glad she was that abortion was a legal option when her daughter needed it.

There have been many other such moments: I was standing in an airplane aisle, waiting to exit, when a man in the opposite aisle recognized me and started virtually yelling to me that he couldn't believe what anti-abortionists were trying to do. As we were deplaning, a woman caught up with me and said, "That man told me you argued the abortion case. I just want to say thanks for all you've done."

A retired Episcopal priest in a town outside Seattle told me that he paid his way through seminary by working at an undertaking establishment. The first two bodies he helped with were women who had died after illegal abortions. He is a pro-choice leader in his community. Men have told me what their mothers and sister have gone through. In Las Vegas, a hotel driver who took me to the airport talked about the pregnancy he and his girlfriend had chosen to end. They were both working, he was also in school, and she had a five-year-old son. They were barely making it, and so decided on an abortion when she discovered she was pregnant. When they arrived at the clinic they found an abortion protester had locked himself to the front door. The driver told me he wanted to punch the protester out; his girlfriend prevailed, and they waited peacefully until the police arrived.

And now after a speech it is almost inevitable that a woman will approach me and tell me a story from her own life or the lives of family members or friends. I never tire of the emotional stories people share with me. Their faces and voices flood back as I write, and I wish I could share all of their stories. They make me believe that people will not voluntarily go backward, will not acquiesce when the freedom of choice is taken from them. First comes determination to act. Then comes action.

11. Remembering the Past, Looking to the Future

The weather has turned cool in Austin; it's a glorious day here on September 22, 2012. As I look out my window at the crepe myrtle blossoms and various colorful plants, my thoughts linger on the 40th anniversary of *Roe*, which will be here soon, on January 22, 2013.

Today's media attention is focused on abortion in the political sphere, with pundits and politicians alike arguing back and forth about whether or not the freedoms established in *Roe* should continue to exist, or should be stripped away. Forty years ago we worked tirelessly to base our arguments on the Constitution, but religious and "principle" arguments have recently dominated discussion more than any rational or logical lines of reasoning.

Every time someone comes to visit and every time I look around my office, I am reminded of that day forty years ago. Just inside the front door is a framed handmade goose-quill pen that was at my place in the courtroom of the US Supreme Court when I arrived there to argue the case. (Since I ended up arguing the case twice, I actually have two pens.) As you walk into the hall-way, there is a signed photo of the 1973 Supreme Court Justices, signed by each of the nine men (eight who were white, and one who was black) who were Supreme Court Justices at the time I argued *Roe*. (Today, a photo of the Justices would include three women, a black man, and a roster of totally different white men, all appointed since *Roe*.) I had to pay for the photo, but the Justices were gracious enough to sign without charging. "Can you get a signed photo if you lose?" visitors sometimes ask." I don't know," is my response; "I've never lost a case in the Supreme Court." Of course, I have to truthfully add that the only case I've argued there is *Roe v. Wade*.

I worry that the impact of my case is weaker today, especially as it is becoming much more difficult for women to access abortion and contraception services. The determination to protect the victories of the past is a constant and crucial factor in increasing women's decision-making ability in many important aspects of their lives.

I wish that I could predict the future, but that is not possible. However, important clues such as the candidates and positions of the Democratic and Republican parties in 2012, the current membership of the US Supreme Court, and the current status of public opinion significantly help us anticipate what's to come. The actions of candidates, pundits, and voters during election season are critical in determining the outcome of the abortion issue in the US.

A few years ago I was wearing a pin on a flight that featured a photo of a coat hanger with a red circle around the edge of the pin and a red slash across the hanger. I was seated in an aisle seat, as I prefer. A young flight attendant came by and paused to examine my pin. She went on down the aisle but returned a bit later to examine it again. That happened several times. Then she stopped and asked, "What do you have against coat hangers?" I explained to her the symbolic importance of that pin, highlighting the fact that the liberties established in *Roe* eliminated the need for women to undergo dangerous back alley or coat hanger abortions.

Billie Jean King, the twenty-time Wimbledon champion tennis player, once said: "How are you going to shape the future if you don't know the past?" I, and others of my generation, must share the lessons of the past with younger generations. There is a saying that rings with truth: "Those who cannot remember the past are condemned to repeat it." I'd hate for us to repeat that past. I was born during World War II while my father was a Chaplain on a US Navy troop transport ship in the Pacific Ocean. I respected him and WWII veterans for their willingness to protect American principles. In the 1970s, Americans were once again fighting to protect American principles, though the battlefield was quite different. Women and men across the country were fighting to end anti-abortion laws, make contraception available, change customs to allow women to run full court—instead of half-court—in basketball, to get credit without having to get the signature of a father or husband, to teach in the public schools while pregnant, and to make many other needed changes. I participated in the battles for women's rights of the 1960s, 70s, and 80s, but few of us remain. The strong Texas women I stood with included Lady Bird Johnson, First Lady of the US with President Lyndon Johnson; Liz Carpenter, Lady Bird's assistant in the White House; Ann Richards, a Texas governor; Barbara Jordan, a black member of the Texas Senate with an attention-getting style of speaking who was later a member of the US House from Houston; Molly Ivins, a quick wit whether she was writing or speaking; and others. I miss the camaraderie of those very special women and the memories of us laughing at events together. It is vital to learn from the perseverance of these powerful women and to fight to defend the rights they worked so relentlessly to establish.

This dynamic group of women provided me with many lively memories throughout the years. Liz Carpenter, Molly Ivins, and I had breast cancer in the 2000s, and we did many events together to benefit efforts against the disease. I'll always remember one of Liz's lines: "I've always heard 'A tit for a tat.' Well I've given up a tit; what is a tat and when do I get one?"

As Robert Caro, the biographer of Lyndon B. Johnson, once eloquently stated, "The power of history is in the end the greatest power."

Time seems relentless in the on-going attacks on the legality and availability of contraception and abortion. For this reason, even though I know many people will be reading this after the election, I can't help but emphasize how important it is to vote for pro-choice candidates. 2012 has been particularly important due to the extreme divergence in the positions of the parties and the top candidates regarding abortion. To quote Nancy Keenan, the president of NARAL Pro-Choice America, "The decision women make on Election Day could mean the difference between our rights defended or our freedoms denied." How true that is!

Recently, I saw a cartoon that I thought was wonderful. Pictured was a button labeled "VOTE." with a finger pressing the button. This expressively symbolized that women can protect themselves by voting against anti-abortion candidates.

In the 2012 election, we had President Barack Obama on our side. On January 22, 2012, the thirty-ninth anniversary of *Roe*, Obama stated, "I remain committed to protecting a woman's right to choose and this fundamental constitutional right." Furthermore, the 2012 Democratic National Platform stated that the party "strongly and unequivocally supports *Roe v. Wade*."

The Republican candidate, Mitt Romney, had held a series of positions over the years, but during the campaign he referred to himself as solidly "pro-life," calling *Roe v. Wade* "one of the darkest moments in Supreme Court history." According to his campaign website, Romney advocated overturning *Roe* and allowing the states to determine laws regarding abortion. Romney's position adhered to the 2012 Republican Party Platform, which stated, "We assert the sanctity of human life and affirm that the unborn child has a fundamental individual right to life which cannot be infringed." However, a Romney campaign spokeswoman recently expanded upon the Platform's definition, saying that Romney "opposes abortion except for cases of rape, incest and where the life of the mother is threatened."

But the 2012 election season wasn't important solely because it decided who would be US President. It was also significant in that it determined who would serve in the US Senate and the House, as well as in statewide and state legislative positions. For example, the Senate Judiciary Committee is responsible for deciding whether to approve or reject a president's Supreme Court appointments. Whichever party has the majority on that committee can determine whether a candidate stands or falls. The battles for congressional seats and state elected positions are especially crucial when anti-abortion legislation has been passed by Congress and state legislatures, as was the case in the years leading up to the 2012 elections. Although those measures did not made the abortion procedure illegal, they certainly succeeded in making it less available and more expensive.

The protection for women's choices established by *Roe* has been diluted by many Supreme Court decisions. Watching the action of the Supreme Court in the years since I argued *Roe* has been like watching the weakening of *Roe* in slow motion. As I pointed out above, the make-up of the Supreme Court is much different today than it was when I argued there. Here is a chart setting out the Justices in 2012, ordered by age after Chief Justice Roberts:

NAME	AGE IN 2012	APPOINTED BY	SERVICE BEGAN
John Roberts	57	George W. Bush	Sept. 29, 2005
Ruth Bader Ginsburg	79	Bill Clinton	Aug. 10, 1993
Antonin Scalia	76	Ronald Reagan	Sept. 26, 1986
Anthony Kennedy	76	Ronald Reagan	Feb. 18, 1988

Stephen Breyer	74	Bill Clinton	Aug. 3, 1994
Clarence Thomas	64	George H.W. Bush	Oct. 23, 1991
Samuel Alito	62	George W. Bush	Jan. 31, 2006
Sonia Sotomayor	58	Barack Obama	Aug. 8, 2009
Elena Kagan	52	Barack Obama	Aug. 7, 2010

The President in office in 2013 will have the sole responsibility of choosing a replacement should one of the justices step down. As a result, the future of the Supreme Court could be significantly impacted by the election of 2012. The current line-up of Justices makes up the oldest Court since the New Deal Era, and it is likely that at least one of the Justices will be replaced in the near future. The ideology of the next Justice who is appointed is critical due to the fact that the current Justices often split 5-4 along ideological lines. Justices Ginsburg and Breyer typically support *Roe* principles, while Justices Alito, Scalia, Roberts, and Thomas vote against such principles. Justices Sotomayor and Kagan's stances are unknown, because they have never ruled on a case dealing with the principles of *Roe*, and were not asked about their stance in their confirmation hearings. Because they were appointed by a pro-choice president, it is more likely that they would vote to uphold *Roe* principles than not. Justice Kennedy frequently serves as the swing-vote of the Court. Each vote is critical. The next Justice appointed to the Court could truly tip the ideological balance of the Court, making the possibility of an anti-choice President in office especially formidable. The importance of electing pro-choice candidates into office cannot be overstated.

The Supreme Court of course has played a major role in undermining *Roe*. The court's decision in *Planned Parenthood of Southeastern Pennsylvania v. Casey (1992)* significantly weakened the protections established in *Roe*. *Casey* involved a Pennsylvania statute that did not make abortion illegal, but set up considerable restrictions. For example, the statute required doctors to inform women seeking abortions about fetal development and alternatives to abortion, thereby seeking to influence them to continue the pregnancy. In addition, it required minors under eighteen to receive permission from a parent or obtain a judge's exemption from doing so. Furthermore, it required married women to sign a form stating that they had notified their husbands of the pregnancy and their desire for an abortion unless certain exceptions applied. If married women did not fill out the form accurately, they were subjected to jail time.

On June 29, 1992, the Supreme Court Justices decided *Casey*, and *Roe* survived the day by a one-vote margin. Justice Sandra Day O'Connor, who wrote the majority opinion, held that it was constitutional for states to legislate abortion to a greater extent than in the past. O'Conner's opinion held that as long as states did not "unduly burden" a woman's decision regarding abortion, they had the right to place limits on access to the procedure itself. Consequently, the Court approved all of the Pennsylvania statute's restrictions except the requirement that applied to married women. Although this opinion significantly hindered the protections guaranteed in Roe, the majority of justices made it clear that Roe should not be overturned.

Since *Casey*, the Court has continued to make access to abortion considerably more difficult. The Supreme Court's decision in *Gonzales v. Carhart (2007)* approved further limitations on a woman's right to abortion as established in *Roe* and *Casey*. The case considered the question of whether or not a law called by the anti-abortion folks the "Partial-Birth Act of 2003" was constitutional under the Due Process Clause of the Fifth Amendment. The Act, which had been signed into law by President George W. Bush, prohibited a form of late-term abortion medically called intact dilation and extraction. The law failed to include the exception that the procedure could be used in order to save the life of the mother The Supreme Court had previously declared a Nebraska law stating that partial-birth abortions were illegal to be unconstitutional in the case *Stenberg v. Carhart (2000)*. However, in *Gonzales*, Justice Kennedy transformed his dissent in *Stenberg* into acceptance, effectively overruling the precedent set in *Stenberg*. The Court ruled that the "Partial-Birth Act of 2003" was constitutional on the grounds that it only applied to a specific method of abortion and thus failed to "impose an undue burden on a woman's right to abortion based on its overbreadth or lack of a health exception." In her dissenting opinion in *Gonzales*, Justice Ginsburg stated," The Court's hostility to the right *Roe* and *Casey* secured is not concealed." And it is becoming more and more visible today.

The responsibility for the fate of *Roe* belongs not only to the Supreme Court and Congress, but also to anti-choice legislatures in a variety of states that have made access to abortion considerably more difficult. Today, the battle over a woman's right to choose is being fought on many fronts, but particularly in state legislatures.

As I write, numerous bills limiting access to abortion are being introduced in every session of state legislatures. As Gloria Steinem once said, "If men could get pregnant, abortion would be a sacrament." Women made up only 23.6 percent of all state legislatures in 2012. Perhaps tellingly, in 2011, ninety-two anti-abortion restrictions were passed throughout the country, an all-time record. As of September 2012, 13 anti-abortion laws had been passed in state legislatures.

Many states passed laws forcing a woman to have a sonogram (oftentimes vaginal sonograms), followed by a twenty-four-hour waiting period, before she could have an abortion. An extreme anti-choice example comes from Arizona, where in April, 2012, Governor Jan Brewer signed into law a bill that redefined when life begins, defining gestational age as "calculated from the first day of the last menstrual period of the pregnant woman." The effect of the change was to give Arizona the earliest cut-off for late-term abortions in the country, because the pregnancy legally begins before conception. Currently, the constitutionality of the law is being argued in federal court.

Here in Texas, Governor Rick Perry, other elected officials, and Texas Health and Human Services commissioner Todd Suehs (appointed by Governor Perry) announced a rule in February, 2012, that formally banned Planned Parenthood clinics and other "affiliates of abortion providers" from participating in the Women's Health Program, a Medicaid program that provides low-income women with contraception, well-woman exams, and cancer screenings. Because of the affiliation with Medicaid, the federal government provided Texas with a 9-to-1 match in program funding. However, because federal law grants Medicaid recipients the right to choose their health care provider, the federal government was unable to continue providing funding to the Texas program once the participants could not have a provider of their choice. The Governor vowed to continue the program with state funds, but never indicated where the state was going to get the 30 million dollars a year that the federal government previously provided, especially in light of major budget cuts. Planned Parenthood clinics were used by approximately 45 percent of the women in the Women's Health Program. After the law passed, those women had to seek care at alternative locations, which were often far away and difficult to get to.

A pro-choice governor, on the other hand, can play an important role in protecting women's access to health care and abortion services. Kathleen Sebelius, who currently serves as the US Secretary of Health and Human Services, was Governor of Kansas from 2002 to 2009. In April 2008, Sebelius vetoed SB 389, the *Comprehensive Abortion Reform Act*, which would have tightened abortion regulations in Kansas. During her tenure as

Governor, the Kansas abortion rate declined 8.5 percent. Instead of trying to stifle a woman's right to make her own decision about her body, Sebelius focused on expanding health services for pregnant women and accurate sex education.

Some states do try to protect women, often by having privacy provisions in their state constitutions; others are considering legislation to add such protection. Referendums may be a way to ensure that a state remains pro-choice. Citizens can support pro-choice measures in their states and oppose measures that would limit choice.

As time has progressed, it has become alarmingly clear that the rights instilled by *Roe* have become comparable to the Cheshire cat in Alice in Wonderland, which sat on a tree branch and disappeared part by part. The protection of *Roe* is vanishing before our very eyes.

12. A Plan to Fight for Reproductive Rights

Within the reach of this book are the heroines and heroes of future pro-choice efforts. It would be impossible to pick each of them out today, and it is unlikely that even they know what role they may play. What is important is to empower the necessary individuals and support their collective efforts. It is time to renew the battle for reproductive rights. We have often been outmaneuvered, outspent, and outvoted by anti-abortion activists, and we need *you* to be a champion for choice. What can you do? Here are some possibilities.

1. VOTE PRO-CHOICE.

The first priority is to elect pro-choice candidates to every level of public office. Be sure you are registered to vote. Volunteer, give money if possible, and most importantly, vote for only pro-choice candidates. If you do not know who they are, you can find out from pro-choice groups. (Refer to feministpress.org for more information.) What most politicians want more than anything else is to be elected and re-elected. Make their pro-choice votes a condition of your support.

Educate candidates who are open to information on the importance of keeping abortion safe and legal. Voters for Choice publishes a guide called 'Winning With Choice." Updated for each election cycle, the guide familiarizes pro-choice candidates with various aspects of the issue and appropriate tactics.

We must always elect a pro-choice President. The President will control future Supreme Court appointments and federal appointments, and have veto power over congressional actions. The next President might fill one or more Supreme Court vacancies.

The importance of having a pro-choice President can be exemplified by examining President Bill Clinton's actions during his terms in office. Only fifty-one hours after his inauguration, Clinton signed several important measures during a White House ceremony, ending the anti-choice policies of the twelve previous years. He commented that he was "acting to separate our national health and medical policy from the divisive conflict over abortion."

That day he swept away the "gag rule," which forbade clinics that received Title X funding from informing and counseling patients about abortion services, even in circumstances when patients specifically asked for abortion information and even if withholding the information about abortion would endanger patients' health. As a result of Clinton's actions, the information about the health care a woman received no longer depended on whether she had independent means or had to rely on Title X-funded care.

The President also reversed the "Mexico City policy" of the two prior administrations that had kept the US from providing assistance to efforts like the family planning activities of the United Nations, which sought to prevent pregnancy in countries that used their own funds to provide abortions for their citizens.

He also lifted the moratorium on fetal tissue transplantation research, research that has the potential to dramatically improve the lives of those suffering from such diseases as Parkinson's, Alzheimer's, diabetes, and leukemia.

President Clinton's successor similarly illustrated the detrimental effects of having an anti-choice President in the White House. On his first day in office, George W. Bush, a Republican from Texas, reinstated the "Mexico City policy." Later, on November 5, 2003, Bush signed into law a bill called by anti-abortion activists "Partial Birth Abortion Ban Act," which prohibits a form of abortion known by medical professionals as 'intact dilation and extraction.' This Act had been passed by Congress in 1995 and again in 1997, but President Clinton had vetoed it both times. The Alan Guttmacher Institute stated that in the year 2000, only about 0.2 percent of all abortions were believed to be "intact dilation and extraction abortions."

When Barack Obama, a pro-choice Democrat from Illinois, was elected President in 2008, he too addressed access to abortion in his first week in office. Obama rescinded the "Mexico City policy" on January 23, 2009, just as Clinton had done sixteen years before. Obama's major accomplishment by 2012 had been the passage of the Affordable Care Act, which includes provisions for affordable family planning services, better access to contraception, and maternity care. As he campaigned for a second term in office, Obama emphasized his pro-choice stance.

Recognizing the danger from anti-abortion groups, some Congressional legislators have been trying to pass new laws that would buttress the constitutional protection of *Roe*. The Freedom of Choice Act would write the principles of *Roe* into national law; through the Act, a woman's range of choices about pregnancy would no longer depend on her state of residence. Though efforts to pass the bill have never been successful, it is important that when the Act does get passed a pro-choice President is in office to sign it into law, rather than an anti-choice President who would veto the bill.

We need a president who will encourage the use of contraceptives both here and abroad. As a nation we should be assisting Planned Parenthood and similar organizations around the world to make every child a wanted child and every mother a willing mother rather than trying to impede the success of pregnancy-prevention programs. Melinda Gates is starting a special effort by the Gates Foundation to make contraception available worldwide.

We need a president who will make a priority of investing in the children who are already here, of seeing that pregnant women who want to continue their pregnancy have access to proper medical care, and of creating an economy where people can afford to have children.

Congress is also important. The only way to get out from under the shadow of presidential vetoes is to have a pro-choice Congress with enough votes to override vetoes. NARAL Pro-Choice America reports that in 2012 the US Senate was made up of forty pro-choice senators, fourteen mixed-choice senators, and forty-six anti-choice senators. With the addition of eleven pro-choice senators, the Senate could be majority pro-choice. The US House in 2012 is made up of 154 pro-choice members, thirty-three mixed-choice members, and 247 anti-choice members. With the addition of sixty-four pro-choice members, the House of Representatives could be majority pro-choice.

The most effective contact with an elected official is a personal call or e-mail, especially if you know or have supported that official. The next most effective is a personal letter, indicating your residence in the official's district. You can also sign petitions and mass letters, giving your address as a voting constituent. It is easier than ever to let your voice be heard through online petition groups, such as Change.org.

The most important thing is to act. True, there are some issues about which elected officials stated a position when they ran, and about which they are unlikely to change their positions absent enormous pressure. But on many issues, those officials want to reflect the position of the majority of their constituents. The problem with the issue of choice is that officials have been hearing more consistently and loudly from our opposition than from us.

2. GET INVOLVED IN SOCIAL MEDIA ACTIVISM.

Social media has the power to engage a person in the most private of places—their own home. The ability to reach millions of people, for free and in an engaging way, is new to my generation: we had to make phone calls and knock on doors. While that is still important, today's youth are easier to reach than ever before. And it's not just young people getting involved—while the most common users are between ages eighteen and forty-nine, half of all internet users are between fifty and sixty-four years old and a third of all internet users age sixty-five and older use social media.

Facebook and Twitter played a key role in the Susan G. Komen Foundation's decision to reinstitute support for Planned Parenthood clinics for breast cancer screening. A grassroots movement of hundreds of thousands of supporters was able to express their outrage in a matter of hours via online media, testament to the power of a few clicks of a mouse.

Another example is the *Unite Against the War on Women* movement. In late February 2012, a Michigan woman and a New York woman were talking on the phone about the anti-woman legislation and rhetoric occurring across the country. They asked themselves, "Why aren't women taking to the streets?" After their conversation was over, one of the women created a Facebook group called "Organizing Against the War on Women."

When she woke up the next morning, almost 500 people were asking to be part of the group. Ten weeks later, *Unite Against the War on Women* held fifty-five events in forty-five states across the country with 47,000 in attendance.

3. BE ACTIVE IN AT LEAST ONE PRO-CHOICE ORGANIZATION.

Joining, or expanding your participation, in established organizations visibly demonstrates your personal conviction to choice. Being on a mail or e-mail list for newsletters and the like is a way to receive consistent and updated information about the latest events and about specific actions that are needed. Many national groups have state and local affiliates, which you can locate online. Collective action is always more effective and powerful than isolated individual activity.

NARAL and Planned Parenthood spend a major amount of time on pro-choice activities. Cecile Richards, President of Planned Parenthood Federation of America and Planned Parenthood Action Fund, has done an excellent job leading the fight to provide and protect women's health and abortion services. I have great respect for her, and she is an inspiration to many. The ACLU Reproductive Freedom Project has been one group fighting the legal battles through its Center for Reproductive Law and Policy. Supporting these groups financially is critical to their success.

Use your own sphere of influence. Make sure that groups you are involved with are vocal in their support for choice. The League of Women Voters and Business and Professional Women/USA, for example, have made choice a priority issue for programs and action. Ask group leaders if you can help set up a program on choice. It costs more money to get inactive pro-choice people to join new organizations than it does to activate the pro-choice groups to which they already belong. In addition, some people can't afford the dues that joining another organization costs. As a result, there is a new emphasis on coalition efforts to activate existing organizations that have a pro-choice position.

4. TALK PRO-CHOICE.

Discuss your pro-choice stance whenever there is an opportunity. Unfortunately, because we are not trying to force our beliefs on anyone and are simply asking to be let alone to follow our own best judgments, many citizens do not realize how many of us are pro-choice. Anti-abortionists tend to be more visible. One way to increase our visibility and to persuade others is by explaining our position. It might be to family members, to neighbors, to colleagues or other acquaintances. It might even be to our opponents, in more or less formal debates.

The opposition has won many battles with the power of language and words. Abortion opponents call themselves "pro-life," " but do not say "pro-life" when referring to them. Say "anti-choice," "anti-abortion," "anti-freedom," "pro-birth," "pro-illegal abortion," "pro-mandatory birth," or maybe "pro-world calamity"— something that indicates the opposition's sole intent of forcing women to go through unwanted pregnancies. Use "pro-choice" or "pro-freedom" when referring to those who believe the woman involved, not the government, should decide the issue.

5. KEEP THE FACTS STRAIGHT.

The opposition has said so many times that abortion is being used for birth control that people have begun to believe it. I have *never* heard any woman, if asked about what kind of birth control she is using, answer, "Abortion." Sometimes contraceptives fail or people fail to use them, but people don't consider abortion a method of birth control.

Similarly, opponents of abortion insist on calling people like me "pro-abortion." I am not, and neither is anyone I know. I never say to someone, "Oh, what a beautiful day! Wouldn't it be wonderful to get an abortion today!" But I certainly am in favor of women—not the government—choosing whether to continue or terminate a pregnancy.

I try to clip or underline good material as I read. For example, on September 5, 2012, I read a letter to the editor of the Austin American-Statesman by Dr. Heinz Aeschbach which emphasized that half of all pregnancies end in miscarriages. He also wrote "Civilizations recognize that sperm, ovums and embryos are living and human but not living, sentient humans. Cultures value humans according to development stage . . ."

6. TURN THEIR TACTICS AGAINST THEM.

Sometimes I wish everyone could watch an uninterrupted one-hour program featuring the leading anti-choice advocates. I think people would be appalled by the vision they have for the world and our lives. It is up to us to turn clinic blockades and other anti-abortion tactics to our benefit. Clinics across the nation that offer abortion services are currently "pledging picketers": pro-choicers pledge a certain amount to a clinic for every anti-choice picketer who shows up. If the antis see us raising money for our cause through their actions, maybe it will offset the fun they're having harassing women and medical personnel, and convince them to stay away.

Assist as a clinic escort, or in other efforts to defend clinics from anti-choice zealots. More people should participate in clinic defense activities to ensure the access of patients and employees and to protect their privacy. I guarantee that if you go to a clinic under harassment and protect a woman seeking services as she struggles to make her way through the mob, you will become more determined about the issue of choice. At first it's frightening, but think of how much that woman needs help at that difficult moment of her life. Clinics that welcome assistance provide training for volunteers; be *sure* to go through the training before your first defense activity. This may be the first time you've ever physically put yourself on the line for something you believe in. I believe that after you do it once you will want to help again and again.

7. NEUTRALIZE THE RELIGIOUS ARGUMENT.

Religious leaders were in the vanguard of efforts to protect the safety and choices of women. We need to reactivate our religious institutions for choice. Be knowledgeable about the position of your faith. A good resource is the Religious Coalition for Abortion Rights.

While it is difficult to draw the line between appropriate and inappropriate conduct for religious groups, we need to be clear about what constitutes going too far. Of course the Pope has a right to order American priests to exhort those who attend their churches against abortion, but when the current Catholic doctrine (among others), stating that life begins at conception, becomes written into law, isn't that going too far?

The religious aspect of the abortion debate troubles me deeply. When I argued *Roe* before the Court, I stated that forcing the beliefs of any church on the population at large was, in my opinion, a violation of the spirit of the First Amendment. We must uphold our basic principles of choice in the way we want to practice our faith.

8. ENCOURAGE DOCTORS TO SUPPORT CHOICE.

Doctors set the stage for *Roe* because they were concerned about the large number of women who were having illegal abortions and often suffering severe medical consequences. Groups opposing abortion have been successful in intimidating some medical personnel although many doctors, nurses, and administrators continue courageously performing abortions despite the personal price they pay.

When possible, select doctors who support choice. Help offset the pressure many doctors feel at being told that their business will suffer if they are pro-choice. An obstetrician-gynecologist in Jacksonville, Florida, told me that he had lost a number of patients because he is pro-choice. On the other hand, a new patient told him she had chosen him precisely because he is pro-choice.

If you're a student, consider a career in medicine or nursing, so that you can yourself be a provider of women's health services.

9. PROTECT WOMEN IN STATES WHERE ABORTION BECOMES ILLEGAL.

One reason to keep abortion legal is to avoid dangerous attempts at illegal abortion. Already people are contemplating the best arrangements for women if abortion becomes illegal. Some doctors, especially women, have begun discussing the practicalities. I hear talk about setting up a new abortion underground to try to ensure that safe abortions are available even when they are illegal. Some people envision an updated version of "abortion tourism", a phenomenon already common for several medical procedures, to help women from a state where abortion is illegal travel to one where it is legal. The necessary equipment, it is said, is disappearing from clinics and being stored in safe places, and some abortion providers are training as many people as possible in the proper techniques. There is speculation about smuggling in supplies of the abortion pill RU-486. I've heard some providers say they would refuse to quit providing services and refuse to go underground. One woman looking for legal options mentioned the possibility of clinics on boats that sail beyond US waters. Once again there will be women volunteering to help other women find places to go, just as they did in the effort in Austin that led to *Roe v. Wade.*

The only way to avoid the horrors of illegal abortion is to keep it legal. That's why we must make its legality a priority. For low-income women, however, many state-enforced hurdles may mean that legal abortion is available in theory but not in reality. Financial assistance is needed for these women. Many local Planned Parenthoods and other organizations have established funds to loan or give money to women who need it quickly. They deserve support.

10. TAKE THE BATON AND RUN.

My generation reacted to the limitations imposed by society and law. The current generation of young women have rarely had anyone tell them they cannot do certain things because they are female. No one has told them they cannot play full-court basketball or be lawyers or get credit in their own names. When we said, "The world is your oyster, all you have to do is get out there and take it," we meant that we had opened many doors previously closed to women. What those younger women may have heard was that all the problems had been solved. But there are still pay gaps between men and women of similar educational achievements; a glass ceiling that seems to trap women at lower levels than men; and a lack of societal structures, such as family leave, to make it easier for women and men to combine family and jobs.

Perhaps because younger people have had a different set of experiences, they would more likely become involved in groups led by their peers. The pro-choice movement needs new blood. Those who have been in the trenches are beginning to age and wear. We need fresh recruits for support and leadership. We need people with new energy and enthusiasm.

Take the baton and run by becoming active in a new version of an existing organization, for example, a NARAL chapter on a college campus or a local Planned Parenthood Young Professionals group. If existing groups don't suit you, you might start an organization that fits your needs and style. When my generation became active in the late 1960s, there were many worthy, hardworking women's organizations, such as Business and Professional Women/USA, Zonta, and the Soroptimists. But we started new organizations and became the leaders.

11. WELCOME SUPPORT FROM MEN WHO ARE PRO-CHOICE.

On an issue such as choice, about which women feel so passionately, many men who also are pro-choice simply aren't sure about their role, so they stay on the sidelines. In the earlier days of the women's movement, women sought to have female leaders in their own organizations, since male leaders presided everywhere else. But men still wonder what their role is in the pro-choice movement perhaps because they have heard the heated discussions about the men leading the opposition groups, yelling at women, blocking their entrance to clinics, and generally being hateful. As I recently pointed out in a speech, seventeen of the twenty anti-abortion picketers who greeted me the night I spoke were men who appeared to be fifty years old and above. "What right do they have to be involved?" women may ask. "Abortion will never be a personal issue for them."

However, the active, visible support by men who are pro-choice, as with any other group, adds valuable numbers and enhances our efforts to involve everyone concerned with preserving choice. Many of us may have said at one time or another, "Men just don't understand." But many of the women who said that went on to have sons, and brought them up to be feminists. Give the sons a role and welcome the men who advocate choice as a matter of principle. We certainly need the help of men-and the majority of our publicly elected officials, for now at least, are male.

12. WORK TO HELP WOMEN AND THEIR CHILDREN.

We must focus on the goal of allowing women *all* choices, including that of having children. While this has always been our underlying principle, we may not have said it loudly and often enough. As part of broadening our message, we should reemphasize the range of choices we want women to have. Women often tell me, "When I got pregnant I decided to go ahead with the pregnancy, but I'm still so glad it was *my* choice."

We need to make contraceptive information and techniques more accessible to men as well as women, and hopefully reduce unwanted pregnancies. We also need to ensure that women can obtain basic reproductive health services. For many of them, family planning clinics such as Planned Parenthood constitute the only source of health care, counseling, or referrals for themselves or their children. Frances Kissling of Catholics for Free Choice has said that if people could sit in on counseling sessions and listen to women tell their stories, the abortion issue would soon be behind us.

In 2010, Planned Parenthood health centers nationwide saw nearly 3 million patients, and over 90 percent of services performed were preventative. They provided breast exams for nearly 750,000 women, provided birth control for more than 2 million people, administered 770,000 pap tests, and administered over 4 million tests and treatments for STDs. You might consider volunteering in some capacity at Planned Parenthood. Few experiences are as motivating as helping the women who seek their services.

It never fails to amaze me that the same people who oppose a woman's right to choose often do not support prenatal care, or neonatal medical care, or women's and children's health care. The antis have chosen to try to force a woman to give birth, but they disappear when responsibility begins after birth. Why don't those who claim to be "pro-life" do more to improve the lives of kids in poverty? Some of them talk about how much our government and nonprofit agencies spend on children or mention the things they have personally done to help poor children and children up for adoption, but in comparison with the enormous need, their efforts are minuscule. Improving conditions for the poor is hardly their exclusive province; there are plenty of pro-choice churches and individuals who do as much as antis do, or more.

13. OTHER SUGGESTIONS.

Here are other things you can do, including ideas from a pamphlet issued by the North Carolina Coalition for Choice:

— Write a letter to the editor of your local newspaper. Focus on women's lives, women's health, and the need for safe, legal abortion.

— Find emerging leaders, women and men, especially younger

ones. Discuss with them the need to speak out for choice and the need for new leadership on this issue.

— Display the symbols of choice on bumper stickers, buttons, T-shirts. Or encourage those who display those symbols by letting them know you agree.

— Come up with your own ideas about keeping abortion safe and legal, and share them with others (including me).

Today more Americans are focusing on the abortion issue and being galvanized into action by national events. The outlook for the Supreme Court, and media coverage of intense anti-abortionists' activities is making women feel more vulnerable than they have at any time since 1973. And the uproar is likely to grow if the Court further limits the rights secured by *Roe.*

I see that uproar expressed in many ways. Not long ago, I was the speaker for a public affairs luncheon sponsored by Los Angeles Planned Parenthood. The event—all 550 tickets—was a sellout, and the volunteers who organized it said that participants shared a new intensity of feelings.

In these economic hard times, students, especially graduating seniors, are worried about getting jobs. When I gave a commencement speech last year, I asked the senior class president what the seniors would like me to say on their behalf to those assembled. His response was, "Please ask our parents not to charge us rent yet." The number of people who are unemployed is high, as is the number of people who are having to work longer hours to survive financially. When people feel economically vulnerable, in the absence of religious fervor they often are more timid about becoming involved in controversial issues, lest that involvement lessen their job prospects. On the other hand, the economic trials of bearing and then rearing an unwanted child could dislocate many more lives.

It will take a great effort from many people to stand up to the challenge. But that's no different from the situation when we started *Roe*. Back then, some were working in the political process, asking candidates to support changes in the abortion laws, voting for candidates who agreed, lobbying state legislators, and trying to get laws changed. They were successful in New York, Colorado, California, Hawaii, Oregon, and Washington before *Roe v. Wade*. Those states were havens for women who could get there before the case, and one hopes that they will continue to be havens if the strength of *Roe* is weakened.

What we proved almost forty years ago is that dedicated effort can make a difference. If we who want to keep abortion safe and legal will pursue that goal we can, I believe, win the important battles ahead.

Our challenges now include getting the majority of pro-choice Americans to vote and to join pro-choice organizations, reframing some of the terminology currently in use and what it stands for, emphasizing the importance of the separation of church and state, and supporting pro-choice doctors and service providers. We must also diversify and turn the issue of leadership over as necessary to a new generation of women and men. And we must promote better services—medical, social, and educational—for the people who are already here.

One of the questions for me personally—and for many of us—is how to sustain the energy level necessary for the seemingly never-ending effort demanded of us.

As a plane taxis out, passengers hear the flight attendant say, "This cabin is pressurized for your comfort. In the unlikely event of an emergency an oxygen mask will drop down from overhead." These days I am more conscious of the need to increase my oxygen and my energy. I laugh more now than I used to. Someone gave me a plaque that reads: "He"—I've inserted "She"—"who laughs lasts." New information and new experiences are oxygen; I am making a greater effort to shoehorn them into my crowded schedule.

The energy of the young women and men who are flooding to defend freedom of choice rubs off on me. As I speak around the country, I meet young professionals who have an infectious enthusiasm for the future and for the defense of *Roe's* principles. But the personal experiences people share with me are my constant—and best—source of energy. A professionally accomplished woman with three children who became pregnant six weeks after her third child was born recently shared with me her gratitude that she had a legal choice. A photographer told me about the experience of a friend of his girlfriend's who began to hemorrhage after an illegal abortion; he feels very strongly that abortion should never again be illegal. A young woman described to me supporting two college friends who faced the abortion decision; she isn't sure she would choose abortion for herself, but she is adamant that the choice should belong to women. These shared personal experiences increase my oxygen and energy, and now they come almost daily.

Hearing about such experiences is energizing because they emphasize the importance of guaranteeing the right to choose. On the one hand, it is unnatural to have reached one's professional peak at twenty-seven, and I do wonder if it's even possible to top that victory. On the other hand, I take tremendous pride in the gift all of us who together won *Roe* were able to give future generations. Americans have had the personal right of privacy for almost forty years, and I am sure they will remain motivated to defend it. Thomas Cabot, who gave money years ago to sustain *Roe* by paying for the printing of most of the briefs, said that, even though he was over ninety years old, it was the gift he was proudest of. I join him in having the satisfaction of knowing my work made a difference for others. And I know too that many have never known the trauma of illegal abortion because of our work.

I encourage you to seek out women and men under forty who are emerging leaders. Talk with them about the need to speak out for choice and have new leadership on the issue. Understand that guaranteeing reproductive rights is not a single issue. It is the cornerstone of an agenda that includes prevention of unwanted pregnancies, human sexuality education, day care, family leave, available health care for everyone, AIDS education, and global population issues.

This book has a final page, but the story of *Roe* will continue. It is the story of women and their continuing efforts to push back the barriers that have limited their decisions and circumscribed their freedoms; it is a story lived daily by countless women and the men who care about them. Increasing numbers of people are rallying to protect not just the words of *Roe,* but what we wanted those words to mean in our lives.

This revision was written as we prepare to celebrate the 40th anniversary of the Supreme Court decision in *Roe* and to share with you the story of our victory in 1973 and the sources of the problems we face today. Moreover, it was written to emphasize the importance of your help in defending and preserving the meaning of *Roe v. Wade.* It was written with the hope that those who read this message will choose to be the heroines and heroes of this cause.

Let us join forces and work together so that Americans, especially American women, will forever be able to make their own reproductive decisions. It's a question of choice.

For a full list of up-to-date resources, see feministpress.org/books/ sarah-weddington/question-choice

13. A Few Last Comments

As this 40th anniversary edition—the revised and updated version—of my book *A Question of Choice*—is being rushed to print, I can't resist the temptation to write a few last comments.

The hard cover version was published in 1992; the soft cover version was published in 1993. In many ways the issues being discussed today are the same. It is now six weeks after the national Presidential election of 2012. On November 6 Barack Obama was elected as the US President. As part of his reelection effort, Obama emphasized his belief that women should have access to contraception and that a decision about abortion should be a decision for the woman involved to make. His opponent campaigned hard for an opposite point of view.

What, then, of the future for women's reproductive rights and choices? This is anything but a new question. Since those euphoric days of the 1970s when we won landmark freedoms for women, attacks on Roe have been relentless. Obama's victory is cause for heart-felt celebration by those who are committed to the principle of women being the ones entitled to reproductive freedom and the ones entitled to make the decisions that most affect their lives. His position as President means that in the very likely event of future vacancies on the US Supreme Court, the person appointed to any vacancy is likely to favor the decision in *Roe v. Wade*. None of the current Justices has indicated plans to leave that Court. However, Ruth Bader Ginsburg, for example, has recently not looked to be in robust health. Nonetheless my guess is that she is keenly aware of her key influence on the future and that she will remain on the Court as long as is humanly possible. Obama's re-election does give us hope against further erosion of past decisions of the US Supreme Court pertaining to constitutional rights such as privacy. However I'm old enough now to recognize that nothing is certain.

Obama's position as President means that he can use his influence with his Administration and administrative officials to continue to work for policies that expand opportunities for women and girls in a wide variety of ways. He is likely to continue and to extend the record he has established in that regard. I believe that he will use his influence with Democratic elected officials to serve the principles that he established as a candidate and, when possible, to seek support from Republican officials for those principles.

The focus is shifting to the states and state legislatures. Anti-choice groups in state after state have sought to chisel away our rights, to limit access to abortion and to smear the good name and work of Planned Parenthood and other groups working to defend women's rights. What we're seeing are increasingly successful challenges by those opposed to abortion under almost any circumstances to abortion being available at all. State legislation covers a wide gamut of efforts to circumscribe the rights that women have had since 1973.

Many of those who worked before the *Roe v. Wade* decision to make that decision possible are still determined to work for its principles, but age has simultaneously made them more tired. The torch will be passing to women and sympathetic men who believe that women are the appropriate people to make the basic decisions that determine the lives of women. It will be on their shoulders to turn back the fanatical forces of the right. It makes me happy to watch as those younger people join our cause. They are the future and I trust them to protect victories of the past and to win future victories. My generation will do all that's possible to support their efforts and, increasingly from the sidelines, we will be cheering for them and wishing them success.

Here's to you, those of every age who are sharing the responsibility to protect victories of the past and to widen the area within which women can make their own decisions!

—Sarah Weddington
December 16, 2012

Acknowledgments

R oe v. *Wade* would not have been won without the energy, determination, and intelligence of dozens of people. While there were too many involved to name them individually, I would like to thank them publicly, along with each of the thousands of others who have fought to establish and retain women's reproductive rights.

I especially want to thank Cecile Richards, President of the Planned Parenthood Federation of America, for her contribution to this book via the thoughtful and insightful Foreword that she wrote and also for the leadership she continuously provides for the movement that we share. We have worked together for many years, but I feel her support deserves a heartfelt thank you here. I greatly admire her efforts on behalf of women.

I also want to say a special word of thanks to those without whom this 40th Anniversary Edition, which has been revised and updated since the first edition of 1992, would never have been accomplished.

Becky Seawright, the Chair of the Board of Directors of the Feminist Press (hereinafter referred to as "FP") is the person who suggested that this book would go "hand in glove" with the purposes of the FP. I am grateful to her for that suggestion and for her help in preparing this effort for publication. I have admired her activism since I first watched her work years ago as the President of the Young Women's Political Caucus of Texas.

Joyce Whitby, the Secretary of the Board of Directors of the FP, was invaluable in the process of writing and getting this book published.

I learned about the history and accomplishments of the FP from Helene Goldfarb, the President of the Board of Directors of the FP, and from Florence Howe, one of the founders of the FP.

I continue to be grateful to those who provided interviews, research, and suggestions beginning with the 1992 edition of this book, including Jan Blackwell, Barbara Vackar, Mickey Dudley, Melinda Morris Freeman, Tom Glick, Barbara Hudson, Dawn Johnson, Frances Kissling, Karen Mulhauser, Peggy Romberg, Tom Santarlas, Elizabeth Snapp, Bill Stott, Jane Stott, Ron Weddington, Jim Wheelis and the other people who worked with Judy Smith and Bea Durden Vogel.

The group in New York who helped with the briefs and preparation for the Supreme Court argument made it possible for the case to be successful. That included Nick Danforth, Dan Schneider, Brian Sullivan, and Dave Tunderman.

I continue to think with fervent gratitude about those who were critical in the writing and publishing of the 1992 edition of this book. Jane Isay, my editor and publisher, was fabulous and worked so well with me. She even came to Austin for several weeks and made it possible for us to complete the book and have it distributed in advance of the Presidential election when Bill Clinton was the Democratic candidate. I was determined to have the book out in time to have an impact on that election because I felt that *Roe v. Wade* would be protected by Clinton appointments and would be in increasing danger if he were not the person making Supreme Court appointments. The entire team at Putnam Publishing, headed by Phyllis Grann, was wonderfully helpful, including their maestro of publicity Marilyn Ducksworth, along with Anna Jardine, Charlotte Gilbert, Sally Hoffman, and Rona Cohen.

My original plan in writing this Acknowledgements section was to include information about a variety of people. Unfortunately, as I began to make a list of the appropriate people to enumerate what had happened to them, I realized that most of them are deceased. I found it too depressing to continue to follow my original plan; in fact, as I contemplate how many of them are likely to join in celebrating the 50th anniversary of the *Roe v. Wade* decision, it is even more depressing.

Instead I'll close by saying that this effort has made me even more aware of the need for a younger group of individuals to become the leaders on the legal front, regarding the provision of health care services, in providing the financial resources for pro-choice groups to continue their oh-so-important efforts, and in creating the public relations strategies needed to protect past victories.

A list of up-to-date resources and an index
appear on our website at
feministpress.org/books/sarah-weddington/question-choice